More praise for <u>How Much Joy Can You Stand?</u>

"*How Much Joy Can You Stand?* helps us to see that we all have passion and inspiration and creativity and genius residing inside us. [Falter-Barns's] book teaches us how to coax it out and live a truly joyful, lively existence!"

—BARRIE GILLIES
Senior Editor, *Fitness*

"Falter-Barns's warmhearted book will hold your hand as you go through the stages of learning to accept the great happiness that comes from following and fulfilling your dreams. Loaded with tips to help you stay focused, confident, and passionate, *How Much Joy Can You Stand?* also revs you up with stories of real people who dared to live more abundantly and joyfully. You'll come away from this book experience with renewed optimism, a greater understanding of how big you're willing to be, and a good sense of how to actually live from your greater, you-based self!"

—PENNEY PEIRCE
Author of *The Intuitive Way:
A Guide to Living from Inner Wisdom*

By Suzanne Falter-Barns

FICTION
Doin' the Box Step

NONFICTION
How Much Joy Can You Stand?

how much joy can you stand?

A Creative Guide to Facing Your Fears and Making Your Dreams Come True

Revised, Updated, and with New Chapters

Suzanne Falter-Barns

Ballantine Wellspring™

The Ballantine Publishing Group • New York

www.randomhouse.com/BB/

Library of Congress Catalog Card Number: 00-190367

ISBN 0-345-43916-3

Text design by Holly Johnson
Cover design by Barbara Leff
Cover illustration by Betsy Everitt

Manufactured in the United States of America

First Ballantine Wellspring Edition: June 2000

10 9 8 7 6 5 4 3 2

In memory of my father,
John Falter,
who lived with joy

Contents

How to Use This Book

This book was written in response to that creeping enemy of self-expression: entropy. If you've ever set out to create something, you know what I'm talking about, for sooner or later, no matter how well it's going, the whole damn system breaks down.

The book is organized into short, pungent little essays to read in such moments of flagging enthusiasm. Each essay is intended to inspire and help keep you going, despite the mental sludge.

Keep this book handy wherever you do the work of your dreams, and refer to its pages often. If this book does its job properly, you'll be up and running in no time.

Why Leap off the Cliff in the First Place?

Whether you realize it or not, you and you alone have something unique to create. None of the billions of other people who populate the earth has your particular talents, knowledge, experience, and dreams. This is your birthright—the gift you have been given. Whether it's creating the ultimate bagel, a thriving dry-cleaning business, a lifetime of exquisite tapestries, or a child, you are the only one who carries its blueprints. If you've ever listened to that small, still voice in the dark recesses of your soul, you know this is true. Somewhere in there, the longing to manifest this gift speaks to you on a regular basis; it's that embarrassing dream you keep coming back to, the one that usually feels so hopeless.

The purpose of this book is to explore the one thing necessary to move you toward that dream, your own creative process—the steps you must take to turn that dream into reality. Understanding the sometimes-fickle, sometimes-euphoric nature of all this creating is key to making progress.

So why does there need to be an entire book about the creative process? Because if you don't know how creativity works, you may never realize any of your dreams, whether they are becoming a fine artist, playing pro ball, or managing a mutual fund. Your creative process informs every decision you make, from conceptualizing, problem solving, and networking to deciding which emotion to express. Creativity is not the lone province of artistic types with dirty fingernails living in picturesque garrets. Rather, the creative process is a lifeblood we all share—a fundamental human property with millions of applications. It is essential to accomplishing anything in life that's uniquely your own; it is the engine that drives your dreams.

Unfortunately, there is one small problem. Out there right now, circulating around the atmosphere, is a carload (an eighteen-wheeler load, really) of out-and-out lies about creativity. And if you're trying to pursue any kind of dream, you can't help but get run over by it once in a while. Hopefully, armed with enough information and clarity, you can dodge those madly careening trucks and see your way to the other side. I wrote this book in an attempt to prevent further roadkill.

I figure, all the lies surrounding this process have persisted because we're basically a doubting, disbelieving breed. We have to make up whatever thoughts we can to keep us from doing the work of our dreams, and so the myths persist. In nearly twenty years of my own creative work, many of them spent encouraging others to express themselves, I've seen more people cling to more lies that render them absolutely powerless than I ever thought possible. They believe these lies will keep them gloriously afloat, yet such lies are nothing more than leaky life rafts that will only hold them up for a while before giving out entirely. Furthermore, hanging out on a life raft is no substitute for swimming. Whether you admit it or not, that dream of yours isn't going away. Far from it. It will badger you relentlessly until you finally give in and listen.

Chances are, your dream has persisted doggedly and continues to chatter at you regardless of how often you shove it aside. Look at how it reappears at odd, restless times like the middle of the night or those first crystal-clear moments of the day—whenever you're unusually lucid and your mind is free of clutter. Its voice carries on year after year, decade after decade, growing fainter at some times and stronger at others, but still refusing to die altogether.

It is almost as if we cannot bear these precious, private visions. The very presence of a dream is incredibly threatening, for to take action and actually follow it requires a freedom we think we do not have—not here, not now, not in this secure, comfort-lined world we've constructed to be as seamless and mindless as possible. Pursuing the dream would mean too much hard work, too many demanding hours, less security, less TV! Worst of all, it would mean exposure and even more mortifying . . . *potential humiliation.*

Yet think of how devastating it would be to come to the end of your life and realize you've missed your chance. If you settled for mediocrity and die with most of your potential unrealized, you would have blown it big time, once and for all. That really is the end of the road; there will be no going back.

This withering scenario should never happen at all, for the pursuit of a dream is actually a simple, straightforward affair. Pursuing dreams requires bravery, discipline, patience, and ingenuity, yet these are qualities every one of us possesses—*if* we're willing to do the hard work dreams demand. *If* we're willing to honor our creative process instead of fighting it. Pursuing your dreams simply means flexing the muscle of your creativity, slowly at first, but then with more vigor and confidence as you feed it the food of your own passionate conviction and it becomes stronger and stronger.

Creativity is that magic seed many of us assume we were born without. Yet it is lying latent, waiting in every single one of us. This book is about tending that seed, so that it flourishes as effortlessly and as naturally as God, Brahma, the Universe, or whoever originally intended.

Contrary to popular belief, creativity is not a temperamental, whimsical, all-too-fragile breeze that may or may not blow in our direction. This book is intended to smash that myth as well. The fact is, your creative instincts are a lot like your underwear: they're right there in the drawer waiting for you to climb into them every day, durable and dependable, and they don't play favorites. Your instincts are on call whenever you need them, as long as you remember to reach for them. That's really all you need to know.

Well, okay, you say. But why bother with all this dream-pursuing, creative hoo-ha in the first place?

Simply because of the joy.

If you can manage to leap off the cliff and trust yourself to fly, you will experience a fine, effortless joy like nothing else. You will experience a larger connectedness with the

Universe and, possibly for the first time, see your place in it and your own unique value to it. You will be doing what you were always, originally intended to do. This is the secret of the whole process. Once you've truly tasted that fantastic fruit of joy, there is literally nothing, not even years of flat-out rejection and failure, that can keep you from its magic. The process of creating the dream becomes too pleasurable to resist.

It may take a while to wade through all your resistance, fears, misperceptions, and basic disbelief in yourself. It may take far longer than you think it should. But if you can just keep going through the process, and trust yourself in a basic way not attempted before, the joy will be yours. Your vision and creative instincts will become stronger, clearer, and more vital each time you connect with them. Your commitment will strengthen, and as it does, the world will cooperate in ways you never would have expected. Little signposts will appear along the way, offering support and encouragement. People will show up, bringing challenges, ideas, or information. Your dream will begin to materialize, the result of nothing more than finally listening to the still, small voice within and acting accordingly.

It is out of my love for this perfectly simple arrangement that I wrote this book. It is also out of my love for you. The joy is available to all of us, right this minute, here and now, forever and ever.

All you have to ask yourself is this: How much joy can you stand?

Try This ...

When the raw stuff of dreams begins to collect, you might want to store it all somewhere. Sprinkle a handful of blank notebooks throughout your life for jotting down ideas and inspirations. Keep a small tape recorder on hand for recording observations. Buy some large plastic boxes for keeping bits and pieces of the raw materials your dream demands. Then designate a specific place for this important cache: the piano bench, an empty closet, or the bottom drawer in your desk.

Once you've begun to collect ideas, materials, odds and ends that pertain to your dream, feel free to dig into your cache frequently and create. The fact is, the more you write, record, and accumulate, the more power you give to your vision.

Now get out there and have fun.

Dare to Be Heard

o you want to be a venture capitalist, write a screenplay, or open a Victorian tea garden like the one you visited once in London and never forgot. So you want to do anything slightly risky that demands a personal vision.

You? . . . YOU? says the voice, as it collapses on the floor in gales of laughter.

Who do you think you are, anyway?

For many of us, this is where the conversation about pursuing our dream begins and ends. Because—let's admit it—we're sensible people. We're not the sort who take huge, wild risks. We're not the slightest bit visionary. We don't have a lot of high-minded thoughts that keep us awake at night, and God knows we don't know the first thing those other, more successful people must have known before they set off to realize their dream. We're just . . . us. Basic. Flawed. Certainly nothing special.

Actually, when you get right down to it, we think we don't really even deserve to have a dream.

Still, we do have this niggling idea that keeps surfacing and resurfacing, begging to be explored, teased out, played with, and realized. We otherwise staid individuals do have to admit to oddly ambitious stirrings we don't completely understand. So we do what we have always done: we ignore them.

After all, we're just not the kind of people who go off half-cocked after some so-called dream, right?

The truth is that people with creative impulses need to create, no matter how "uncreative," sensible, logical, and otherwise unimpulsive they consider themselves. People with a pressing idea have an obligation to express it. And yet we almost never do. We subscribe to a weirdly common belief that no one wants to hear what we have to say. No one wants to know about our great new idea, patronize our business, attend our productions, or give us any kind of a break. *No one.* We feel as if the world were just waiting to flatten us with some great, universal sledgehammer.

This is the soft, dark underbelly of all dreams, the part

that's hovering in the shadows, hoping to derail you. And this is the first and seediest demon you will have to confront. The really annoying part is that the demon is you. All that imagined rejection is nothing more than your own twisted projections. When examined in the cool, rational light of day by other, more benevolent people, your own contribution usually merits a much greater response than you could ever imagine.

I will never forget the first time I performed my cabaret act—a two-woman show in which my partner and I wrote and sang all our own music. For months and months we'd worked on the act—composing, harmonizing, writing lyrics, choreographing moves—all the while convinced that what we were doing was good but strange. No one in their right mind was actually going to like this stuff, though we might get some polite applause. In fact, we only kept going because we were having fun.

Then our opening night rolled around. As we stood on the stage singing our first number, a curious thing happened. People began to smile. They nodded and sat up a little straighter as if they were actually listening, and then a miracle occurred: they laughed. All of them. Loudly, even. The audience got the first joke in the lyrics, then another, and another.

They laughed in places I hadn't even anticipated. Like some fantastic flying machine lumbering into that sacred moment of liftoff, the act was working. At that moment I fully understood the impact of what my partner and I had created, and it shocked me. I was someone worth listening to. People actually wanted to hear what I had to say.

The common disposition among us is a painful sort of shyness. People get embarrassed when called forth to be themselves for even a millisecond in front of others. The core belief is that since nothing I say matters to anyone, I will end up looking like a dork. This is precisely the feeling that keeps people from feeding their dreams.

Oddly enough, that sniggering voice of doubt never really goes away. Years pass, and you get somewhat used to it, as you learn to test the waters more and more, and eventually the voice slides from an obnoxious bellow into more of a background drone. Witness the famous acceptance speech Sally Field made on winning her second Oscar: "I guess you really do like me, don't you?" Observe the fact that Truman Capote was once quoted as saying he'd never written anything he thought was *really* good, not even *Breakfast at Tiffany's*. Jane Austen wrote of her work, "I think I may boast myself to be, with all possible vanity, the most unlearned and ill-informed female who ever dared to be an authoress."

The point is this: No matter what you take on, insecurity is part of the job description. It's not possible to blaze new trails and forge your own path while remaining on familiar ground. If you want to start a business, you take on financial risk. If you want to move to another part of the country, you plunge yourself and whoever is attached to you into the unknown. If you want to try any endeavor you care about, you're going to have to kick it out of that cozy little nook it has carved in your soul. And you're going to have to stand there and watch your dream as it takes its first baby steps. This is not an experience for people who crave comfort.

Writer Raymond Carver likened publishing his stories to riding at night in the backseat of a driverless car with no lights on. And yet such vulnerability can be a valuable part of the creative process. My old acting teacher, Allen Schorr, insisted that serious doubt is actually a very good sign, a signal that you're being completely honest and vulnerable in your work. Mark Twain said of *The Adventures of Huckleberry Finn*, "I like it only tolerably well . . . and may possibly pigeonhole or burn the manuscript when it is done." As for me, I only know that I got through the first novel I published by convincing myself no one would ever read it. I was sure that this was yet another little piece of my own personal weirdness that no one would ever have to sit through. And yet a major publisher actually bought it.

Daring to be heard, then, is simple. It's recognizing your cascades of self-doubt for what they are: a whole lot of hot air you've cooked up for absolutely no good reason at all. Then it's mustering up the courage to trust yourself for five minutes anyway, because maybe you really do have something important to say. And ultimately, it's having one of those defining little epiphanies and saying, "What the hell." Daring to be heard means recognizing that if you put your voice out there, all you're going to get back is a yes or a no. The days of public stoning are long over; so is being pilloried. In fact, a large part of the world won't even be paying attention, no matter how loudly you scream.

Daring to be heard, ultimately, is something great you do for yourself. It's giving your poor, withered soul some fresh air and sunshine. Daring to be heard means stretching out languorously in the luxury of a strong opinion or basking in the joy of planning an endeavor you've always wanted to start. No matter what your medium, the dream is yours and yours alone to realize in your own particular way. With the dream comes the chance to represent yourself in the world in a way that truly matters. Daring to be seen and heard becomes the chance for perfect freedom.

It becomes your chance to fly.

Try This . . .

Take a pad of paper and a large, fat Magic Marker (big, black, and permanent works wonderfully well). Unplug the phone, get family and roommates out of the house, and close your door. Then spend the next half hour gloriously scrawling out whatever opinion or idea or invective you've wanted to hurl in your life but didn't. Scribble it all out on that pad, as fast and furiously as you can. Don't stop. Don't judge. Don't even think. Just spew. If you run out of paper, get more! Just keep on going until you've said everything you had to say. If you find yourself crying, yelling, and pounding the pillows on your bed, all the better.

I find this exercise to be particularly useful after stressful family visits or bad days at work.

How to Get the Fire in Your Belly

irst of all, the title of this chapter is deceptive. There really is no "way" to get the fire in your belly about anything, much less the arduous pursuit of a vision. The fire is born through solitary activity requiring not only balls-to-the-wall honesty and extreme patience but the willingness to chip away for years at work that the world at large may never even see.

Passion is an elusive beast, and it appears to land on certain people almost whimsically, through some act of God. This would explain how a fifty-five-year-old New York City doorman I once read about in the *New York Times* was able to put himself through law school at night (a task that included an average of four hours of sleep a night for six years) while the rest of his buddies were content to open doors for other people for the rest of their lives.

The difference between him and the other doormen was not the dream, for you can be sure he wasn't the only guy opening doors for executives with expensive suits and heavy briefcases and fantasizing about what their lives were like. The difference was that this doorman chose to act. Not only did he choose to act, he chose to do it *no matter what*. The fact that he had to live on next to nothing for years while he paid for his education didn't matter. The fact that he studied until one o'clock every morning and then got up at five for work didn't matter. The fact that he was the only person in his class with gray hair and middle-aged spread didn't matter. Even the fact that his career would be shortened by his age didn't matter. What mattered to him was one thing: the single-minded and absolute pursuit of his dream. He was going to be a lawyer, *no matter what.*

Not surprisingly, after sending out more than a thousand résumés, he was hired by an associate who was impressed by his tenacity and passion. "I may not get more than ten years from him," this new employer said, "but they're going to be ten excellent years."

What this story has to do with the getting of passion is everything. For passion isn't something one "gets" at all; it is something one merely allows. That doorman knew he wanted to be a lawyer, and so he stepped out of the way and let his desires take over, no matter how much work that might entail. He didn't doubt, he didn't avoid, he didn't fill the world with a carload of sputtering excuses, and he didn't sweat the details. He merely let this wild, riderless horse take him on a fantastic ride toward the horizon while he simply surrendered. He listened, he heard, and he said yes. His willingness was truly stunning.

When I think about passion, I am also reminded of Filomena, a remarkable student I taught once in a continuing-ed class about personal essay writing. Filomena was severely disabled with a rare neuromuscular disease that had left her curled in a wheelchair, only able to write by typing with a stick held between her teeth. As life would have it, though, Filomena was the only student in the group of twenty who showed up every single week with her eight pages of essay material faithfully written. Furthermore, not only had she never written creatively before, but English was her third language. What I got from the other students was the usual passel of excuses; what I got from Filomena was the story of her life.

Perhaps it was that this young woman's life was about to end, or maybe it was because most of the time she was housebound in the care of immigrant parents who did not even speak English. Whatever the case, the class became Filomena's confessional, and the pages she wrote were nothing less than the naked truth about how it was to be dying in your mid-twenties. Each week, as we took turns reading her assignments to the class (Filomena's disease had severely affected her ability to speak), the feeling in the room palpably shifted. Here was grace, and we were fortunate enough to witness it. By the end of the semester, not only were the other students finally gaining enough courage to write, but several had started a support group with Filomena, to encourage her to finish her autobiography before her death.

For each person in the world who pursues her dream, there are hundreds, if not thousands, who only talk about it constantly. Or they think about it constantly. They make lists of great titles for books they could write or accumulate impressive amounts of sheet music. They stand around at cocktail parties regaling whoever will listen about an idea they have for the next great sweeping trend. Or they are perennial students who see themselves as having to study well into the next century before they can ever "fully know their craft." Every one of these people likely has a small, fitfully started, precious piece of work stashed deep in a corner of a closet.

For such people, that corner holds an abandoned beginning, evidence of a wonderful moment when their head and heart filled to a point they could no longer stand and they had to sit down and work. Ideas poured out of them, thoughts congealed wondrously, everything made fantastic sense, and like the Darling children under the influence of Tinkerbell's magical pixie dust, suddenly they could fly.

The next morning, however, flush with the false impression that creating would always be so easy, free, and liberating, they expected another miracle. Yet the creative process does not always deliver miracles on cue. They might have been forced to sit and think for a while, and so they might have gotten frustrated. They might have sketched out a few ideas they hated, erased them, and drawn up an entire page of ideas they also hated. Next, the phone rang, and they avoided their project for a good half hour. When they finally looked at what they'd accomplished that night, they had little more than one flimsy page of mediocre work.

Proof! screamed a voice out of nowhere. *That's PROOF! This dream business is totally out of control. What do you think—you're Donald Trump or something?* Back to good old comfortable resignation. Back to hanging out. Back to the tube and a Bud. In other words, back to reality.

The truth is, if you persist into a third day, a fourth day, and a hundredth day, that precious fledgling piece of work might be nurtured into something great. The creative process is not computer software that provides all the answers at the click of a mouse. Rather, it is a sensitive beast who comes to sit by your side and befriend you only after you've stroked and fed it every day for a good while. This beast demands your care and nurturing, it wants to build up your trust, and it craves your love, because in truth, that beast is only you.

Because they cannot give themselves that critical extra bit of love, people don't create. They lie terribly to themselves, insisting they can't do it, deciding that they haven't got anything worthwhile to say, pretending that their dreams don't matter. But their dreams do matter. Every unpursued dream leaves the world a tiny bit paler and life a little less rich. Every untold story means one fewer lesson passed on to someone else. Every abandoned idea means one more strike against hope.

A fire in the belly is a champion for the ridiculous. It keeps you going day after day, stroke after stroke, step after step. You have to keep going in order to honor yourself. The fire gives you the courage to fly in the face of a world that values products more than people and the bottom line more than somebody's tender dreams.

The fire in your belly comes only when you're willing to

work at your dream for no good reason. You don't pursue the dream because you'll be famous someday, because the work is going to make you rich, or because it will make for better cocktail banter. You design, teach, invent, or serve because this is what you are meant to do.

Getting the fire in the belly means simply surrendering to the truth.

Try This . . .

You have three minutes. Make a list of everything that you are truly passionate about. Include anything you can think of, from eating imported chocolate to having great sex to fly-fishing on the Snake River. Then think about what characterizes those experiences. Do you go into a trance and lose track of time? Does the experience leave you feeling like a better, stronger person? How often do you let these passions into your life? Are there any you need to pursue now?

Keep this list and return to it whenever you feel the need to stoke your fire.

Can It Really Be So Simple?

 would like to suggest something radical.

What if that movie you've always wanted to make, the one you've spent hours silently directing as you chugged home from work on the train, the one you've often fantasized about devoting entire vacations to but still haven't written a word of, the one you just *know* Jodie Foster would agree to star in, were already made. What if the movie were sitting out there in hyperspace, fully formed, just waiting for you to calm down enough to sit down, listen up, and start typing. What would you think?

Initially, you would probably think I am nuts. And yet I say it is entirely possible.

Inspiration is delightfully unexplainable. The closest any of us can come to naming its source is to say we honestly have no idea. Yet whenever you get yourself to sit down for a moment and actually listen, something is usually right there in front of you, waiting to be expressed. Of course, the tricky part isn't expressing, it's listening.

Often in the past, when I sat down to do something creative, I would hear an absolute cacophony of marching orders:

Okay, smarty pants—think of something. You're not thinking of anything. . . . What's the matter, stupid? . . . Don't use THAT idea. That's as old as the hills. Who wants to hear about that? Come up with SOMETHING BETTER . . . NOW. . . . See? (sigh) . . . Pitiful.

It was like trying to compose a symphony in the middle of a jackhammering construction site. So no wonder it takes people years to get to the point where they actually sit down and start something.

Meditation helps significantly to quell these critical voices (and we'll talk about that in a later chapter; see "How to Pray and Work at the Same Time"). But you make the single biggest inroad when you learn to accept the fact that those snarling pit bulls in your head will always be there, on the attack, ready to destroy whatever fragile endeavor you set out to pursue. They will continue to insist that what you have designed, planned, or invented isn't really exactly right.

They will demand that the project be redone hundreds of times, until your precious creation is as limp and chewed over as a dead dishrag. And they will have you convinced that nothing you do, *nothing*, will ever amount to a hill of beans in this world. And it won't . . . if you listen to them.

First, you have to know these voices for what they are—a mere smoke screen, set up to distract you. A meaningless test, as it were. Then you must simply allow the voices to do their thing and understand that their presence is an integral part of your creative process. Undoubtedly, the voices will blabber on for a time, while you valiantly hang in there, trying to hear the feeble cries of creativity behind all the fracas. Over time, though, the pit bulls will subside. Their protests will gradually grow shorter and shorter, as the voice of your work becomes louder, and you will begin, ever so slowly, to see the value of your undertaking.

So eventually, when you listen, you will hear more and more input that is productive. And while you may be deeply suspicious that creativity could be so simple, you will begin having more fun, and so you'll go with it. Fairly soon, you will be able to sit down and actually tune out the pit bulls and tune in to the creativity channel directly. And so, finally, you can begin to listen in earnest.

By listening selectively, you will tap into that greatest of all possible teachers: your instinct. Although you may study technique, have the help of big-time professors and consultants, and get lots of pointers on how to use your tools, nine-tenths of your creative work still comes directly from your gut. So when you quiet your mind and concentrate hard enough, the guidance is usually there, turning your hand this way and that, moving you to blend unexpected colors. It takes you down alleyway after alleyway and into the offices of people you'd never expect to meet. It catapults you into entirely unexpected landscapes again and again and again. And all because you've simply learned how to listen.

At such times this process can feel almost as if you were entering a trance. For when you are truly engaged in any creative act, day-to-day, mundane thoughts melt away as you begin to work. A more powerful force takes over. The simple expression of the soul pours through mind and body as time disappears. Work is completely absorbing. Then you happen to look up and notice that three hours have passed, and what you've created is pretty damn great. And that's when you know bliss.

Of course, mistakes are an important part of the process as well. God knows, I've gotten it wrong more often than right. Yet the beautiful thing is that those mistakes are usually guided, too. They're simply part of the creative journey called "my own line of cosmetics" or "some recipes that will eventually be a cookbook." If you surrender to the process fully, the mistakes simply become part of the work, prompting you to retackle whatever went wrong until eventually, after extensive reworkings, you hit it dead-on.

I had my own experience of surrendering to the process the first time I ever led a How Much Joy Can You Stand? workshop. I had the idea of giving each participant an unusual creative material—a box of rubber bands, a roll of tinfoil, a bar of soap—and then giving them forty-five minutes to create something with it. The pit bulls didn't like this, of course, and swarmed all over my idea protesting and sputtering. Still, I persisted and handed out all the materials. At the appointed hour my group returned, and every one of them had something unique and beautiful in hand, except for Sari, a journalist who'd been suffering from paralyzing writer's block. *See!* snarled my pit bulls, as I saw the untouched bar of Ivory Soap in her hand. *Just what we thought.... This exercise is for the birds!*

After the entire group had presented their work—all to much applause, laughter, and general celebration—Sari got up and hesitantly walked to front of the room with her bar of soap still in its wrapper. She stood there silently for a moment while I began to roil in self-doubt. Then, to make matters worse, Sari began to cry. Finally, she cleared her throat and spoke: "I can't believe you gave me the Ivory Soap," she explained, "because when I was little, my grandmother and I used to make up commercials about it. My grandmother always used to say to me, 'Remember, Sari, we are the creative ones in the family. Never be afraid to use your imagination.' " Sari paused and swallowed. "Now I remember," she said, "why I have to write."

By this time I was crying, too, of course, as was the rest of the group. And what I finally understood at that moment, in the deepest part of my soul, was that this whole process was guided and all I had to do was trust.

If you are patient enough, and work and work at your dream, always striving to be utterly faithful to your voice and your path, you will eventually succeed. For you will have brought into being that elusive image you've been carrying around in your head for far too long. You will have given birth to a great, creative wonder and can now reap the joys of parenthood.

It really *is* this simple: the work is out there, waiting for us to heed its call and fall under its spell. Conveying your dream requires only this: your listening heart, give or take nothing.

Try This ♦ ♦ ♦

If one must have a head full of snarling pit bulls, one might as well schedule them. Pick a time each day when you plan to do your work, and allot the first fifteen minutes strictly to the pit bulls. In other words, schedule your screaming self-doubt right into your work session. Give them lots of room to really raise hell, and try to sit back and observe while they do. You might even write down a few of their more choice objections. Then, once these voices of doubt have had their rant for the day, they should go away and mind their own business, leaving you free to get busy.

The End of Struggle

Somewhere, a long time ago, someone started a rumor that art and writing and any work isn't truly great unless it has been suffered over copiously. Writers should drink heavily and gnash their teeth when they write. Ballerinas should bleed. Entrepreneurs should spend every last penny they own and then work like hell while digging themselves deeper into debt. The thought is that for creativity to be valid, it has to be soaked in fresh struggle.

Balderdash.

What makes a ballet wonderful or a business take off is the simple outpouring of the creator's soul. And if that person is truly doing his job, that process will involve an immense amount of effort but not a whit of struggle. Effort is the clear-minded application of one's abilities, whereas struggle is nothing more than a whole lot of unnecessary lather.

It's like this: You decide to open a great little Italian restaurant. You've got your chef lined up, your investors loosely in mind, and you've done the business specs and found that there's a legitimate need in a certain part of town for decent Italian. You've even gone to the extra lengths of getting a few of the old family recipes from your cousin in Naples and a hot tip on where to buy superb extra-virgin olive oil in bulk. So you're off. Every day after your regular job, you start to put in a little time on the restaurant.

Within a few months two investors are on board, and though you still need a third, you begin to look at rental properties and talk to designers. Day one, day two, day three, day seventy-five pass. You continue to make progress, albeit slowly. Some days go spectacularly; others don't.

Just when you find the fabulous little storefront of your dreams, with exposed brick walls and an incredible kitchen, one of your investors drops out, claiming he's overextended. But then another backer miraculously shows up a week later, and she's got a cousin at the Liquor Control Board. You sweat, plan, crunch numbers, and dream. You keep finding recipes and talking to your chef. You're on the verge of signing a lease when disaster strikes again: your other original investor quits, citing tax problems.

About this time you have lunch with a friend. He asks you how it's going, and you say, "Fine, thanks. It's harder than I thought it would be, but I'm getting there." He asks, "How long until you open?" You answer honestly, "Six months, a year. Who knows? I just lost an investor." A worried look passes across your friend's face, and you can feel that quiet reserve of strength suddenly becoming marshmallowlike in your gut.

Enter Struggle.

"Bummer," he says with concern. "Yeah, I know," you sigh, as you stare at your lunch. Other restaurants seem to spring up overnight and are started by people with money to burn—no one is more aware of that than you. Silently, you begin to wonder whether maybe this restaurant thing isn't such a great idea to begin with.

At this point you have a choice: You can look at your progress as lousy and something to obsess about, or you can see it as part of a larger process over which you have little or no control. You can choose to struggle, or you can simply forge ahead and open the restaurant.

If you are a struggler, you will begin to brood over whether this project is "really happening" or not. In very little time, your mind will become a cluttered mess of conflicting messages with emergency alarms going off all over the place, as the once clear and beautiful voice of your project slowly fades away, unable to be heard.

You may stop pursuing the dream then, until you realize that this work is a unique creation, unlike any other one you or anyone else has ever attempted, and so it may take a little longer. In fact, your dream may take a *lot* longer. Yet that's no reason to quit. If anything, it's the reason you need to get right back to work.

The point is this: The work, in and of itself, does not demand struggle. Your dream demands discipline, honesty, patience, enormous effort, and a fair amount of heart. It demands that you give of yourself or not even bother. And it demands that you love life and people enough that you wish to give back the gift you were given. That is all the work requires.

Struggle, on the other hand, is something people bring to the party—one of those quotidian, human responses, like the urge to tear open someone else's pile of birthday presents. And ultimately, struggle is really nothing more than a complaint, a way of saying, "I don't want to work this hard. Therefore, let me make a major drama out of it and maybe I won't have to." Basically, struggle is your ego, having its nasty little way.

And actually, when you are truly connected to what you should be doing, struggle is the farthest thing from your mind. All you really want to accomplish is that task set before you, and you'll do pretty much anything to make it happen. Look at Gun and Tom Denhart, who started the children's clothing company Hanna Andersson in their living room. The Denharts' mission was to re-create the high-quality, 100 percent cotton children's clothing from Gun's native Sweden for American consumers. They were so dedicated to communicating the quality of their fabric that they personally cut and glued one-inch squares of the material into seventy-five thousand catalogs themselves. For the Denharts, this was just another labor of love, a natural part of building a business that only eleven years later earned $50 million in revenues.

Struggle is the refuge of people who cannot face their own brilliance—people who, for whatever reason, must stay hidden away at all costs. They are the wanna-bes who sign up for classes diligently but stop coming halfway through. They're the dabblers who start a million projects but never finish any of them. Or they're people who simply refuse to stick with anything they care about and suffer from anorexia of the spirit, which they complain about loudly in an attempt to appease their wounded hearts. Just like the rest of us, these people sorely wish their work to be loved, so much that they can't even show it to the world.

Yet at the same time, struggle should not be confused with the need to take a break. Sometimes, after you've patented sixteen inventions in a row, it might be appropriate to take a few months or even a year off. Still, there is no need for struggle. You can simply realize that the work may not be flowing for a reason—sheer and simple exhaustion. And then you can begin the process of refueling, observing, and allowing yourself plenty of unstructured time to do nothing more than daydream and wonder, which, in turn, becomes a different sort of creative act.

There is so much sweetness to be found in the disciplined doing of your work. It is an undramatic, everyday sort of life, but so rich and full of pleasure that after a time you cannot *not* do it. What is there for you is simply the uncovering of yourself, an inch at a time—the finer, better part of you that knows no limits and wishes only to share its own intrinsic genius. This is the part of you that knows the joke about struggle.

It is the strugglers who work hard at struggling; it is the rest of us who work hard at our work.

Try This . . .

Take a pad of paper and at the top write "Good Reasons Why Not." Then list every single excuse you've used to avoid pursuing your dream. Make sure it's an exhaustive list. Really think about it; take a few days to be certain it's complete. Then put the list away for at least one week.

Schedule a time (and write it in your book) when you will look at this list again. Make sure that you will have no distractions or interruptions when the appointed hour arrives. Sit down with your list and go through each excuse. Then, with every ounce of honesty you've got, cross out every single excuse that you know in your heart is bogus. Be relentless. The amount of honesty you bring to this step will determine the exercise's effectiveness.

What you will be left with are a handful of items on the list that are your karmic lot in life. If you want to pursue this dream, you'll simply have to deal with them.

On the other hand, you will finally understand that you do, indeed, create your own destiny.

Vulnerability for the Faint of Heart

am a person who has never been cool. Although I devoted about three-quarters of my life to the pursuit of cool, it just never gelled. I was always too tall, too awkward, an emotional slob, and worst of all, I was constantly being told that my speaking voice sounded exactly like Miss Jane Hathaway's on *The Beverly Hillbillies*. I couldn't imagine a less cool person to be compared to.

Somewhere in the vicinity of thirty, I gave up the pursuit of cool. What prompted this was that I finally walked away from a long, fairly tortured relationship. The minute I dredged up enough courage to leave, my entire existence changed. Suddenly my life went from being about the pursuit of cool to being about the pursuit of nothing. It was as if

I had been stripped clean. After all the tears and regrets, all I was left with was my plain, old, unglamorous self.

So every night after I came home from my job writing toothpaste commercials for a big ad agency, I'd take out a pen and a notebook, and I'd sit on the couch and wait. Slowly the voice of my inner self—that tender, emotional, wiser, more real other person—would begin to express herself, and I'd find myself making notes. As if by magic, the changes I was going through found their way into words, and these words began to be song lyrics.

Though I'd always sung in an on-again, off-again way, I'd never written a song in my life. Yet now I found myself hearing quasi melodies and rhythms; verses somehow snapped neatly into place. Without knowing how, why, or even what, exactly, was happening, I became a songwriter. And what was driving those songs was an entire aspect of myself I'd always longed to express but never had.

Eventually, I began to feel the tiniest urge to do something with the stack of songs on my desk. But what? Obviously, I wasn't a *real* songwriter; I was only someone who'd written a few songs that were probably not only terrible but completely ridiculous. At least that's what my thinking process told me. Still, the small voice within kept on demanding that I take them out into the world. But how? I didn't have melodies for them, so what was I supposed to do? Call up ASCAP and plead my case? Stand on the street with a sign saying SONGWRITING PARTNER WANTED? I wasn't about to do something serious and official like run an ad. I ended up doing the only thing I could think of: I went to a psychic.

The psychic was amazingly straightforward. "What are all these songs, and why are you hiding them?" she demanded. She went on to describe a collaborator for me in detail—a tall jazz pianist and composer who was a friend of someone I knew. We would have an uncommonly good vocal blend if we chose to sing together, she said. Three weeks later, I was sitting in the apartment of a tall jazz pianist and composer introduced to me by a friend. This woman's understanding of my lyrics was so full and precise, and her music for them so achingly beautiful, that the only thing I could do when I heard them was cry.

There I was—the tall, skinny, vulnerable me—written out in chords that expressed something deep and essential I'd always wanted to say. There was the voice I'd been shutting up for all these years, finally given some room to breathe. Here was an entirely new and rich way to bring myself forth in the world. I was amazed, moved, and suddenly filled with passion. My scribblings really were songs after all—and not only that, they were good! Getting the songs out there suddenly became the most important thing in the world to me. It was as if, for the first time, I felt myself to be as completely and fully alive as God intended.

Carey & Falter, the act that our songs turned into, never played Carnegie Hall but did play New York's small, backroom cabarets for a wonderful three-year run. We developed a small following of core devotees who never missed a show. We lost money and worked our hearts out, practicing between three and four hours every night after our jobs. We infuriated our bosses, confounded our boyfriends, and worried our parents, but we couldn't have cared less. For two restless women in their thirties, this undertaking became an act of pure and wonderful defiance, a thousand defining moments squeezed into one forty-five-minute cabaret act. And what this had to do with vulnerability was everything.

In our own minds, we were flying high without a net. And although neither of us had ever done anything like this, we operated with a weird sort of confidence—the same confidence children display when they learn how to ski: They don't think or analyze. They just point the skis down the hill and go, usually in a straight line. So it was with our act. Whenever a question came up, we'd just look at each other and operate on instinct. We were completely and totally in what the Zen Buddhists call "beginner's mind." Because we didn't realize how little we actually knew about creating a cabaret act, we acted with a marvelous, creative certainty that came entirely from our guts.

Furthermore, we were completely passionate about our work and driven by the delicious freedom of expressing our true selves for a change. There was joy to be found in even the most mundane technical rehearsals and midnight stamp-licking sessions. We'd already done the hard part, coming out of our own particular closets, so now the rest of our work was painted with the pure and simple happiness of doing what we were truly meant to do.

What we learned was the power of our voices—not our singing voices (which did, in fact, blend uncommonly well) but our *voices*. Our presence. Our essences. We discovered that we had weight in the world and that the simple sharing of ourselves, our true selves, was in and of itself quite moving.

When author Frank McCourt won the Pulitzer Prize for *Angela's Ashes*, he told the *New York Times*, "I learned the significance of my own insignificant life." It is a shock when you realize the value your own inner secrets hold for others. Yet it is true. The public wants to be moved, delighted, and struck by your bravery. They want to see you succeed, and they crave your initiative. If you are an artist, people long for the depth of your expression; if you are a businessperson, they hope to be inspired by your vision and creativity. And no, the public doesn't want the canned version of a good idea; they want *your* good idea, the one that can only come from your own particular set of DNA.

When you think about the great success stories through history, every one of them came about because people were dreamy enough to believe that they could actually do something in their own weird way. Consider Benjamin Franklin, Abraham Lincoln, Amelia Earhart, and Bill Gates. Lincoln did not free the slaves because it was the easy thing to do, nor did Gates start Microsoft on a whim. Franklin did not run around in a rainstorm hoping to attract lightning for kicks. And Amelia Earhart didn't fly the Atlantic because she was looking for publicity. These people did these things because the small, still voice insisted they must.

These people embraced their own vision, saw the perils, and leaped anyway. They didn't sit around licking their wounds and guarding their most intimate feelings. They probably didn't even consider their feelings, or they never would have leaped at all. And they certainly didn't fret over outcomes like being electrocuted or starting a war. Being truly vulnerable means having uncomfortable feelings, facing risks, and barreling ahead anyway. Vulnerability means plunging headfirst into the fear, the uncertainty, and the great stew of the unknown for no good reason other than that it's what you have to do. Vulnerability means allowing yourself to take on the difficult and rise to the occasion, not because you ought to or because of some guarantee that everything will turn out okay. You confront these challenges simply because you must.

And here is the wonderful payoff you receive in return: the secret of real vulnerability is that it becomes your greatest source of strength.

Once you're out there in the thick of it, the tender part of you that so feared public excoriation will rise up bigger, better, and stronger, ready to do anything to defend the honor of your endeavor. This is all the support and brilliance you will ever need—unbelievable fortitude, determination, and bravery that seem to come from nowhere. And yet they will come from you, a natural and powerful aspect of yourself that has always been there, even if previously asleep. As with anything, your vulnerability strengthens with use, melding into your core beliefs about yourself and feeding your reserves. And slowly the walls of steel behind it will reveal themselves—walls of steel you probably never even knew you had.

At adventure programs all over the country, people pay large sums of money just so they can tap into these reserves while hanging upside down off a belay line forty feet above the ground. Such reserves are real and present in every one of us, yet the only way to reach them is straight through your tenderest parts.

It is not until the beast is unleashed that it can prove its speed, and so it is with the power of your dreams. It is not until you take on risk that you will find out what you are truly made of. And believe me, you're made of far more than you think.

In your vulnerability lies not humiliating goofiness but that divine thread that links us all together. In your vulnerability also lies your power. Simply put, it is where all dreams truly begin.

Try This . . .

Find some old photographs of yourself, preferably from your most awkward, zit-riddled teenage years or even earlier, when you were still a wild, free little being, full of thoughts and feelings.

Do not choose pictures in which you're smiling politely for the camera. Choose the ones where the camera caught you unguarded and exposed. Choose photographs that remind you of a time and place that mattered deeply to you, an experience that can still stir your emotions when you look at the pictures.

For maximum effect, make oversize copies of the images. Then hang these pictures in the place where you do the work of your dreams.

Where to Look for Inspiration

nspiration is everywhere. Most of the time, though, we can't see it. And it isn't even that we don't look; rather, we don't know how to look.

We are living in an era that lacks gratitude. Humor is ironic; disillusionment is the status quo. To wander outside and spend a moment enjoying how softly the snow outlines a sapling is considered a pretty pointless, nerdy thing to do. To be hip, you must be fast, furious, and powered up by the latest technology, whether it be antidepressants or computer modems. There is no time for reflection, so don't even bother. "What's it going to get you?" goes the popular thinking.

No small part of our dilemma comes from our addiction to things—sneakers that flash, toys that beep, a ceaseless parade of gadgets that all seem designed to counteract each other. These are short-lived technologies, all of which are around to keep us entertained, distracted, totally comfy, and ultimately utterly bored. Like television, new technologies provide us with too much stuff to contemplate, and so we contemplate nothing. We walk outside to get somewhere, instead of simply to take a walk.

Yet it is in such simplicity that ideas are born. I used to live in New York City precisely because I could step out my door and be bombarded with sensations, feelings, spectacles, and insights. Once, someone left an old, upright piano in front of the empty lot across the street from our apartment. In the space of one short day, I saw someone doing tai chi next to it in the rain, a very large man doing a Jelly Roll Morton impression for his laughing wife, and a very somber little girl in a Christian Dior coat playing "My Country, 'Tis of Thee." A week later someone came along and smashed the piano into smithereens. The following afternoon the scrap-metal man came and cut off all the strings, and his friend the scrap-lumber man took the wood. It was the life and death of an abandoned piano, in three short acts. I never could have written it so perfectly if I'd tried.

There are tremendous riches around us all the time, but we must tune ourselves in to see them. Imagine how it is when you live near a mountain. Every time you see it, it seems completely different. Sometimes the mountain is blazing gold, burnished by a brilliant sunset. Other times it is a forbidding block of black on the horizon, and it appears truly menacing. Still other times the mountain can be the palest lavender, baby pink, or soft gray after a snow; sometimes it disappears altogether in a storm. Your view of the mountain is continuously changing, and you can never predict what it will look like next. From this perspective, the view out your window becomes even better than television for pure, spontaneous entertainment.

When I lived in New York, I had the opportunity to know the artist who pioneered white-on-white, minimalist painting. One evening I asked this man, whose one-man shows include New York's Museum of Modern Art, how he began, and he told me he started out as a guard in the Museum of Modern Art. His real goal at the time was to be a jazz musician, but standing there, day after day, looking at the work on the walls began to get under his skin. Then he found that he was drawn to the materials in an art store window he passed every day on the way to work. So pretty soon he took some paint home and began to experiment.

When you look at his work today, this all makes perfect sense, for what he does in so much of his painting is make us question the way a piece hangs on the wall or what its basic components are made of or even why it exists. His work truly is about art as an idea—an idea you might have plenty of time to consider when standing guard in a great museum hour after hour after hour. For me this is an ultimate example of finding your joy in your everyday surroundings.

The world around us, whether it's the haphazard poetry of city street life or the scattering of autumn leaves in a mountain forest, is the single greatest creative resource we have. The workings of this world are seemingly random, yet their interplay is fantastically complex and perfect. Whether you believe in God or not, you can't help but find inspiration in the chaos of life. So it is here—in plain, old, boring "everyday" reality—that the best ideas begin. As the old chestnut goes, you've got to use what you know.

To do this, then, begins with gratitude. You've got to perceive the life that unfolds around you as the rich source of information that it is. You've got to look at the perfect upheavals, coincidences, and crises of your life and the lives of those around you as what they really are—truly miraculous. You have to cut the stifling backchat about "my painfully boring existence" and begin to plumb it for raw material. For this is where you will find the solutions to a million different creative problems and possibilities. You will find a treasure trove of connections and vast networks of supporters. You will uncover stories that have to be told and opportunities that must be seized. Such rich material will not be far away and unreachable but literally right in front of you.

All that has to be added is your particular take on all this raw material. In fact, this is what makes any creative work great—the presence of you in the act of creation. It was Beethoven's massive fury with his deafness that made his Ninth Symphony the masterpiece that it is. Edward Hopper was unafraid to convey the isolation in his own life, as well as in everything around him, which he painted with unflinching dedication. Carolyn McCarthy, who was a licensed practical nurse until her husband and son were shot on the Long Island Rail Road, was unafraid to fight for gun-control laws, which landed her in the House of Representatives. Each of these people was committed to one thing: giving us his or her take on the world, as honestly and fully as possible. And that is why their work endures and succeeds, and continues to make an enormous difference today.

The world really does want to know what you think. All you have to do is tell the truth—your truth—in all its glory. If you see unfairness and injustice, then that is what you must express. If you see rage dissolve into sweet forgiveness, then that must be your message. If you see a better way to make a mousetrap, then you must make it. Whatever it is that speaks to you must be passed on to others. That is your responsibility as a member of society.

As Bruce Springsteen once said, "If you're an artist, you try to keep an ear to the ground and an ear to your heart." Well, the same can be said for all of us. Here is where you will find true inspiration.

Try This . . .

Make these lists:

> Ten Things I Love about My Life
> Ten Things That Are Uniquely "Me"
> Ten Things I Know That I'd Like to Share
> Ten Things I Could Fix or Change in the World

If You're Looking for Something Else to Do . . .

Use a camera (a disposable one will do) and begin to shoot pictures of people, places, and events that are evocative for

you. These should be places you'd like to keep a little piece of because they move you. Have the film developed and place the photographs in an album or a box, anyplace where you can visit them frequently and have your juices stirred a bit. When you're feeling uninspired and your dream seems dead in the water, take a look at your pictures.

The Luxury of Not Knowing Your Dream

ome of you may not know yet what your dream is. You may sit silently while your friends go on at length about their plans to start a heli-skiing company in the Andes. You may change the subject when asked directly about your life plans. And you may brood about the fact that you're just not finding "that thing" and be paralyzed by not knowing what you want.

Well I say take heart if you don't know what your dream is yet; you are actually in rich, fertile territory. Furthermore, you have less of a problem than you think you do.

We live in a culture of doers—people with big plans and ambitions, and 401(k)s set up to feed every minute of those dreams. So woe be to those who can't get right out there and start pushing their own personal agenda. And herein lies the problem. We've been conditioned to think that it's *bad* when we do not know what our dreams are and that we're *wrong* not to be hard at work already. We think that if we don't know exactly what we want to do in life, we're doomed to failure. A thick overlay of shame obscures the simple truth that, for better or for worse, we just don't know what we want to do yet.

If we can drop the histrionics and self-criticism for a while and allow ourselves to explore, we can indeed locate those dreams. And we might even have some fun in the process.

Too often we get lulled into thinking that there is only one Perfect Dream out there with our name on it, and no other one will do. Then our minds gnaw away at the possibility that if we do happen to tease out a dream, it's not that perfect one but some half-baked substitute. We assume we're so hopelessly flawed, we can't even get our dream right. And we assume that the Perfect Dream is like a whimsical stroke of fortune that may or may not choose to land in our laps. We figure that the Perfect Dream will just find us magically, that we'll wake up one day with a sudden, unexplainable urge to start a B&B in Tahiti or study rocket science with the mission-control guys at NASA. We forget that we are actually steering the ship.

In truth, there is no Perfect Dream. There are only impulses—some that lead to major discoveries and successes, others that lead to nothing, and still others that may only become important later in life. Furthermore, we are the ones who choose to act on those impulses and craft dreams from them. To do that, you have to give yourself permission to hear those impulses in the first place. Then you have to give yourself the freedom to explore them with an open heart.

I have learned a lot about this from my friend Beverly. Beverly appeared in our very small town in upstate New York on a Saturday in December, having just driven in from Portland, Oregon. She had quit her job as an architect, given up her apartment, left her boyfriend behind, and driven across the country to spend the winter in a small, rented house among strangers in the middle of nowhere. All she had was enough savings to last until spring and some vague plans about doing something with paper or maybe puppetry.

I kept pestering Bev about exactly what she was doing all day. "How are the puppets coming?" I'd ask hopefully. "Oh, I'm not really doing puppets," she'd say. Or she'd look up at me blankly and then say, "I'm actually fooling around with fabric." After a while it became clear that Bev didn't really know what she was doing and that she was totally comfortable with that fact. The question was, Could *I* be totally comfortable with that fact?

Bev was doing something radical. As she put it, she was giving herself "the gift of having the freedom to wonder." Unlike most of us, Bev had survived a life-threatening form of cancer at age nineteen. The experience neatly prioritized life for her, so that when the call came to get out there and explore for a while, she was able to muster up the guts to leave her career behind and do it.

Bev has since starred in a play, started a gallery, created art installations with paper sculpture and natural materials, and traveled down a number of creative roads to pursue exactly what that thing is that she is looking for. Glasswork calls to her. Puppetry still does, too, and maybe even writing. To keep the quest going, she has taken on several different part-time jobs to support herself. She continues to live her dream just by having the willingness to try anything and everything that interests her. As Beverly puts it, these days she is living life as "the real me."

What I love about this story is the total permission that Beverly gave herself. She managed to pry herself loose from the clutches of others' screaming doubts. She managed to change her life in the face of all of her friends' demanding to know why—*why why why!!!*—was she doing something so open-ended, vague, and downright strange.

If we feel stuck without a dream, the question we must ask ourselves is, What are we not letting ourselves explore? And why won't we let ourselves explore it? What is it about the adventure of trying new things that has us so frozen? Is it that we're afraid we won't be brilliant? Or that we're afraid we *will* be brilliant? Are we worried that if we choose a dream, it won't be the "right" one? Or are we afraid of all those questioning voices around us that demand updates, specifics, and status reports? Do we believe our own harsh critiques and feel we must look "together," polished, and professional all the time? Or can we just be authentic and look like the messy explorers that we are for a while?

To find your dream, you must begin the search, regardless of where it will take you or how it will strike anyone else. You don't necessarily have to move across the country, nor do you have to quit your job. But you must begin to probe and explore, as Beverly did, for yourself and yourself alone. This is the true luxury of not knowing your dream: you begin stripped naked, with no expectations to meet, no mettle to prove, and no agendas to work from. And so you get to bask in the freshness of a new creative undertaking. And you get to feel how that project fits inside your own skin. If things work and your project ignites, then congratulations. If they don't, then you get to sit back and ponder what might be a better fit. And you get to try again.

Your pursuit is not necessarily to find the "dream" but to track down, step by step, that which feeds your soul and fills your heart. Your mission is to locate that very food you've been hungry for for so long. Once you have tasted even a small bite of it, you will become closer to your purpose on earth. And you will be nurturing yourself as God intended, which always brings a marvelous sense of fullness.

Permission is critical. Can you give yourself permission to fool around with some dreams and see what happens? Can you give yourself the chance to just try something . . . anything?

Can you give yourself the opportunity, as Beverly did, to live life as "the real you"?

Try This . . .

Create some time when you will be free from interruptions, and then sit back and answer these questions in a notebook:

□ When you were little, what did you want to be when you grew up? Try to write down as many different things as you can.

□ When you got out of school, what were you going to do "someday"?

□ While waiting in the ATM/checkout/gas station/bank line, occasionally your mind wanders to a great idea. What is it?

□ List five things that you really want to do before you die.

□ Whose permission are you waiting for? (Please be ruthlessly honest.)

The Boring Truth about Living Your Dream

A common misperception is that if you want to pursue your dream, you have to know exactly what you're doing all the time. Just look around at all those other, more successful people out there. They move through life with a crisp smile and an unwrinkled shirt, and when you ask them how their work is going, they always say the same thing: "Great!" It's actually kind of nauseating.

The truth is that none of us ever fully knows what we're doing. We make projections, lists, sketches, and plans, but things seldom go as we wish. Life is unfortunately unplannable; it's a fluid, random conglomeration of stuff, people, conditions, attitudes, needs, ideas, and circumstances that careens down the road like an overloaded wagon, ready to mow down anything in its path. You have to be ready to leap out of its way at any time, and with you comes your project, trailing intentions.

That's when you wind up by the side of the road, licking your wounds and cursing your decision to get involved in the whole thing in the first place. And then you remember how little you know. You think about how much all those other people seem to know. Finally, you remember how insecure this whole situation feels. And then . . . well, hell, why not just quit? Because, after all, if you want to make your dream work, you have to know what you're doing, right?

Absolutely, categorically, unequivocally wrong.

The very nature of creating something is that you almost *never* know what you're doing. Sure, you know some technical stuff, and you can put together a reasonable-looking product. You probably even know most of the steps involved. That's the easy part. But the real meat of the creative process, the inspiration that will set your project on a path of its own, is far more complex and elusive than that.

The popular belief is that inspiration "strikes" us, like a lightning bolt from the sky. Actually, it's the other way around. In reality, we strike inspiration much the way miners strike gold. By ceaselessly working, reworking and reworking the old territory, sooner or later we'll run into a little nugget of something wonderful, something better. The more we dig, the more we'll find, until—if we're very lucky and very persistent—we hit the mother lode. In reality, creative work is no different from swinging a pick. For every day of incredible divine intervention, there are probably ten spent sifting through the dirt.

This is the bad, boring news about going after what you want: just as with any job, there are many times when the work is unexceptional, difficult, and downright demanding. Yet these are also the days when you hunker down and keep on doing, because there simply isn't any other way to get where you're going. And herein lies the difference between average dreamers and people who go after their dreams. Successful people are willing to put up with the hard work because inside of it they find a joy like nothing else on earth. But average dreamers do not know this joy yet. Average dreamers find their joy in tangible rewards and get stopped when they realize that all that hard work may ultimately "be for nothing."

When you set out to undertake the work of your dreams, it is critical that you understand something: the reason so many people abandon their fledgling musical comedies, antique stores, and medical careers is that they expected it to be perpetually fun and interesting. "But this is my dream!" they think lustily. "It *has* to be fun." Then the minute the dream gets challenging, which it inevitably does, they quit. As if it had suddenly turned into the wrong dream or, more likely, as if there were something wrong with them—some weird defect all those other, more successful people never, ever suffer from. In fact, there isn't a thing in the world wrong with any of these people; it's just that they don't understand that pursuing your dream takes effort. *And just because it takes effort is no reason to abandon it.*

Each day spent digging puts you that much closer to the gold. And over time, if you keep at it, a curious thing happens: you begin to love sifting through the dirt. Some of your happiest moments can come during the seventh and eighth rewrites of a novel, when you're reinventing your character's peculiar walk for the umpteenth time. Happiness can be found in the small hours of perpetual sanding you've put in on a fine piece of furniture, when the wood grain begins to be as smooth as silk, and you begin to feel the rightness of what you set out to do. Finally, you can understand all those curious twists and turns you took and see the larger, greater picture that they form. And this is when all your doubts about your goal begin to blow away, like so much dust in the wind.

This is also the point when you come close to sensing the divine in your work. It does not arrive heralded by trumpet-blowing cherubim or even in a seamless blast of nonstop inspiration. Rather, the divine steals over you in the small, humdrum hours of your undertaking—during the checking, refining, editing, and polishing. The divine creeps in during yet another unexceptional night in your workroom, exactly when you least expect it.

As you climb inside the fantastic nautilus of your creation, you begin to understand why Zen masters spend entire lifetimes perfecting the tea ceremony. It is the sheer poetry of creating something from nothing and working on it until it is truly and absolutely right that ultimately keeps you coming back.

This is the magic that can only be born of hard work, and this, ultimately, is realizing your dream.

Try This . . .

Buy or create an oversize calendar for your dream, then hang it in the space where you do this work. Make a mark on each day that you actively work at your project. You can add qualifying remarks, describing how the work went, or any other notes pertinent to your process. You can go the kiddie-reward route and paste on Superman stickers or gold stars whenever you've pressed through a lot of resistance or achieved a breakthrough. Or you can cut out faces from magazines and catalogs and tack them on the calendar to describe the emotional climate of each day's work. You can write one-word descriptions or stick up summarizing poems or quotations on self-adhesive notes. The important thing is to put a little bit of yourself on that calendar each day that you work at your dream.

Your calendar should be a big, visual journal of the pursuit of your dream, a constant reminder that you are giving yourself an important gift and that you are, indeed, making progress.

How to Pray and Work
at the Same Time

By now, I can hear what you're thinking.

Sure, you make it sound easy . . . but this is NOT going to be easy.

. . . But I haven't GOT any intuition!

How am I supposed to know what's emotionally honest and what isn't?

But I really HAVEN'T got any time . . . REALLY!! HELP!!!!

First of all, remain calm. Or perhaps more accurately, try to get calm. Calmness is essential to this entire process—calmness plus trust in that key element, yourself.

I guarantee that your intuition is there—always has been, always will be. But you're not going to find it until you become still and learn how to listen. Then, and only then, will you begin to hear your inner guidance at all and tap into your own vast wellsprings of trust. For me this has been accomplished in a number of ways, the most important being through meditation.

By meditation I don't mean anything particularly mystical, nor do I mean a "right" way to meditate as opposed to a "wrong" way. What I mean is methodically stilling the voices in your head for even a few minutes every day—whether it's first thing in the morning, on the train while coming home from work, or whenever you can grab a regular bit of time. Meditation could mean silently counting to yourself as you rhythmically inhale and exhale. It could be finding a mantra, a meaningful little phrase or affirmation that you chant or repeat silently to yourself; or perhaps staring into a design or the flame from a candle. Meditation could also mean prayer, a walk in the woods, feeding the birds, or having a long, thoughtful run. You must experiment and play with the calming process until you find the combination or the method that is inherently right for you. What is important is the stillness you create and the regularity with which you do it.

Creativity Meditation

Here is a guided meditation you might consider recording on a tape recorder and playing to yourself. Be careful not to rush your reading of the meditation. Give yourself plenty of time to enjoy it.

Begin by sitting in a comfortable position with nothing in your lap. You can be seated in a chair or on the floor with a cushion or against the wall. Do not lie down. Close your eyes and begin to breathe rhythmically.

Relax your head and your shoulders. Feel the tension drain from your face. Relax your chin and your mouth, and your neck. Breathe. Relax your shoulders and the tops of your arms. Feel any tension melt away as you really let go. Breathe. Relax your chest and your arms and let the tension drip out of your fingertips. Relax your belly and give a sigh. Let your hips go and relax your buttocks farther into your seat. Let go completely.

Relax your legs, your upper thighs, your knees, your calves. Relax your feet and feel any tension you may still have leave completely now, pouring out of your feet into the floor. Let yourself sink into your seat completely and breathe.

Now imagine yourself in a beautiful, natural place . . . a beach, the bank of a river, or a glade in the woods—any place that is serene and special. See what is around you and take in all the details. Smell the smells and feel the breeze on your skin.

In the distance see a house. Begin to walk toward it. This is the house where you do the work of your dreams.

There is a path to the door of the house, and you take it. When you reach the door, open it and step inside. Notice the entryway around you and the front hall. There is a staircase, and you walk to it and begin to go upstairs. Notice what kind of house this is. Is it lavish and ornate? Simple and rustic? Does it seem like a place of possibility?

Walk up to the second floor and begin to go down the hall. There is a door at the end of the hall, and you open it and step inside. This is your studio, where you do the work of your dreams. Look around you and notice what materials are in your studio. Are you alone, or is there someone there to help you, like a spirit guide or someone you know?

Go to the place where you do your work and just sit with your work for a few minutes. Then ask your work what it wants you to do next.

Ask your work if there is anything it needs from you to further assist your progress.

Ask your work whom you should ask for help and where you will find them.

Ask your work for any other help you may need solving particular problems.

Ask your work what else it would like to tell you about your dream.

Ask your work what lessons it is meant to teach you right now.

Allow yourself to feel the full power of divine assistance in your dream and know that you are truly not alone in this process. Also know that you can go back to this place whenever you wish, for guidance, inspiration, or simply to create. This is the place where you do the work of your dreams, and it exists solely for you.

Feel free to stay as long as you wish. When you feel you have gained all the comfort and insight you need for the moment, prepare to leave. Thank anyone present in the room with you and thank your dream for its presence in your life. Put the room back in order as it was and leave it, closing the door behind you. Walk down the hallway, descend the stairs, and head outside.

Begin your walk along the path back to the beautiful spot where you began. Again, notice the sights and smells of this special place and everything about it that you love. Find your way back toward where you began.

When you are ready, move your hands and your feet gently and prepare to open your eyes. You might want to make a few notes about what you learned during your meditation. If things are not clear or obvious now, they will probably become so later.

As you meditate, life itself will become increasingly quiet. The nervousness of the everyday with all its attendant anxieties will take a new place, subordinate to the great reservoir of calm you are now building at its center. From calmness you will be able to tap into all those lovely creative juices; the more you plumb the depths of calmness, the greater this resource will become. Ultimately, you will find that the work itself becomes the meditation, putting you directly in touch with your spiritual connection almost every time. Like some character out of the Bible, you will be doing what you do, not because it brings home the bacon but because it has a higher, spiritual purpose. You will, indeed, be heeding your calling.

I had my own brush with this divinity when I was in my twenties. At the time, I was coming home from work every night and meditating for one or two hours in an attempt to soothe my work-weary spirits. After a good year of this, I experienced a miracle. I was on a vacation in Scandinavia with my husband when his back went out. He was lying on the floor of our hotel room on a tiny island in the middle of the Norwegian fjords, unable to get up. There were no doctors or hospitals, or even painkillers around, so I decided to give him a backrub, hoping this might do some good.

Ten minutes into the backrub, my hands began to get extraordinarily hot. Fifteen minutes into the backrub, I could actually feel the pain in Larry's back begin to dissolve and travel up my arms. I was operating completely intuitively, in a semitrance state I often fell into during my meditations. Somewhere around the twenty-five-minute mark, I sat back somewhat groggily, and Larry stood up, his back completely healed. "How did you do that?" he asked, and I honestly had no idea. All I could figure was that it had something to do with my desire to help him and my ability to tap into the great intuitive guidance I'd found through meditating.

Within a month I seemed to be surrounded by people who needed healing. Then came the day I got a call from a friend who had been stricken with a rash all over her body a few hours before an engagement party in her honor. I went to visit her, and as I laid my hands on her, I felt an overwhelming urge to speak. So I did, moved by my usually dead-on intuition. My words went on and on, but when I had the urge to say that her transition would be signaled by the death of a family pet, I suddenly stopped.

My friend opened her eyes and looked at me. "Go on," she demanded. "What else?"

"Well," I said, drawing in a breath, "the transition will be signaled by the death of a family pet."

Her eyes widened in amazement. "Our dog died this morning," she told me.

I went home and meditated and basically told God I would do this healing work only if I didn't have to market it, that this was not to be a career path for me but rather an experience of proof. To me, it was proof that I was, indeed, an instrument of God and that my work was and always would be an expression of that, no matter how it manifested itself. It was proof that I have since come to understand applies to us all.

I made room for stillness and spirit in my life, because it felt too good not to do it. I literally could not resist its healing embrace, and I urge you to do the same. Once you've gotten in touch with all this lovely, spiritual energy, you must invite it in often—every day, if possible, through both meditation or prayer and regular work on your dreams. Please notice that I'm not talking about that other, more mundane work you've filled your life with up until now. What I'm talking about is soul work, the pursuit of which every day, or nearly every day, fills your life with incredible equanimity and joy. Like chocolate cake, the more you taste it, the more delicious it becomes, until, quite literally, you simply can't resist.

It is precisely this deliciousness that leads people to give up their jobs on Wall Street to become sheep farmers or sell the split-level in suburbia and head off to serve in the Peace Corps in Bosnia. There is a sense of rightness about your dream, and the more you allow this feeling into your life, the stronger it will become. This could be the reason why so many people shake their heads regretfully and mutter, "I could never be that disciplined." What they're really saying is, "I could never allow myself to wake up and hear the calling I've been successfully ignoring for years. I really couldn't stand that much joy."

It's as if we can't bear to be that good to ourselves. It's as if we've always been told to keep it small and carve out only a modest chunk of satisfaction for ourselves. Whether or not you believe in God, your meditation will serve you by honoring that lost piece of your self. And once honored, that self will not sit silently by. For this reason such regular scheduling should never be seen as "having discipline," that militaristic-sounding condition that makes pursuing your passion sound like some sort of bondage and deprivation. Rather, all it really means is giving your soul a little space to fool around every day. And so that so-called discipline magically turns into freedom.

It is obvious to me that we avoid our creative undertakings simply because we've lost touch with that other, more powerful part of ourselves. We think that we haven't got any intuition or that, if we do, it's flawed. We think we're too busy to bother listening; we insist that there really is no possible space we can work in or that our toddler, aging mother, needy spouse, or frantic boss is more deserving of every spare minute we have than we are.

Our heads are filled with animated conversations about why we can't stop to feed our passion, instead of why we can. We're convinced that our circumstances are different— *really! Honestly! They ARE!!* We insist that we are special, and so we, and we alone, are the only people on the planet to whom none of this applies. We're convinced that there's never enough time, money, or inspiration to do the work or that there's no point because "none of it will ever see the light of day, anyway." We're convinced no one will care a whit about what we want to contribute. Most of all, we're convinced that we're right.

What we've forgotten is that this special work of ours is prayer, and I don't necessarily mean the religious version that happens in a church or a temple. Pursuing the dream is the prayer of simply living as we are meant to live. Inherent in this is the understanding that we are not alone but connected to the pull of the Universe. For it is in our work that we can finally surrender into God's infinite and comforting embrace. Doing our work means realizing that we do not know all the answers and then relaxing blissfully into our semi-ignorance, simply doing what God has given us to do.

So there is more at stake here than the swing of your moods and whether you'll ever actually get down to work.

What pursuing your dream is really about is your place on earth and the benevolent demands of your own personal version of God.

The world awaits your vision. So when will you find it in yourself to share?

Try This . . .

Begin to walk. I have found that a long walk first thing in the morning clears my head and supports my own work incredibly well. And by walking, I mean moving at a brisk pace for at least twenty minutes in comfortable shoes, down a road or around a neighborhood that offers some kind of pleasure. You can take a walk to work or a meander through a country field; choose the same route again and again or vary it, depending on your mood.

As you walk, use the time to connect with God or whomever or whatever you recognize that great protective force to be. I find myself giving thanks and having conversations. Sometimes I make up a short affirmation and repeat it in rhythm with my steps. Sometimes I just daydream, and as I do, fine ideas for my work come along. Whatever the case, I hope you find, as I have, that these spiritual walks feel so wonderful, you just can't not do them. (The bibliography at the back of this book includes some books on walks of this type.)

Do this every day or as often as you can. Your work should blossom accordingly.

Expect a Miracle
or Two

here comes a moment in the midst of every creative project when the whole damn thing looks
impossible. The moment usually arrives when
you're on a roll, busily generating ideas, feeling
the fun straight down to your toes. It is that terrible moment when you realize you cannot go another step
until you've located another half a million bucks by next
Friday or wrangled an hour-long interview with Salman
Rushdie on film. Damn your good ideas. What only a moment before seemed like a happening, no-problem project,
now, in an instant, has become blatantly impossible.

This is where commitment comes in.

First of all, commitment is not some coat you put on and
take off, depending on the weather. It's a promise you make

to yourself that must be renewed every single day, and always in the context of work. In other words, you sit down, do the work, and thereby reaffirm your commitment. If the work has taken hold of you, you *have* to reaffirm it—it's unavoidable. For you may find yourself thinking about your project at odd moments. A bridge for a song might come while you're waiting in line for a bagel; a sudden solution to a marketing problem might dawn on you in the bath. You find yourself living your project in a most natural but unexpected way. And in your commitment to it, you find yourself solving the impossible.

Yet commitment also happens on days when such solutions are not flowing. Then you sit with yourself for a while, computer glowing quietly in front of you, waiting and listening. You might make a few false starts. You'll come up with a few ideas that don't feel particularly connected to anything, so you'll delete them. Then more silence. You might be tired that day or simply need a break. And ultimately, you'll take it. You simply can't solve the problem on this particular day, but you don't worry. You know your commitment isn't going anywhere; you know you will be back in that chair the next day, waiting and probing for more wonderful stuff. Having an off-day does not in any way affect your overall dedication to the project. And this is where the miraculous part comes in: miracles do show up, almost as rewards to your commitment.

One day, while working on a novel, I wrote myself into a corner when I decided one of my characters had to make cream of truffle soup shortly before he killed himself. Now, anyone who's been around truffles knows these exotic mushrooms are hard to find—having a season of about fifteen minutes during which they are uprooted by trained pigs—and so they are also hellishly expensive. Having never tasted a truffle, though, I realized I couldn't write about one until I had. The problem was, all I had to spend on this particular research was a twenty, even though a healthy bunch of truffles ran somewhere in the three-figure range. Still, off to the local gourmet grocery I went, dubious but willing to try.

I arrived just as the black truffle season was sputtering out, so the person behind the counter offered me white truffles in a jar, in precisely the quantity I was looking for. "How much?" I asked. He inspected the jar and replied "$23.50." Amazed and relieved, I told him to wrap them up, which he was doing when his boss appeared and much whispering ensued. The young man seemed crestfallen as the boss walked away. "What happened?" I asked. He looked at me dolefully. "The price was actually $235.00," he said, "but since I quoted

you the lower price, that's all you'll have to pay." Miracle achieved, research accomplished.

Now, I don't mean to get dangerously cosmic here and suggest that all you have to do is wish for something and it will magically appear on your doorstep. But it is my belief that if your path is straight and true, and you're really listening to your instinct, the world will fall in line to support your dream, no matter how outlandish your needs may become.

It is almost as if the world wants us to succeed on our chosen path and will do whatever is necessary to point us on our way. The story is told that Grandma Moses painted her first large painting because she was wallpapering the living room and ran out of wallpaper. Using the brush she'd painted the floor with, she created a quick landscape of butternut trees by a sunny lake and put it up to cover the gap. An elderly relative loved it and began to encourage her, and so her work as a fine artist began in earnest.

My husband, Larry Barns, realized his dream of buying a New York City apartment building even though he didn't have nearly the money such a purchase usually demands. Still, he found a building whose price had been slashed twice, since all the tenants were striking and a squatter had taken over the owner's apartment. Everyone he went to for advice told him not to buy the building. A crooked estate lawyer demanded cash in a paper bag just to show it to him. And he couldn't even get in to see all the apartments because the tenants had changed the locks. Nonetheless, after two years of looking, he knew this was the building he wanted, despite its many problems.

Larry went ahead and bought the building anyway. As it turned out, the tenants ended their strike after he sat down with them and gave them new leases. The squatter turned out to be his old girlfriend, a woman he'd been living with a year earlier who'd moved out one day, unannounced, and disappeared. When she found out who her new landlord was, she not only gave up the apartment willingly, but they sat down and had the talk that completed their relationship. And so Larry ended up with the building he'd always dreamed of at a price he could afford.

The founder of Sears, Richard W. Sears, began his business while he was employed as a station agent at the Minneapolis and St. Louis Railroad. One day an unclaimed shipment of watches turned up. After a few weeks it began gathering dust in the claim room, so the enterprising Sears did a little market research, found out the wholesale cost of the watches, bought the freight himself, and began selling watches up and down the railroad line. This led to his forming the R. W. Sears Watch Company. Interestingly, Alvah C. Roebuck was the watchmaker who originally did all his watch repairs, so eventually his company took the name Sears, Roebuck and Company.

The point here is that quirks of fate are part of the plan. Complete happenstance, lucky coincidences, and total accidents *do* occur—and for good reason. For I believe such occurrences aren't really accidents at all but traffic signs giving you the right of way. They happen almost as rewards to your single-minded dedication to your project, showing up to affirm your path and give you that little goose of encouragement you've been needing.

Now, I know someone somewhere is reading this right now saying, "Yeah . . . *right!* I'm gonna decide I need half a million, and it will just magically show up in front of me. . . . What kind of fruitcake book *is* this, anyway?"

All I have to say to that is, bend your imagination a little. So what if this is only my opinion and not some scientifically proven fact? Such thinking can only help you with your own particular vision. One of the things I love most about life is what a mystery the human brain is. The truth is, we really have no idea how these so-called coincidences occur—whether we have some sort of extrasensory skills that can predetermine them or whether they really are acts of God or even whether they are completely random.

The key is to receive such synergy as a gift, for if nothing else, it will provide critical ballast the next time your impetus begins to sag. "Hold fast to your dreams," said Walt Whitman.

And while you're at it, expect a few miracles, say I.

Try This . . .

Before you decide you're one of those people for whom miracles never happen, pull out your journal or notebook. Then make a list of miracles that have happened in your life—unexpected twists of fate and chance encounters that led to important relationships and opportunities. Think hard about what you'd set out to do when your miracle occurred. Record all the details: what you thought was going to happen, what actually did happen, where this led you, and any other outcomes you can think of.

You might be surprised to find you've experienced more miracles than you ever thought possible.

Now make a new list—the miracles you want to have

happen. Feel free to be as fantastic as you like in assembling this list: write down even the miracles that you think have *no chance* of occurring. (Be careful you're not just coming up with any old miracles; choose the ones that really seem right for you and your cause.)

Then tuck that list away in a drawer or a file and forget about it. Don't be surprised if some of those miracles do, indeed, come true.

Why Geniuses Have Genius

s far as I can tell, true genius is a fairly simple affair. What geniuses do is straightforward enough: they recognize their gifts, and then they fully and completely embrace their craft.

By this I mean that they live it, twenty-four hours a day, for most of their adult life. The stories abound. I read somewhere that the English painter Lucien Freud rarely leaves his London studio, except to visit the National Gallery during his favorite off-hours, between eleven P.M. and five A.M. To prepare for a role, actor Daniel Day-Lewis will do things like live in a small box for days to re-create the physical limitations of a character with cerebral palsy. The great mezzo-soprano Marilyn Horne told a *60 Minutes* interviewer that she does not speak while on tour, not even a word, until each night's concert has been given. Painter Andrew Wyeth does not wear a watch, for fear that any sort of schedule will interrupt the flow of his painting.

These people have achieved success because they surrendered fully and completely to their passion. Their topmost priority in life is their work, and they give themselves to it without question. Geniuses do not wake up some days and "just not feel like it"; long ago they passed the threshold where one is controlled by such fleeting thoughts. Their work is the love of their life, a pull they are physically unable to resist. This is how Matisse entered the final, most incredible phase of his career while an invalid, creating masterpieces of color and simplicity from his sickbed. This is how Michelangelo created *David*, working inside wooden walls he constructed around the eighteen-foot-high block of marble, sleeping in his clothing, stopping only for occasional bread and water, even working by torchlight at night. What geniuses know is out-and-out surrender to their creativity.

Once success begins, the issue of responsibility also emerges. Some geniuses keep creating on a certain level because it is expected of them, but others recognize the sacredness of the creative process and remain true to the call. Consider the Nobel Prize–winning Japanese novelist Kenzaburo Oe, who quit writing fiction at the height of his popularity in

Japan and around the world. Oe, who wrote almost exclusively about his brain-damaged son in his novels, felt he'd said everything he had to say in his fiction. And so he stopped, with the same bravery and total respect for honesty that had made him a success in the first place.

Similar stories are told about the legendary airplane designer Clarence L. "Kelly" Johnson, who founded Lockheed's underground technology think tank the Skunk Works. In their book *Organizing Genius*, authors Warren Bennis and Patricia Ward Biederman cite one story in which Johnson returned millions of dollars to the air force after deciding his team could not build a hydrogen-powered plane. Johnson did this freely, despite the considerable financial loss such a move meant for Lockheed.

Geniuses will also surrender to all the emotional demands of their work, no matter how frightening or challenging they may be, even if they entail public excoriation. Orson Welles will always be considered a genius, and *Citizen Kane* will always be one of the great movies of all time, but not because either was polite or well liked. In fact, *Citizen Kane* (a scathing, thinly veiled portrayal of William Randolph Hearst and his mistress, Marion Davies) was screened only briefly after it was made and won only one Oscar (for best screenplay). The movie was hidden away in the RKO vault for more than a decade because the studio was afraid to release it widely. The film was openly booed at the 1941 Oscars each time its name was mentioned, and Welles retained semipariah status for the rest of his career. Yet when you look at *Citizen Kane* even today, it is almost overpowering in its freshness. It remains a unique, haunting portrait of a character that, like the best of Shakespeare, simply refuses to go away.

The treatment of geniuses has been the same throughout history. The impressionist movement began in a tent outside the Academy in Paris, bearing a sign SALON DES REFUSÉS, or EXHIBIT OF THE REJECTS. This is how Manet, Monet, Renoir, and Degas first showed their vision to the world, after academy officials refused to exhibit their work. Parisian crowds laughed at the paintings and were particularly scandalized by Manet's *Olympia*, a portrait of a common woman, most likely a prostitute, painted utterly realistically to mock the academy's neoclassical "divine maidens." In fact, *Olympia* had to be hung high, so as to keep it safe from the walking sticks and umbrellas people hurled in its direction. Yet today these works are among the most beloved of all paintings, while neoclassicism long ago stopped drawing huge crowds.

Genius is brash and audacious. It smashes convention with delight and refuses to be ignored. It defies the social animal in all of us that's trained to be polite, clever, and adorable, and it chooses the path of raw veracity every time. Genius exists for itself and the sheer joy of its release into the world, and yet it exists for us as well. For we need its power and its roughness, just as we need the tranquillity of the everyday.

Geniuses have genius because they simply have no choice. Their gift is prodigious enough that they won't have a moment's peace until they have ridden its wild horses straight into the sun. All of us, in fact, have a touch of this genius. Whether our gift is baking bread, assessing environmental hazards, teaching children, or powerhouse investing, it's never going to be enough just to dabble a little here and a little there. If you wish for full satisfaction, you must give yourself to this work completely, 100 percent. This does not mean that you have to quit your day job and go live on the street while you pursue your goal. Nor does it mean that you must live like a hermit and eschew normality. But when you are able to work, you must dive into your pursuit with bravery, gusto, and out-and-out abandon. And above all else, you must work!

Do not hold back or quibble over details. Do not doubt your process or be afraid. Open the floodgates and let yourself disappear into your vision. Turn yourself inside out and risk complete exposure. Dig into the raw material before you

as if it were raw clay, craving your touch. No matter what you do, do it as fully and completely as you can. And like so much butterfat, the work that has the highest concentration of "you" will rise to the surface first, crying out to be tasted.

No one has ever celebrated a genius who only took things halfway. Indeed, the world looks to geniuses not just for vision and inspiration but to take comfort in the pure audacity of celebrating life as fully as possible.

This is the province of true creative genius, a place of no boundaries, no restraints, and no taboos.

Try This ...

Visit the local bookstore or library and find some books about geniuses in your field who inspire you. As you read them, keep a notebook handy for recording observations that can inform your path. Photocopy images of your heroes and hang them in your workplace. Or pick some pertinent quotations and create a screensaver for your computer with them by using customizable screensaver software. Subscribe to any magazine that publishes success stories and trade information on people who've achieved dreams similar to yours. Keep a file of news clippings for easy reference.

When Talent Does and Doesn't Matter

nother prevailing belief about talent in our world is that you've either got it or you don't. And if you don't, you might as well shell peas in the corner of a grocery for the rest of your life.

Well I, for one, say, "Phooey."

It may be that some of us lucked out in the gene pool more than others. Talent is a real and undeniable aspect of the success of many great achievers. There is a reason Yo-Yo Ma was at Juilliard by the time he was eight. It's no mistake that Bill Gates quit Harvard to invent MS-DOS. But let's talk about all the successful people out there who *don't* have extraordinary talent, for in some ways their rise is even more spectacular.

Take Madonna, for instance. Now, Madonna has a fine voice, and she can certainly dance, but one could argue that it took more than talent to achieve her superstar status. For one thing, the woman is a human dynamo. She has no fear whatsoever about asking for what she wants. Furthermore, she is unafraid to reinvent herself continually to stay fresh and fascinating to her fans. Madonna's genius is in her awareness of what people want and her ability to provide it.

In other words, if you haven't got it, invent it.

We can be fairly sure Madonna never stood around twisting her hair and saying, "If only I could sing like Aretha Franklin." Actually, Madonna didn't even set out to be a singer. She came to New York to be a dancer, drifted into drumming, and was discovered by two French promoters at Danceteria, a disco that was the epicenter of the New York club scene in the early eighties. "You should sing," they said, and so she did. Several voice lessons later, she got her first major record deal. And as the A&R person who signed her said, she just had that certain something, that superstar quality. Yet that quality wasn't in her voice or her packaging; it was in her presence. Madonna could sit in a chair and project the essence of a star, which I attribute to two things: crystal-clear vision and a will of steel.

You don't have to have talent to be a star, but you absolutely must believe that you will be one, come hell or high water. And so you must also have an indomitable will. Your road won't be easy. You'll certainly endure rejection after rejection. You will have to work harder than you ever thought imaginable. You might even go the route Madonna did in her early days, sleeping in abandoned buildings and eating from garbage cans. Or you could choose the safe route and get a nine-to-five job, but here your will must be even stronger, to save you from that cozy, sleepy stupor of security that can undermine creative resolve. At any rate it won't be easy, and God knows it won't be fair.

Yet whoever said life was fair to begin with?

Think of all the incredibly talented people out there right now who don't even have enough faith in their abilities to pick up a paintbrush or face a blank spreadsheet. I'd wager there are far more of them than the tiny minority of the less talented whose wonderful audacity keeps pushing them forward. I would also wager there is room in this world for both, so ultimately, talent is not even an issue.

However . . . since this is an imperfect world, talent occasionally *is* an issue. Say you want to be a singer. If you really don't have a perfect "instrument," as the voice teachers call it, you will face frustration, and it will be commensurate with the size of your dream. If you want to be Madonna, you at least have to be able to carry a tune, feel the beat, and sound pretty musical. And you have to be willing to work your tail off to make your voice and your entire persona into something salable. You have to be willing to do whatever it takes to make your dream happen. And ultimately, and perhaps most important, you have to be willing to fail.

You have to love yourself so much that even after years of voice coaching, dance lessons, head shots, costume fittings, demo tapes, videos, practice gigs, mailing lists, cold calls, business letters, auditions, rejections, constant practicing, and the endless grind of just trying to find an audience, you can walk away quietly when the time comes, knowing you did what you had to do. If it doesn't work out, you'll have to be able to make your peace with your inability to become the next Madonna—and perhaps, in doing so, see that following your dream really wasn't all about the satisfaction of your ego and whether or not you went on worldwide tours attracting millions of fans. What it was really about was the nourishment of your spirit. You gave yourself a profound gift, and that you didn't "succeed" was not even entirely true, for you may even have discovered that great universal secret: *The doing of the work is where true pleasure lies.*

You will have grown in subtle and important ways, and so you will hopefully scan the horizon for the next dream you can appropriate and the next adventure on which you can set off. In this way, you can never lose; you can only grow, through perseverance, sweat, and the happy broadcast of your own fantastic dreams.

Try This . . .

Test your will by checking off those things that apply to you:

- ☐ There are things I want to do in life, and I'll get to them . . . in my nineties.
- ☐ If given a choice between putting in some time on my business idea and rotating my tires, I'll go with the tires every time.
- ☐ I'd probably write the great American novel if I didn't have a television.
- ☐ I can no longer open the guest-room closet because it's full of all the craft projects I started but never finished.
- ☐ I'd like to do something creative, but I haven't got a creative bone in my body.
- ☐ I definitely had more will when I was younger.

☐ I could do a better job than any of the so-called super-stars in my field. I just don't feel like it.

If you checked any of the preceding items, chances are you need to reexamine where you stand with your will. Take a minute and complete the following lists. Feel free to be brutally honest.

☐ What I'm Afraid of Finding Out about My Dream
☐ What It Will Mean If I Succeed at My Dream
☐ What Will Change If I Succeed at My Dream
☐ People Who Support My Dream
☐ People Who Do Not Support My Dream
☐ What I Will Gain by Pursuing My Dream

Read This in Case of Emergency

nlike the rest of life, an emergency in your creative process is inevitable. When you set off on the long road to realizing your vision, you can expect some major traffic jams ahead.

This does not mean that you have to get off the road altogether.

It simply means that great things are seldom created without some breakdowns along the way.

"Why is this?" you might ask. I contend it is because we are only human beings—and pretty limited ones at that. We're insatiable when it comes to praise, accomplishment, and looking good. And we're pretty damn pitiful when it comes to hanging with something for the long haul and having a little faith. Bottom line: We enter most creative enterprises from the mind-set of "I'll try it, but my results better be brilliant *now* . . . or else."

This is sort of like trying to master origami in an afternoon; it's simply not going to happen, no matter how hard we try. And not only that, by rushing the process, we never get to experience the thrill of gradual mastery.

Something almost chemical happens when you try, try, and try, only to master something after long and committed effort. The voices of doubt are thrown into happy submission, and for at least ten minutes you can actually be a hero in your own mind. Enough of these small triumphs and you might even accumulate some serious self-esteem. It's a slow win, but it's a real one, the rewards of which are yours forever.

In the meanwhile, you will inevitably bog down. It may be that your project gets off to a fantastic start. You're clear-headed, inspired, full of ideas, and tear home from work each night, eager to get to it. That's the first week, or the first month even. Then you have a bad day. The boss calls you names. Your computer crashes. The promised promotion goes to someone else. You limp home, licking your wounds, and instead of turning to your project for a bit of soul healing, you crack open a beer and turn on the news. "I've had a helluva day," you justify. "Don't I deserve a night off?"

What you forget at such a moment is the power your work has to restore your wounded spirit. "Give me a break," you sigh. Well, okay—we all *do* deserve a night off once in a while. But the disaster happens the next night, when you consider how easy it was to slough off your project the night before. "Still recovering," you murmur to yourself, as you head off to happy hour. Two months later there's half an inch of dust on the work that was originally intended to save your life. Years later you still have a dim memory of that book you were going to write, and that memory is soaked in resignation and regret.

When we feel like quitting, we confuse concentrated effort with backbreaking labor. The view from the downy, soft contours of our overstuffed armchairs is definitely biased. Indeed, it seems virtually impossible to get up and make phone calls, prepare financial projections, test recipes, or do anything. *I can't. I just can't. I'm too tired. I'm too weak. I can't even think straight. I JUST WORKED ALL DAY! How can I possibly create???* At that moment it seems that the effort is just plain more than we can bear.

There are always going to be moments in your process when you think yourself straight to hell. You're going to be convinced you're too tired, too uninspired, or too depressed. A million other temptations will beckon. The mere idea of sitting at your desk will seem impossible until you actually sit down and do it. Thinking about it is what will immobilize you—just thinking about it. The actual work, if you can get yourself to begin, will probably be relatively easy.

Alex Forbes, a friend of mine who is a professional singer/songwriter, calls this The Wall. In the course of nearly every song she writes, she hits a place where she just can't go on. Any spark of inspiration in what she's already written has somehow died, and finishing the song now seems impossible. And yet she knows she cannot just walk away and not return. So Alex sits there, noodling around, waiting for something to happen, trying not to despair.

The Wall is the place all of us hit sooner or later; it can feel terrible, yet it can also be the place of the greatest rewards. For what Alex has found is that if she can just hang in there and press through her resistance, what lies on the other side is usually a breakthrough—an incredible bridge section that lifts the song to a whole new place or a lyric that really gets at the heart of the matter. Every so often, however, The Wall wins. When this happens, Alex is forced to confront the fact that the song she's trying to write is really just a piece of useless fluff that doesn't deserve song status. In these cases what The Wall demands is some serious soul-searching and truth telling. So she has come to realize that not every creative impulse needs to be pursued to completion. Alex now sees The Wall as a productive and important part of her own process.

Yet here you are, still sitting in your comfy armchair. And the work is still sitting on your desk, staring you in the face. So it becomes simply a matter of hauling yourself out of the armchair, *even when you don't feel like doing it,* and getting to it. For it's been proved again and again: all you have to do is do it. Soon enough the creative process will draw you in once again, warming you, enriching you, soothing all your dark defenses, welcoming you back home.

It's simply a matter of staying on the truest course.

Try This . . .

The next time you need to work on your project but "just don't feel like it," give yourself the gift of a few minutes to consider why.

Perhaps these questions will help. Answer honestly—they're for you.

1. What would you rather be doing right now?
2. If you were doing that other thing, how much would your life actually improve?

3. What's the bottom-line truth about why you are avoiding your project?
4. What are you afraid of?
5. How will you feel if you don't go back to work?
6. How will you feel if you do?

How False Modesty Kills Dreams

ecently on the *Today* show I saw a boy named Paris Goudi, not more than twelve years old, who was skillfully juggling balls in front of an impromptu street audience. The host couldn't help but ask, "Gee, aren't you nervous juggling on national TV?"

The boy's eyes never strayed from his efforts—five balls that he was now juggling behind his head. "Nope," he said simply. "This is my home. This is where I belong."

Amen.

We should all be so supremely confident that we can say the unthinkable before an audience of 3.5 million. And this was the unthinkable. This kid did not have some megawatt agent wrangling him a spot on national TV. Chances are, he didn't have a PR person or even a manager. The network crew just happened to bump into him on a sidewalk in New York, but then, Paris Goudi already knew national TV was his home. And more important, he put that knowledge into his speaking.

Much has been said about the power of our words. In her excellent book *Jesus CEO*, which examines Jesus as the extraordinary leader that he was, Laurie Beth Jones notes that in Isaiah 55:11 God said, "I declare a thing and it is done for me. My word accomplishes that which I send it out to do." This is a simple statement of fact. Our words are our messengers. And it isn't just God who can make this happen. So it is with all our words: we really are what we speak. *Really.*

In leading my workshops, I often hear people present work to the group with a preamble: "This probably stinks, but . . ." or "I know this isn't any good, but . . ." or "I tried, but this was the best I could do . . ." This is a weird human reflex I like to think of as The Parade of False Modesty. It's that automatic urge to publicly denigrate anything you've created—regardless of whether you secretly think it's good—in order to save face should the thing bomb. And whenever the Parade of False Modesty begins, I find my interest taking a major step back. It's as if these people were actively willing me not to like their work, no matter how wonderful it is.

The Parade of False Modesty immediately snatches a little joy from its intended audience, just so that person can avoid the squirming vulnerability that comes with true self-expression. Just so he or she can squeeze into the paradigm of cool for a moment, because these days self-confidence is not totally hip. Self-confidence is a self-loving way to be, which in our ironic age almost never flies.

You will never achieve what you set out to do unless you can get squarely behind it, believe in its power, and actively speak that belief. You will never make anything happen if you have to keep hiding behind false modesty. And you must remember that although this work comes from you, it is not yours alone to kick, punch, and mutilate at will. In fact, your work belongs to the rest of us as well.

This is why you have to watch your speaking, for if you constantly insist that your work or your life is inadequate, the world will respond accordingly. Rather than seeing you as the witty, urbane individual you hope to be, we will hear your denigrating words and take that deadly step backward. We will feel robbed, and rightly so, of the chance to see your work for itself. And since we will smell a self-made loser, rather than pay serious attention, we will simply pass you by.

The reverse is also true. People who have the self-respect to speak kindly of themselves and their work are usually rewarded with success. Walt Whitman not only self-published the initial editions of *Leaves of Grass*, he also wrote his own reviews, describing himself as "large and lusty, a naive, masculine, affectionate, contemplative, sensual, imperious person." Not unlike Paris Goudi, Whitman knew he belonged in the public eye and had no problem saying so. And so, rather than bragging, like Jesus he simply stated a fact. And in doing so, he introduced himself to us as a person whose gifts we all might share.

When you step forth and express yourself, the audience hears one thing: how generous a gift you are willing to give. Think for a moment about your own speaking. Are you more in the "Oh, it's really nothing, just a little something I scratched out. It's probably terrible" camp, or are you more like Paris Goudi? When someone compliments your work, do you immediately jump down her throat with a list of its imperfections? Or do you say thank-you and allow the appreciation to sink in for a moment? Giving others the chance to appreciate you is, in fact, another way of giving back to them. It completes the cycle that all this giving generated in the first place, which is what your loving audience demands.

So what this all boils down to ultimately is your sense of generosity. Can you actually bring yourself to clothe your dreams in the respect and love they deserve? Can you speak of them as the powerful, wonderful creations that they are? For they are your children in a sense. Or do you have to defeat them with your words, so that they, like you, stay small and limited?

Will you give the gift or not? Although the answer may ultimately lie in your actions, it truly does begin in your words.

Take a look and see. Are your words delivering the message that you want?

If You're Looking for Something to Do . . .

Unplug the phone; kick out kids, spouses, and neighbors; and give yourself some peace and quiet. Then get a large pad of paper, several pencils or pens, and a very comfortable chair. Pour a little tea, if you like, and put on some undistracting, soothing music. Then make a grand, master list of all the beliefs that keep you from moving forward with your project.

Here are some limiting beliefs that have come up in my workshops: "I'm not qualified." "I have to do this every day or not at all!" "I'll offend too many people." "My mother will never forgive me." Press through the voice in your head that's trying to distract you, and be relentless with yourself. *Keep going until you have at least twenty-five limiting beliefs.*

Proof That Rejection Won't Kill You

The first time I wrote a novel, I heard a monotonous hum in the background the entire time. It was my mind chanting, *The first time this gets rejected, I will die. The first time this gets rejected, I will die.*

Somehow, I managed to finish the thing and put it into the hands of a few people I knew in the publishing business. The first rejection rolled in from the sister of a friend, a six-month publishing novice who was a secretary to a famous editor. "Well, first of all," she began, "the whole thing needs a major haircut."

A haircut! A HAIRCUT!! sputtered my indignant mind. *Why don't we just shave it all off and go bald?* "Hnnh," I said, as noncommitally as I could.

"Yes, and some of these characters, Suzanne..." her voice trailed off in dismay. "How shall I put this? They were just... well... trite."

TRITE... TRITE???!!! Now my mind was under siege, and emergency help was running in from all directions. Somehow, and I don't remember how, I managed to wind up the conversation and get off the phone before she finished her critique, whereupon I broke down into racking, heaving sobs. My book had been soundly rejected—hated, even.

Yet I did not die.

Ultimately, I signed with a literary agent who did his best to sell the book, but no one wanted to buy it. Every couple of weeks or so for an entire year, another elegant, cream-colored rejection letter with my name neatly typed on it would slip through the mail slot. For a while they just accumulated on my desk, but then one day I shored up my soul, sat down, and read them all, one by one. Immediately I began to understand something about rejection: *it's nothing personal.*

Seriously.

In fact, almost every one of the twenty-seven rejection letters I got had a different reason for not buying my book. Some editors wanted the book but couldn't convince their bosses or their marketing teams to buy it. Others loved the writing but not the plot. Some didn't like the characters or the fact that the book didn't have a stronger social relevance. But not one of them said a word about me personally. No letter said, "How can you send me a book by such a loser?" or "What kind of idiot wrote this thing?"—all of which seemed entirely possible to my warped thinking. The bottom line was that my book was rejected by every single publisher in New York, but not only did I survive, I managed to keep on writing.

What I learned from this experience was nonattachment. This is quite literally the difference between those who achieve their dream and those who don't.

For every person who cannot put his or her dream in place, there is a whole lot of silent screaming going on: *Help! I might finish it. Help! It might succeed. Help! I might finally be someone and have to answer for myself in the world. HELP! Recognition will probably destroy me.* The sad thing is, it isn't us the world is waiting to recognize; it is only our work. This is where nonattachment comes in.

First and foremost, *we are not our work.* We are living, breathing people who create businesses, art, ideas, and babies. But these are not, and never will be, the stuff we're made of. Still, somehow, in the process of caring a hell of a lot

about something, and pouring all your sweat and blood into it, you can get terribly confused.

When a performer goes out on a stage, he may feel the audience is judging every aspect of him and his life. In fact, all that poor audience is doing is waiting to be entertained a little. They aren't commenting on the actor's looks, politics, hairstyle, or intelligence. These are really the farthest things from their minds. When they applaud, they are just telling a performer that they liked what she did at that particular moment, in that particular place. That's all. The rest, quite honestly, they don't even care about, nor should they be expected to.

So it isn't up to me what the world thinks of me; the world will think what it thinks, and I have no control over this. Indeed, my job is simply to do the work and send it out there. That is all; end of story. It isn't up to me to make the world like me, any more than it is up to me to determine the fate of my creative undertakings. In fact, I contend that the more honest, provocative, and truly vulnerable I am with my work, the more vocal will be those who despise it. However, by the same token, my honesty will genuinely touch more people as well.

What we have to keep remembering is to release these gifts as easily and as effortlessly as they were given to us in the first place. Not because they will make us rich, nor because they bear any significance at all. We must release these gifts simply because they flowed through us and must now be given away—whether to the public at large or even just to someone we love. And should we decide to go public with the work and it gets rejected once, or even hundreds of times, we simply need to follow our instincts and keep on releasing it until we sense that it is time to stop. Perhaps our work will be appreciated; perhaps it won't. That we created it in the first place means we have grown in the process—which is crucial to do in our life.

Each project we undertake is merely another milestone on our own particular path, a signpost that has to be passed in order to reach the next one. We all have our share of scathing reviews, bitter rejections, and out-and-out failure, but ultimately who even cares? The bigger question is, can you go to bed comforted by the thought that you came a little closer to accomplishing your vision? Can you say to yourself, I did my work—my real work—today?

Creativity is a selfless act, demanding that you give of yourself simply for the sheer love of giving. We cannot give our work to the world expecting any kind of reward. That this simple act requires courage is merely creativity's gift to us in return.

Try This . . .

Take a moment and assess: How exactly do you handle rejection? Are you a quitter? A pouter? A take-it-on-the-chin type? Are you someone who seeks revenge? Or do you avoid rejection altogether by never starting anything in the first place?

If you're not sure, try writing down at least three times you suffered rejections. (They can be work-related or personal.) Then carefully reconstruct exactly how you handled each experience. What is the status of those efforts today? Was anything learned?

When to Run, Not Walk, from Helpful Advice

There are people out there who would like to see you realize your dreams, and there are people who would not. The latter group of so-called friends come in all guises—family, coworkers, even teachers. For whatever reason, they relish defeat and take comfort in helping plant the seed of yours as well.

Avoid them at all costs.

Once you have begun the pursuit of your vision in earnest, you will be tempted to share it with the world. This could be news of your very first sale as a Realtor or perhaps some early bottles of wine from your own small vineyard or maybe the manuscript of your first novel. You lug all 2,500 pages of it into your office, drop it at the feet of that guy

across the hall who kept saying you could never do it, and stand back to enjoy a moment of smug satisfaction.

"There," you say with a smile. "Want to read it?"

The guy across the hall is the wrong person to show your precious work to at this moment, for he is not, and never will be, your ally. And no matter how victorious you may feel at the huge progress you've made, your creative self is still painfully fragile. All this so-called friend has to do is shove it with his toe and say, "Yeah, sure ... when I've got some time," and suddenly your dream deflates a tiny bit.

And then, God forbid he does get some time. He'll return the manuscript, saying only, "Pretty good. . . . I mean, I didn't believe a word of it, and I thought the plot was pretty dismal, but hey, what do I know?" Chances are, the manuscript will find its way to a dark corner under your desk, where it will sit collecting dust far into the future.

It is my belief that the only people truly qualified to give opinions of your work are professionals: the investors, dealers, agents, critics, publishers, managers, directors, producers, admissions boards, licensing bureaus, and bureaucratic chiefs—in other words, people who get paid for their opinions. Everyone else will have an opinion, of course, but that by no means implies that you should listen to it.

Still, we are gluttons for punishment. In some sick way we *want* the guy across the hall to hate it, so that ever-chiming voice of doubt can be right for once. Then we're off the hook! No one else ever has to see the work! All the hard work, risk, and discomfort are over! Blissfully, we can sink back into our armchair, assume permanent couch-potato position, and just forget the whole damn dream business that started all this in the first place. So we're defeated, we smirk, reaching for a fistful of chips. Who gives a damn? At least we can relax for a change.

As you and I both know, it ain't that simple.

The guy across the hall hates our book, and so we've just died a thousand small deaths. And yet the phoenix can and will rise from the ashes, as we proceed to do what we should have done in the first place. We go to the library and research agents, managers, licensing bureaus, or whoever the gate-keeper is for our chosen field. We locate books and professional organizations where we can find information on how best to approach these folks, learning whatever etiquette may be required. We get the education we need to make the mark, and join clubs or enroll in classes that help us learn how to market our efforts. We network, calling everyone we ever knew, asking whether they happen to know anyone who might be helpful. And then and only then do we pass our creation on to maybe one or two trusted, true friends, *the kind who honestly want to see us succeed.* (You know who these people are, and if you don't, start looking for them. Everyone needs at least one ally.)

Our supporters will have ideas for us, and many of them may be of value. If they happen to be proficient in our chosen field, then so much the better. But remember one thing: they are not, and never should become, our gods. Treat their opinions as nothing more than what they are—opinions.

My father, John Falter, was an artist who, as a very young child, exhibited a natural talent for draftsmanship. When he was fifteen, his parents took him to the nearest big city and showed samples of cartoons he'd been publishing in the local paper to a successful syndicated cartoonist there. "This boy will never be a great cartoonist," the man decreed. "He draws too well." My father so revered this man's opinion that he basically wrote off cartoon work.

Even though he became one of the most important illustrators of his generation, a small part of him always longed to do cartoons. A number of times over the years, he submitted cover ideas to *The New Yorker*, each with legitimately funny concepts, but they were always turned down. Perhaps the cartoonist was right, but maybe he wasn't. What's certain is that my father never felt confident as a cartoonist after this prediction, despite his success as an artist. He never published another cartoon.

The opinions of mentors and teachers need to be treated with a degree of caution, as well. Far too often they teach not to inspire and encourage their students into working but to snag a precious audience and feed their ravenous egos. Beware of teachers who make denigration a key factor of teaching: constructive criticism should never be confused with public humiliation. In fact, criticism can never even be heard by a student unless it is delivered in a gentle, soul-informing way, a way that acknowledges the student's own innate gifts.

Also, beware of classes where the teacher sits back and turns the students into teachers. These free-for-alls can turn into slash-and-burn sessions that are more about competition than anything else. I remember an advertising copywriting class I took once, taught by an award-winning creative director, in which the students (90 percent of whom had never worked in advertising) were challenged to "find the holes" in each other's work. By midsemester 50 percent of the class had stopped coming. By the end only three of us remained. It is safe to say not a whole lot of learning went on there.

True self-expression demands incredible vulnerability,

and so we must treat our work as the precious gift that it is. The urge to share may be wonderful and irrepressible, but we need to be smart about it. For this is not ours, this thing we have created; it's divine work that has been put in our hands, however briefly. To be careful stewards, we must proceed with open eyes, fully cognizant of the minefield ahead. Only then will our work find the souls it was intended to touch, and only then will our job be complete.

Try This ♦ ♦ ♦

Make two lists:

1. People Who Support My Project
2. People Who Do Not Support My Project

Notice whether some people you really were convinced were your supporters make their way onto the opposing list as well. Be honest here, and these lists will be useful tools for getting the support you need.

Then Try This . . .

Begin a "Support" file filled with encouraging notes, E-mails, and letters you collect along your path. These could be messages from supporters, parents, kids, colleagues, and professionals—anyone who was genuinely touched by what you're doing and wants to support your efforts. The file can even include rejection letters from people who see and state the value of your work. Feel free to plunge in and read them whenever your morale needs a boost.

In Praise of Failure

ne reason many people never get around to pursuing their dream is what psychologists and other analytical types call "fear of failure." Essentially, they are so paralyzed by the mere possibility of failing that they do backflips to avoid such a catastrophe. Well, to any of you who might be feeling this way, I have only a few choice words: Get over it already.

Not only is failure an essential part of your progress; it is unavoidable. No matter what you set out to do, sooner or later a failure will occur, whether it be a complete and total belly flop at the outset that redirects your course or a later one, after you've become an established success. Basically, experiencing failure is like arguing with your spouse; nobody wants to do it, but sooner or later it's bound to happen. And handled intelligently, failure won't be a disaster at all. Rather, it will yield all sorts of important information about your well-being and your conduct in life.

Although it may seem a gross generalization to say that nobody can avoid failure, it's true. More often than not, failure is simply the smashing of our expectations. It is the rerouting of our vision onto a different course. And although we hardly like the experience, it is wonderful in a way, because it shakes us out of our smugness. It reminds us how little we actually know about this path that we're on. It pulls us back up to the job of reinventing ourselves, returning us to the essential work of creation. If our egos will just let us get on with it, failure calls us forward once again, as creators.

There is a wonderful story about Stephen Crane. His novel *Maggie: A Girl of the Streets* was found to be too realistic and grim for commercial publishing of the 1890s. So, unable to find a publisher, the author published it himself but sold only a hundred copies. Unfortunately, Crane had spent his entire savings on the book, so he was forced to burn the remainders for fuel. However, one of the few copies that was left reached William Dean Howells, who then helped Crane get another manuscript, *The Red Badge of Courage,* published. After its success, *Maggie* was republished to roaring success.

Michael Klepper and Robert Gunther's book *The Wealthy 100* tells the story of one of the wealthiest men in U.S. history, Cyrus H. McCormick. A farmer's son, McCormick dedicated his entire adult life to the development of a horse-drawn reaping machine, a project his father had begun. After several years of refinement, he finally got the design right. Then he spent nine years trying to convince farmers, who had been harvesting their fields by hand with scythes, that his invention actually worked. There were no buyers. The panic of 1837 followed, and McCormick went bankrupt; the bank repossessed everything except his reaper, which it decided wasn't worth a dime. That was fortunate, since McCormick was not about to give up.

After two more years of doggedly dragging farmers out into fields and demonstrating his machine, he finally sold one. Four years later, he'd sold fifty of them. He tried everything to market his invention—money-back guarantees, payment plans, and testimonial advertising, which was unheard of then. Six years later he'd sold three thousand reapers. Then he demonstrated the machine in Europe and, before a skeptical crowd, harvested seventy-four yards of wheat in seventy seconds. After a moment of stunned silence, the crowd began to cheer wildly. McCormick took home international medals and the accolades of the press. By the time of his death, thirty-three years later, McCormick's reaping machine had enabled him to amass a fortune of $10 million and launch a company known today as International Harvester.

There is a similar story about Michelangelo at San Lorenzo. Michelangelo (who had been regularly beaten by his father for wanting to be an artist) began the church at San Lorenzo in Florence after establishing himself as Italy's preeminent monumental sculptor. As William Wallace relates in his fine biography *Michelangelo at San Lorenzo*, Michelangelo was originally hired to design and sculpt all the statuary on the church facade. Another architect had been hired to design the church itself. After two months of working with the architect, however, Michelangelo decided only he himself could design a building magnificent enough for his sculpture. Yet at this point in his life, Michelangelo had never designed any architecture. Michelangelo won the commission and, thinking big as usual, declared that he would "domesticate the mountains" and create "the mirror of architecture and sculpture of all Italy."

He set out to create a facade for the church that included twenty enormous columns, each made from a massive piece of marble. Each piece would have to be hauled by horse-drawn sledge, cart, boat, and finally on foot, from the other end of Italy. Four years later Michelangelo had opened a new quarry, built roads to it, designed a massive crane for hauling the marble, devised a pinion system for moving the loads around steep, twisting mountaintop roads, and employed an entire army of three hundred quarrymen and stone movers.

Michelangelo personally spent more than eight months just checking out veins of marble. He was nearly killed when one of the columns, because of a faulty iron ring, smashed to the ground as it was being lifted out of the quarry. And this was only one of seven columns he quarried; five more disappeared en route. Only one column actually made it to San Lorenzo, where it still lies today, covered with moss in a ditch near the church.

Later that year the pope who commissioned the work died, Michelangelo's contract was terminated, and the project was given to other designers to complete more simply. Michelangelo wrote to the Vatican: "I am not charging to this account the fact that I have been ruined over the said work at San Lorenzo; I am not charging to this account the enormous insult of having been brought here to execute the said work, and then having it taken away from me. . . . I am left with two handfuls of toil and a striving after wind."

When he wrote this, Michelangelo did not know he was going on to spend the last third of his career as one of the world's great architects, nor that the facade of San Lorenzo would always remain unfinished out of respect for what he had begun. All he knew was that he'd tried architecture and failed miserably. Yet the architectural triumph of the Medici Chapel still awaited him, as did St. Peter's. At this moment, Michelangelo's sense of failure was the same as anyone's. It seemed like a hopeless situation from which nothing good could ever be derived.

History has proved, however, that Michelangelo's failure was anything but complete. Indeed, the facade for San Lorenzo took him into an entirely new era in his career. So, like all failures, it was simply a rearrangement of plans, a sudden and unexpected blow to expectations.

Most failure is not an end in itself but a beginning disguised as an end. The only true failure would have been for Michelangelo to have stopped caring and stuck his sculpture into a facade he considered unworthy. The only true failure would have been for him to have arrested that part of himself that refused to acquiesce. That would have been the death of his vision and a strike against his almost unbearable passion, an emotional force so powerful that the townspeople gave it a name: Michelangelo's *terribilita*.

More recently Lorelei Rodgers, president of The Lorelei Collection, a successful jewlery design business she created out of the ashes of her previous career, took my workshop.

Like a lot of people in the early nineties, Lorelei had been laid off from her job as a sales rep for a large jewelry company. At the time, she was devastated, even though a small voice in the back of her head kept reminding her that she didn't really want to sell jewelry . . . she wanted to design it. Yet Lorelei had no design background or education. All she had was an intense interest in color and enough savings to live on for a few years. So she began.

Lorelei's early designs were dismal things made out of wood, crystal, and hardware wire, and they tended to fall apart. Still, she gamely started plugging them. Sales contacts politely declined. Friends would say things like, "Not bad for a first try." A major retailer finally took pity and stocked some of her pieces, not one of which sold. Then Lorelei stumbled onto using Czech glass beads, and things began to look up. She got some technical instruction and went over to the Czech Republic, where she connected with a local glass manufacturer who took a week off from work to drive her around town, looking for a source for beads. Not long after that, she exhibited at her first trade show and received an order so big that her entire family and most of her friends had to sit around the dining table assembling earrings night after night.

Lorelei continues to go out on branch after branch after

branch to build her business, never looking down to notice the dizzying heights from which she could slip or stopping to weigh the many attendant risks. As she puts it, "What was important was that I stuck with my idea in the beginning and just kept giving myself time to keep trying new designs. I always knew this could work because I wanted it so much." Lorelei now has a small factory with a staff of six, producing about fifteen thousand pieces of jewelry per year. She considers herself extraordinarily lucky. I consider her wise, for she honestly knows the truth about failure and persistence.

There really is no such thing as failure. There is only the rearrangement of plans and the surrender of ego. There is only the twist in the road we never expect. As long as we remain true to our vision and ourselves, we simply cannot fail. That is all we have to remember.

Try This • • •

Make a list of the ten most important failures in your life and what they led to. Were they true failures, or were they simply a rearrangement of your plans? What did you learn or gain? Did you ever make use of these "failures"? Have you forgiven yourself yet? How can you make use of them now?

The Benefits of Wishing for Too Much

As a nation, we are constipated wishers. And who can blame us? Most of us grew up in homes where epithets like "Be careful what you wish for. You just might get it!" were constantly being hurled in our faces.

Be careful what you wish for. You just might get it. What exactly does this mean, anyway? I interpret it to mean don't bother to consciously desire happiness, challenge, and growth, because you—oh, worthless one—couldn't begin to handle it.

I also interpret it to mean that some believe we are doomed to a life of fruitless wishing for fruitless pursuits that would probably be so stressful (even if they did come true, which they won't) that they'd end up killing us.

Well, excuse me for living.

I am a passionate believer in wishing and think we should all do far more of it. And yet there is a definite art to it, which I have learned not only from the occasional wish come true but from a thousand or so wishes that have been dashed.

The magic is this: My wishes only work when I really believe I deserve them. On the other hand, if I don't believe, I usually don't receive.

An example. From time to time, in a casual, backhanded sort of way, I've wished for a million dollars. It's a Pavlovian response, an automatic answer when the subject of wishing comes up. Sure I'd love a million dollars. Who wouldn't? But in the very next second, I also inevitably have the thought that I'll never get it. A million dollars just doesn't fit in my radar screen. It's too vast a sum, too huge a gift. It doesn't seem possible, not given the little person I really, actually, secretly am. And so my wish dries up and blows away, another fruitless thought.

The truth is, I could never accept a million dollars unless I believed I'd done something spectacular enough to merit it. So when I look at it, I don't really want the cartoon suitcase bulging with bills. What I want is work that's worth a million dollars to the world. Then my wish feels stronger, more plausible, truly worth wishing for. It seems like something I might even deserve.

Recently I was looking through the paper and saw an ad for a one-night-only benefit performance of unpublished songs by the late Jonathan Larson, the creator of *Rent*. I have been a huge *Rent* fan and immediately thought to myself that I had to see it. Then I noticed the cost of a ticket: $150. Without further ado, I turned the page, but the wish had already been made. I'd connected with my deep desire to go. I didn't question that I deserved to be there. I could even see myself walking into the theater, ready to soak up every last exhilarating ounce of it. I'd only tossed the idea because of simple financial logistics, so as far as I knew, I wasn't going. Then I promptly forgot about it.

Three days later, on the afternoon of the performance, a friend called, offering me a free ticket to see the show. We had orchestra seats that night, and I learned once again the power of deep desire. I was merely confirming the fact that you really do get what you want in life.

When my wishes haven't worked out, it's been because they came from my stomach instead of my heart. Actually, I really have no idea from what part of my body the wishes came, but they felt like stomach wishes, because they were so incredibly gluttonous. For instance, when I published my first novel, my wishes had me lounging on David Letterman's couch, languidly tossing out bons mots while millions watched and adored. My wishes had me lunching with Sting, turning down screenplay offers left and right, and raking in major literary awards, not to mention escaping from my horribly crowded book signings through a back door to my waiting limo.

The reality of publication included a handful of tiny write-ups in tiny newspapers, book signings where I read to three people to whom I was related, and a book that almost immediately went out of print. So much for wishing from your stomach.

What I learned was that these wishes were all about me! me! me! and not about them! them! them! It took me several years to get it: at the end of the day, the point of publishing a novel was actually not so I could have my fifteen minutes in the public glare, but so I could offer my readers something they might find moving. The point was to give these people a gift.

My wishes have since changed accordingly. I'm learning that wishing for success is not enough. For me to be authentic and feel deserving, my wishes have to be linked to how they serve people. So going on *Letterman* becomes not about

delivering bons mots but about reaching readers so I can share my books with them and do the work I'm supposed to be doing. Our wishes are actually as organic to the process as the work itself, and that is why they pertain to us.

In setting out to do our work, we have to keep reminding ourselves that we're in the business of giving gifts. In order to give these gifts to those for whom they are intended, we have to get them out into the world. Wishes help this process, because they force us to focus on exactly what we want to have happen. And although we ultimately have little control, we do have our wishes. If they come from the heart and not the stomach, and if we truly know we deserve them, then big things can and do happen.

Which brings us around to the title of this chapter. Say you spent your vacation shooting color pictures of turtles in the Galapagos, and they're really great. They are by far the best thing you've ever shot, even though you've been nursing your amateur photography habit for years. Everyone who sees them is struck by their power, and all around you the feedback is positive. So what do you do with them?

Your secret wish is that some magazine like *National Geographic* will buy them, but of course, you know this is completely unrealistic. *(Not a chance in hell! Forget about it! I shot these on my vacation, for God's sake!)* On the other hand, your brother-in-law the dentist said he'd hang one in his waiting room. So you figure that's about as good as it's going to get, there's no point in submitting them anywhere, and you plod off to your brother-in-law's, negatives in hand. Right?

Wrong, wrong, wrong.

Instead of leaping to the chintziest of possible conclusions, try sitting there for a while and thinking about where this work really needs to go. Try to connect with the tiny, hopeful shred of self that's still in there, desperately trying to make contact. Forget about your ego for once and feeding the gluttonous maw of your self-defeat. And while you're at it, try to cut through any overinflated stomach wishes that may have you feeling a bit bloated. If you can, let yourself really, truly wish for something as deeply as you ever have. Something that is of real importance to you.

It's a frightening prospect, getting what you want. Even more frightening is letting yourself believe that you deserve it. Yet this is what separates the people who achieve their dreams from the rest of us. Their passion for their vision is so strong that they are naturally audacious about it. It never occurs to them to wonder whether they're good enough to sell their pictures to *National Geographic*. These people just naturally think big, so they're more concerned with getting the right pictures in the right places. For them, deserving success isn't even a consideration.

The same can be true for you—but again, only if you think you deserve it. Listen to your instincts about where your work needs to go and whom it needs to reach. Perhaps the audience for it will be small and select. On the other hand, perhaps it will sweep the nation. Be a good parent to your work and have high hopes for it. You deserve it, as do those the work is intended to reach.

By all means, wish for too much. The results may truly astound you.

Try This . . .

Buy yourself a special blank notebook, one you really like. Personalize it by sticking a favorite image on it or writing some key quotations or notes in a visible place on the cover or inside. Then take your notebook to a favorite place: a hammock, a coffee bar, a beach, a park, anyplace that resonates with your spirit. I like to make my wishes on long train rides.

Start writing down your wishes in your book—the really true ones you haven't given yourself much time to acknowledge. Let them flow however they do—in lists, words, or even as detailed scenarios. Try not to judge them or get into how you'll implement them. Instead, just let them pour out of you, one after another. Make a regular habit of connecting with your wishes, and when they materialize, make a note of that in your book as well.

Why Power Is More Than a Trip

There is one ugly question that really drives this book. It's a simple question, yet for some reason it's one that no one ever wants to hear.

How big are you willing to be?

Not how big are you going to be, but how big are you willing to be, emphasis on the word *willing*.

The power with which you waltz through this life is absolutely and completely in your own hands, and it can be tremendous. Your mind can gain infinite wisdom and prosperity, and your body can produce extraordinary health and strength. Your mind and body will do this all for you, but only if you are willing.

If you aren't willing to think and be big, what you get is what many of us have: substantial debt, bad backs, annoying children, excruciating jobs. And with that comes a passel of longing for other people's homes, lawns, jobs, lives, kids, and credit ratings. In this country especially, we believe in the power of more money to lubricate the wounds. We see a larger house as the panacea to a stultifying marriage. We imagine a big vacation to be the thing that will finally bond our families. Yet all those problems are quite solvable within the confines of our too-small, inadequate homes whose lawns are crawling with crabgrass. All it requires is for us to give up being small and whiny and finally start to get big.

The process begins with a question: What is it that you get from your current arrangement? You're definitely getting something. Inadequate jobs are excellent places to hide. Lousy marriages are wonderful protectors of the soft part of your heart. (God forbid you actually be with someone who means something to you. You might get hurt!) And having no money excuses you from all those nasty adult responsibilities, like paying taxes, investing in IRAs, and saving for college tuitions.

The mind is wonderfully literate this way, for it truly will produce whatever it is that you want, and by this I don't mean surface desires but those that dwell in that deep place far within. For here is the seat of your power, the place you visit in visualizations, prayer, repeated mantras, chants, dreams, and through other methods that tap into your sub-

conscious. Although I do not know exactly where this big, black place is, I know when I'm in touch with it.

When I have found that place, my desires run as clear and unimpeded as water in a stream. They're not weighted down with the freight of a million doubting thoughts. They're not scrambling over a mountain of mental logistics. They simply are. *I want to lead workshops. I want to write novels. I want to have a wonderful marriage. I want a son and a daughter.* They are simple moments of truth we take possession of, know in our soul, and don't let go of, no matter what. And they are forces that drive us, through thick and thin and past obstacle after obstacle. They are, in fact, that still, small voice that never, ever gives up.

So why aren't we all walking about like the studly bastions of power we actually are?

Simple. We don't think we're worth it.

We stick ourselves in so-so jobs because this is all we assume we can handle. We believe that the ho-hum salary that goes along with such a job is all we deserve. Like anorexics, we refuse to allow ourselves more than just barely enough money or health or love or sex or creativity to stay alive because deep down inside we are ashamed. We figure we are guilty of a thousand unmentionable sins, so why even bother trying to emerge?

Furthermore, we are afraid. Our power is like a huge and unnatural tool to us—a roaring chain saw, when we're accustomed to using a nail file. Yet when it is handled with care and precision, the things that chain saw can and will do for us are amazing. All that is required is that we wake up, open our eyes, and start taking responsibility.

I received perfect proof of this in an E-mail from Barbara, a reader in Minnesota. Barbara was working as a legal secretary for a high-powered general counsel who got promoted to president of the company, which meant a quantum leap in work for his support staff. When this happened, Barbara had the distinct thought that there must be a better way to make a living and scratched out some notes on starting a business that would help people organize their households. She put the notes away and for four years didn't think much more about them. Then Barbara started to burn out.

Not long after that, Barbara quit her job, unsure of exactly what she would do next. A small miracle promptly followed. As a thank-you gift from her boss, she received a day at a spa. So, as she tells it, "There I was, eating my lunch in this lovely spa, reading *Spa Magazine*, and I find an article about a woman in Washington State who does exactly what I [had] thought about doing five years earlier—organizing people. This was my epiphany, and there was no stopping me."

Barbara tracked down the woman in the article, spent an hour on the phone with her, and then set up shop. Her business, now a few years old, is going strong, and she is living life as the truly powerful person she was meant to be. By having the courage to live up to her potential, and walk away from the stress (and security) of an unsatisfying job, Barbara gave herself permission to be big. Her story is impressive.

We must allow ourselves to see what is in front of us and not merely ride along on the old, popular interpretation. We have to listen to what people around us say and concentrate on what's coming out of their mouths instead of what's about to come out of ours. We must constantly assess and evaluate from a place of deep clarity, a place that is unaffected by politics, favor, trends, or the ephemeral meanings of coolness. Use those old first-grade rules for crossing the street: Stop, look, and listen. All of these are things we were designed to do.

Our power demands that we act deliberately. It has no time for sidestepping. We must be unafraid to be utterly honest, to honor our gut feelings, and to say and do the unpopular when necessary. We have to give up our addiction to other people's opinions and surrender to the freedom of acting with strength and courage. We will have detractors, just as detractors always collect around anything new and powerful. That won't change. What does change when you start to live from your power is that you care progressively less and less about those voices of doom and all their vicious barbs.

You will start to see the humor in others' petty concerns. You will actually begin to delight in people's taunting names for you, or the lacerations of the press, because along with power come massive amounts of perspective and commitment. You will be able to see another person's snipes and snideness as a sad expression of his or her own weak character. Because your ability to empathize will be heightened, little anyone says or does will hurt you.

Your power will carry you through whatever you undertake, just like Luke Skywalker's protective "Force." Although you may not always succeed, you will remain relatively unscathed in the process. Your projects may "fail" on a public level—they may not elicit many sales or become critical hits; but for you they will always be precious and sacred—acts of creation that you truly believed in and loved. Behind any failure will still be substantial joy and pride.

Best of all, you will know you are living as you were meant to live, at your maximum potential. The nagging thoughts of "I should" and "I really ought" will dry up and disappear as you move deeper and deeper into your correct place on earth. The work that lies ahead will no longer seem intimidating. You will look forward to ripping into it with your chain saw. As you merrily smash conventions and see the ripple effect of your power at play, you will connect once again with that core happiness that comes from knowing your vital place on earth.

Whether you realize it or not, you were hardwired for power long ago. Plugging into that power requires no more than simply letting go of the fear, deciding you're worth believing in, and doing that which comes naturally.

The small voice will tell you what to do. All you have to do is listen. Whether you know it or not, the Force is already with you.

Try This . . .

Spend one week treating yourself as the truly powerful person you are. Get up an hour early each day and take the walk you've been meaning to take. While you are walking, connect with your spiritual guidance (see page 76) and create an affirmation for yourself that confirms your sense of power. (Affirmations are little statements that help you create what you want in life. When said repeatedly, they seep into your subconscious, where all manifestation begins. An affirmation can be any phrase that expresses what you want to have happen. They are always positive, proactive, and phrased in the present tense. They also work well for calming fears you may identify as holding you back. One of my personal favorites is "It's safe to trust my power." Another one I've used for several years is "My work moves millions of people around the world.")

At least three times during the appointed week, take yourself to a place that feeds your soul—a museum, a forest, a concert, anyplace that calls to you. Make a special point of taking care of yourself that week. Don't have the usual glass of wine every night and see how much better you sleep. If you smoke or drink copious amounts of caffeine, make a decision to stop for the week. Nurture yourself with food that's good for you. For one week cut out junk food and venture into whole grains and fresh produce, and drink water instead of soda for a change. Unplug the television and let your answering machine pick up the phone. After your life is free of the usual distractions, make a point of doing the work you were meant to do for at least five of the seven days this week.

At the end of the week, take yourself out for a sumptuous meal and assess how your feelings of power have changed.

Why You Are Here

f there is one final thought I could leave you with, it would have to be this: Remember why you are here.

I would suggest that it is probably not so you can do the hang thing in front of old *Seinfeld* reruns or compulsively keep house or cruise catalogs. You and I both know there's something bigger on the Universal agenda for you, and you have already been called upon many times to fan those smoldering embers. Otherwise, you probably wouldn't be reading this book.

Well, I'm telling you once again. Make a fire and this time let it rage.

Your purpose in life is sacred territory; it is the beloved idea you wish you could get to if you just had the time, the project you started once but stopped when it scared you. Your purpose in life is not necessarily that useful, responsible, taxpaying thing you do every day from nine to five. It is bigger than that, for it is predicated on what pours from your soul when you bother to open it up. And it demands every ounce of courage, love, sweat, and perseverance you've got. Your purpose in life remains in the hands of God, until you decide to live dangerously and reach for it.

There are no guarantees as to the results, for purposes aren't always necessarily about results. Your purpose in life may actually be to start restaurants that fail. But you must start them, and go through all the marvelous crenellations of that process, in order to grow in the ways you were intended to grow.

Your purpose is simply about the fulfillment of your own private destination as a person in this lifetime. Therefore, it's the quality of the ride that counts, not whether you "get there." I even question whether there really is a "there," for the act of creating is, in and of itself, such a splendid, soul-enriching thing to begin with. Create what you envision, then toss it out into the world. If it catapults you to huge financial rewards and screaming success, if Oprah, Montel, and the rest of the world clamor for interviews, then that's

basically gravy. Your project will already have provided you with the juicy steak of fulfilling your vision.

Dream your dream, then dare to stake your claim on it. What you will receive will be all the riches of the world—yourself, as originally intended.

How to Make Time for Your Soul

☐ *Unplug your television.* Even better, completely remove it.

☐ *Cancel your subscriptions.* Get rid of anything you don't read.

☐ *Make regular "soul" time every day.* If you're a morning person, get up one hour earlier and dig into your projects. If you're a night person, stay up one hour later.

☐ *Say no to your boss.* Leave at 5:00 or 5:30. Chances are, you'll find that you're more valuable than you thought you were. Also, you'll probably find that you work with increased efficiency. Offer to come in one hour earlier, if need be, to leave time for your evening classes, projects, events.

☐ *Don't waste your lunch hour eating.* Bring lunch to work, eat it briefly at your desk, and then get out there and do what really matters to you.

☐ *Stop agreeing to do things you don't truly want to do.* This includes volunteering, meeting friends and family, and serving on committees.

☐ *Redesign your work schedule.* Create one day or several afternoons a week to concentrate on the things you really want to do in life. Explore flextime alternatives in your workplace. Consider telecommuting, working from a home office, or going freelance with your company. If giving up corporate benefits seems impossible, get in touch with self-employed advocacy groups like Support Services Alliance to find out about their various insurance plans for members.

☐ *Put the kids to bed earlier.* Establish "grown-up" time, a time zone when all children are in bed (even if they're only looking at books or listening to tapes before going to sleep) and the adults get to have a little room to breathe.

☐ *Multitask.* Fold nurturing practices into your routine, such as meditating or praying while you walk, or practicing an instrument while dinner cooks. Rather than stare at work on the train, take a book you've been

wanting to read. Books on tape are especially good for this.

☐ *Rethink your routine.* Jot down your daily routine, then reevaluate it. Does reading the newspaper from beginning to end do as much for you as working on the furniture you keep wishing you had time to refinish?

☐ *Cut corners cooking.* Take advantage of gourmet take-out and grocery-store fast foods, such as prewashed salad, precut vegetables, and premarinated chicken.

☐ *Let the answering machine pick up.* Better yet, get on-line and encourage friends to E-mail you instead of calling.

☐ *Create your own sanctuary.* Make a room of your own, preferably with a door. Hang a DO NOT DISTURB sign on it and don't let others interrupt you. Family and friends will honor your request to have some time for yourself only if you do, too.

☐ *Quit volunteering so much.* Cut your list back to only those things that truly enrich you. Give other people a chance to do the rest.

☐ *Divide up the housework.* Hand over the laundry and vacuuming to your mate. Teach your children to do dishes, cook meals, and mop floors. And be willing to give up control of the end results. Read Patricia H. Sprinkle's book *Children Who Do Too Little: Why Your Kids Need to Work around the House (and How to Get Them to Do It)* for terrific pointers on how to make this happen.

☐ *If you can't relax your standards, delegate.* Hire local teenagers, professional housecleaners, or even a temp service to help you clear out your desk, answer correspondence, pay bills, organize closets, walk the dog—whatever you can give up that makes more time for you.

☐ *Do something you truly love.* Once you've created this time for yourself, use it wisely. Take on the challenges and dreams that really will improve your life. Chances are that once you start, it will be very hard to stop.

How to Start a Joy Group

First of all, let's ask the obvious question: What is a Joy Group?

A Joy Group is a regular meeting every few weeks or even once a month with some like-minded others who have dreams to pursue and would like to put the ideas in this book to use. A Joy Group is your way to travel your rutted roads together, drawing inspiration from one another's successes and finding reassurance when the going gets tough.

Okay, you say, but *why* start a Joy Group?

Because at ten o'clock at night when you're sitting alone in front of your completely bogged down screenplay and you've just gotten rejection number twenty-three on your other screenplay, it's nice to know that you're not alone and that you actually do have some supporters out there.

Because when you find yourself cleaning the fish tank instead of calling potential investors, it helps to know that someone is waiting for you to make those calls.

And because when miracles finally happen and the earth moves and you achieve your dream, it's the sweetest thing in the world to share that with friends who really know what you've been through.

Along with reading this book to get the wheels turning on achieving your dreams, you may also need real, live, human support on an ongoing basis. The perfect way to make that happen is with a Joy Group. By showing up regularly at Joy Group meetings, you will have an automatic schedule imposed on your dream. You will also be forced to be accountable for your progress.

For a large chunk of my professional life, I worked with a career coach in New York City. A career coach is sort of like a personal trainer for your soul. I saw mine twice a month for support and guidance on reaching my goals in my career and my personal life. The main reason I hired a coach, however, was that I desperately needed to become accountable for my dreams. I needed to show up somewhere regularly and report what I'd done to a person who cared. Yes, my coach and I did a lot of exercises and talking and probing of my soul. Yet it was mostly by his presence in my life and his willingness to listen that he was able to move me from being a frightened wanna-be writer with half-baked resolve to a published novelist who wrote faithfully every day and totally changed her life.

There is no question in my mind that we need supporters like coaches and Joy Groups and just good friends to tackle our dreams.

When a good support system is firmly in place, the obstacles no longer seem so big or daunting. You will still feel like quitting occasionally, but now you'll have a friend to call who will be able to talk you through it. You'll have a place to show up where your excuses will not necessarily be tolerated, and your triumphs will be celebrated. You will be supported, possibly for the first time, by others who truly care whether your dream is getting any closer. Furthermore, your group will be tuned in to the truth of exactly what your vision requires, so there really can be no escaping—not if you truly want to achieve your dream.

For those of you who've used the lack of a deadline or support in your life to allow your dreams to languish, starting a Joy Group may be the best thing you've ever done.

Here are a few key questions to consider in helping your group take shape:

How Do You Start a Joy Group?

First of all, locate some interested friends you trust—honest-to-God supporters who are really in your corner and who will expect the same from you. (Before you choose them, read the chapter titled "When to Run, Not Walk, from Helpful Advice" and do the exercises at the end of the chapter.) If you're not sure you know anyone who fits in this category, post a sign in a local bookstore, at a church or temple, or on the bulletin board on my Web site (see page 166). Chances are that others who've read this book will already be primed on what such work requires.

Each member of your Joy Group should have a copy of this book, which can be used on a chapter-by-chapter basis to prod discussion or bring up issues to work on each week. Joy Groups can morph and manifest themselves in many ways, so the key to running a successful one is to stay loose and allow the group to create itself and change as it needs to.

Who Gets to Run the Joy Group?

As long as there is someone to rally the troops and make a few phone calls, really supportive Joy Groups tend to run themselves. Although it is important that there be one person to set up the logistics of the group and serve as its central contact, most major decisions should be made collectively by the group itself. The job of being the key contact person can rotate within the group.

At the first meeting the group should decide how often to meet and where, and (very important) whether to include food or not. Together the group should choose how much of the book to use in this work and how much time to devote to each member's progress reports. Most of all, members should understand their terrifically important role as dream nudgers and supporters and do their best to protect and nurture their group as a whole.

Each Joy Group will have its own particular character, and the job of its members is to express that quality. One group of writers I was in always met in slightly seedy New York bars with checkered tablecloths and decent burgers. Drinking beers and chewing the fat over "the business" was really important to our little group. Yet another support group I was in always wanted to meet in light-filled public places, where we sipped decaf coffee, bared our souls, and closed each meeting with a prayer. Both groups worked because they reflected exactly what the people in each group wanted and needed.

What Does a Joy Group Do, Exactly?

Support each other, of course, which usually requires breaking the ice. You might want to do this by having everyone come to the first meeting with a "no-name tag." This is an identification tag you make for yourself that expresses your essence *without using your name*. It doesn't have to be a sticky, white rectangle or even a tag at all, but it does have to express what is unique about you, and it does have to be comfortably wearable throughout the session. You could spend that first meeting by having everyone present their no-name tags to the group and state their dreams. Then you could decide the details of how the group will work.

After that, each meeting's agenda is up to you. Discussing a chapter or an idea from the book at the beginning of each session provides a nice bit of grounding. You might use the exercises at the end of each chapter as homework, or you might not. A different person in the group can make these choices each week, or you can decide as a group how you wish to proceed. (At the end of this chapter, I've included a sample Joy Group meeting agenda, which you may use or ignore.)

If you do decide to discuss a different chapter each week, look for ways that its central themes show up in your life unexpectedly. For instance, if the group decides to read and discuss the chapter "Proof That Rejection Won't Kill You," don't be at all surprised if some rejection comes your way that week. Consider this your opportunity to observe firsthand just how you handle it.

The bulk of your support group session time should go toward the support of one another's dreams. Each member should get a chance to fill the group in on his or her progress since the last meeting. It helps if these updates are timed, so each person gets an equal opportunity, but this isn't absolutely necessary. The art of good listening should be practiced by the group while each member is sharing, which includes not interrupting when someone else is speaking. Also, the group should adhere to that old dictum from twelve-step meetings: You're not there to "fix" anyone or psychoanalyze their problems. Whatever frame of mind Joy Group members show up in is perfectly fine, as long as name-calling and chair-throwing don't ensue. All shares are valid, whether miserable or euphoric, and it is the job of the group to lend thoughtful, solid support but not provide therapy.

In other words, offering reassurance is okay, but playing shrink is not. If Mary says, "I'm kind of bummed today. So and so just said my marketing plan stinks," an appropriate response would *not* be "Mary, I think you're avoiding the core of your pain. Have you tried pounding some pillows?" A better response might be to empathize: "Mary, I think I know just what you're going through. Rejection *is* hell." Joy Groups are a good place to bring your suffering, because this is where you'll find supportive friends who understand.

The same goes for criticism. Our goal here is not to be John Simon and be ruthlessly critical of all work discussed in order to be "helpful" in some misguided way. We don't listen to someone's idea for a new kind of ice cream cone and say, "Yes, but what about the fact that extremely high amounts of sugar cause cancer in lab rats?" Even if you're a paid professional, please refrain. What's sorely needed in all support groups is genuine support and encouragement, *no matter where each person is in his or her process.* We want to treat others' fragile dreams as we would like our own to be treated: with care and respect. What we want to say is something supportive: "Great idea for an ice cream cone!

I've never heard that one before." We want to look for the things that really work about one another's ideas. This is how everyone's ideas, including our own, get to blossom.

In any Joy Group there is only one rule I'd insist on. At the end of every meeting, each support group member must clearly state what he or she will do before the next meeting—and then be held accountable for it. Please write your promises down so you don't forget, and then do yourself a favor and make them happen. If you find it hard to keep your promises, try to find out why. Do you tend to over-promise? If so, it's okay to make smaller promises. Is your time cluttered up with other demands? Maybe you need to let go of other things and make your dream a bigger priority. Or are you simply succumbing to couch-potato-itis? Here is an excellent opportunity to really get clear on why you're not fulfilling your dream and then do something tangible about it.

It is the group's job to remember your promises from week to week and provide support so you can fulfill them. It might be helpful to keep a running log of these promises in a notebook; someone could be appointed at each meeting to write them all down and then bring the notebook to the next meeting. The point is not to put a lot of pressure on members of the group but to set goals in a clean way. No one's keeping score here, and your Joy Group is not a competitive playing field. No one is "wrong" if he can't keep his promises. Each member will be learning about himself and his abilities to follow through and be compassionate, for true support requires gentle but steadfast honesty. If someone is chronically unable to keep her promises, the group (who can certainly empathize) should not be afraid to point this out. Such difficulties are merely human and simply need some examination and sorting out. They are also opportunities for the group as a whole to learn.

A Joy Group is a place where you and your dreams will be taken seriously and treated with proper respect. Remember, this is God's work you're doing here, and it is the purpose of a Joy Group to support that.

At the end of the first meeting, members might want to exchange telephone numbers or E-mail addresses so they can provide or get support during the ensuing week(s). You might want to close your meeting with a prayer, a pep talk, a cheer, or even a cold beer. Or you might simply want to say good-bye.

It's all entirely, gloriously up to you. I only ask that you make your support group as fun and freeing, and as supportive, as you possibly can.

How Often Should the Group Meet?

If it were up to me, I'd say support groups should meet every week. That's how one puts dreams in serious motion. On the other hand, if you don't feel the need to progress so fast, by all means meet less frequently.

For those of you who claim you "really do want to meet regularly" but you're "just too busy," again I say, check out your priorities. What exactly *is* sucking up all your time? Is it something that will improve your life in the long run, or is it just that your dream is a bit intimidating to dig into? Perhaps rereading the book would be helpful here.

Finally, whether you meet once a week or once a month, don't blow off your meetings. Your Joy Group will only work if everyone is clear in his or her commitment to show up reliably. Those who attend sporadically need to examine whether they really want to be in the group—and whether they really want to make their dreams happen. After all, these meeting are about your soul, so treat them with respect.

How Big Should the Group Be?

It depends entirely on the format of the meeting. If you prefer a smaller group and want to meet for ninety minutes, then limit the group to four or five people. That way, you each get ten or fifteen minutes for progress reports, with some time left over to discuss ideas and issues from the book.

On the other hand, maybe you'd like to start a much larger group at your church or in your community. If you've got a large enough meeting space, you can have a different person facilitate the meeting each week, pick a topic, discuss it as a group, and then have a chunk of time for sharing at the end. Not everyone may get a chance to share, but the quality of the shares will undoubtedly ring a bell with others in the room. This is how twelve-step groups have operated successfully for years. And in this way, your group can truly be unlimited in size.

Be open to changing the guidelines of your group as its members naturally ebb and flow. Any size is the perfect size for a Joy Group as long as it continues to meet your needs and move you along on the path of your dreams.

Does the Group Have to Meet in Person? Can It Meet On-line?

It helps to have a hand to shake and a face to which to connect, but it's certainly not critical. If you want to create an on-line group, consider using a list server. These are private lists that connect groups of people with ongoing E-mail conversations. You can send your E-mails either to individuals on the list or to everyone in the group, who, in turn, can respond to you individually or via the group list. It's a great way to stay in touch with everyone's ups and downs—and an excellent way to reach out and get as much support as you need.

Two good places to start in the search for a list server are at www.listserve.com and www.lsoft.com. (Check out its L-Soft EASE Home Services Program.) List servers do charge a fee, but divided among a dozen or so participants, it can cost less than a dollar per month for each person.

My own Web site, www.howmuchjoy.com, now has a bulletin board for starting on-line Joy Groups. There is also a link to my teleclasses, which are classes you take on the telephone. Undoubtedly there are many other on-line variations and telecommunications possibilities that can be put in place that I am not aware of. I invite you to see what you can create.

Why Does This All Sound So Unstructured?

Because it is.

Believe it or not, you are far more capable of creating exactly the type of group you want and need than I am. In order for you to have any real commitment to this group, you, yourselves, must create it first. If this sounds intimidating, relax. These guidelines are driven by the same engine that drives the book—an innate faith in your own creative process and the knowledge that God is already supporting your dreams, whether you know it or not. Your Joy Group will undoubtedly grow and flourish exactly as it is intended to.

By creating a Joy Group, you are not only doing something extraordinarily kind for yourself, but you are also supporting the world at large, and that is the best part of all. In this way, you not only get to achieve your dreams; you get to see others flourish as well.

So go forth and conquer, and while you're at it, give birth to a raft of new dreams.

P.S. And don't forget to keep me up to date on your Joy Group. Send me a photograph of your group and a little information about you and your dreams, and I'll post it on my

Web site. Mail your information to Joy Groups, P.O. Box 142, Essex, NY 12936.

Sample Agenda for a Joy Group Meeting (For Use <u>Only</u> If You Feel Like It)

The group gathers. And after the necessary milling around, small talk, and general all-around greeting that goes on, the meeting begins.

1. *Some sort of opening ritual (optional):* A member (appointed at the last meeting) shares something with the group that he or she finds to be inspiring—a quote, a poem, a story, a news item, a song. Or perhaps the group shares a prayer. On the other hand, maybe you all huddle, cheer, and then order a drink.

2. *Discussion of a preselected topic from the book:* The same person who opened the meeting chooses something in the book he or she would like to discuss—an issue or an idea, or even an exercise. That person might share some personal experience he or she has

had that's relevant, and the group, in turn, shares their own related experiences and comments.

3. *Updates on dreams:* Each person reminds the group what he or she promised to do at the last meeting regarding his or her dream. (Check the notebook where promises were logged for this.) Then the person updates the group on recent progress. The group offers support, ideas, and so forth.

4. *Making of promises for the next meeting:* Each person makes a promise as to what he or she will accomplish by the next meeting, which is logged into a notebook by the member who will bring this notebook to the next meeting.

5. *Appointment of member who will open the next meeting:* The date and location for the next meeting are chosen. Anyone who knows that he or she won't be able to attend (for some *incredibly* good reason) says so now.

6. *Some sort of closing ritual (also optional):* More huddles, more cheers, more prayers and exaltations. Do whatever it is that sends you off into the night (or day) with the necessary spark in your spirit.

A Final, Important Word about Joy Groups

There is one last thing to consider before you go leaping off to start your Joy Group:

If you are a woman, think about having a group exclusively for women.

If you are a man, think about making it for men.

There is tremendous power and a certain freedom of expression present when we get together with members of our own sex. And this isn't just because we women feel we can finally pull up our panty hose in front of one another, or because you guys can finally get down and dirty about the Knicks versus the Bulls. It has to do with connecting on a deep, personal level, which must be present for any Joy Group to truly do its stuff.

Now this is not to say you must start a women's or a men's Joy Group. If you live in a less populated area, or you simply have a lot of friends of the opposite sex you want to have in your group, then by all means disregard what I'm suggesting. On the other hand, if you can arrange things with your own sex, do it. We should all have one corner of our lives where we can connect with our own sex, where our behavior and choices are not affected even the tiniest bit by the opposite sex.

I had the great privilege of attending a women's college and experiencing the freedom that comes from unself-conscious brainstorming and talking. There is just something so rich, and comforting, when women—or men—get together as a group. That is why the bulletin boards on my Web site (www.howmuchjoy.com) are set up so men can find one another to start men's Joy Groups, and women can start Joy Groups for women.

I believe the power we draw from our own "sisters" or "brothers" can truly help move us toward action.

A List of Inspiring Reads

Books

This list of books contains all kinds of different takes on work, spirituality, and the pleasures of being your own person.

The Artist's Way, Julia Cameron (Tarcher Putnam).
> Ideas and exercises for discovering your artist self. This book is the established classic in this relatively new area of self-help. Also contains methods for starting your own Artist's Way groups and salons—an excellent support tactic.

The Back Door Guide to Short Term Job Adventures, Michael Landes (Ten Speed Press).

A fat, rich compendium of all sorts of transient jobs, from working at a Club Med to interning at the Center for Investigative Reporting. It's also peppered with wonderful, inspiring quotes. Perfect for feeding souls that are tired of the same old thing.

Conversations with God, Book 1, Neale Donald Walsch (Putnam).

Excellent spiritual insights into how to live the life you want to live.

If You Want to Write, Brenda Ueland (Gray Wolf Press).

My favorite book about writing—written years ago but still in print and still as fresh, true, and insightful as ever. Very good for getting over yourself.

Jesus, CEO: Using Ancient Wisdom for Visionary Leadership, Laurie Beth Jones (Hyperion).

One of my all-time favorite books. The author had the brilliant idea of applying Jesus' teachings to the world of modern business, and it totally works. Whether you're a CEO or simply someone with a desire to do things differently, this book is an amazing, powerful tool.

Mastery: Interviews with 30 Remarkable People, Joan Evelyn Ames (Rudra Press).

In-depth interviews with highly successful people like Marilyn Horne, Henry Louis Gates Jr., financier J. Peter

Steidlmayer, and juggler Michael Moschen about exactly how they have achieved mastery of their crafts.

The Nature of Personal Reality, Jane Roberts (New World Library).

If you can get over the fact that this book is channeled (i.e., that it was delivered through the slightly tipsy person of Jane Roberts after she had gone into a trance), there's much to be gotten here. Contains no small wisdom about the nature and power of our thinking process.

The Path: Creating Your Mission Statement for Work and for Life, Laurie Beth Jones (Hyperion).

A subsequent book by the author of *Jesus, CEO* that really takes on the question "What am I going to be when, and if, I ever finally grow up?" It's a book that really needed to be written.

The Spirited Walker, Carolyn Scott Kortge (Harper San Francisco).

Prayer-Walking, Linus Mundy (Abbey Press).

Two great books that teach you how to take walks and meditate at the same time. Both very motivating.

Take Time for Your Life, Cheryl Richardson (Broadway Books).

A thorough and thoughtful examination of what it takes to live life as a truly powerful and satisfied person, by

one of the nation's top personal coaches. Cheryl's program of exercises teaches us about "extreme self-care," which always includes the pursuit of your dreams.

The Wealthy 100, Michael Klepper and Robert Gunther (Citadel Press).

Fascinating tales of trials, tribulations, unbelievable luck, and fortitude behind the richest Americans in history. Rags-to-riches immigrant stories that will stir the soul.

E-Newsletters

Here are some fun, readable, free electronic newsletters that will definitely help move you farther on your path.

The Innovative Professional's (TIP'S) Letter

Personal coach Philip Humbert's fat, worthy weekly read. In it is good, solid encouraging advice for developing the leader in you, especially if your dream leads you toward business and entrepreneurship. Subscribe at www.philiphumbert.com.

The Joy Letter

My own E-newsletter that accompanies this book. It's published every two to three weeks and contains a brief message from me as well as a column, "Living the Pas-

sionate Life," an interview with someone, famous or obscure, who is doing the work of his or her dreams. A Q&A column and exercises also appear from time to time. Subscribe at www.howmuchjoy.com.

Take Time for Your Life

Cheryl Richardson's wonderful weekly newsletter, which includes a short essay by her on topics such as handling fear and how to program your brain to solve problems more efficiently. She always includes a "Take Action Challenge," too. Subscribe at www.cherylrichardson.com.

Acknowledgments

Although it appears that I wrote this book, in a curious way I didn't. I just sat down one day to noodle around with "something inspirational," and an entire book poured through me at lightning speed. The manuscript was completed in just under two weeks. That said, the obvious acknowledgment here should be to God, who was clearly the source of this material.

However, during the last several years I spent writing, rewriting, publishing, and republishing this book, I got terrific support from the following people who believed in what I was doing and helped me to improve it. I wish to thank Margie Livingston, Michael Levine, Alex Forbes, Dr. Robert Akeret, Vicki Psihoyos, Tom Kulaga, Dolly Shivers, Henry

Dunow, Marcia Menter, Laurie Dowdeswell, Kathryn Reinhardt, Dick Bond, Andrea Costa, Sari Botton, Amelia Sheldon, Fauzia and John Burke, the participants in the How Much Joy Can You Stand? workshops, and Beyond Words, the small press that originally put this book into print.

I would also like to acknowledge Joanne McCall for helping me find my audience. I offer my deepest thanks to David Chalfant, my excellent agent, and to Leslie Meredith and the staff at Ballantine Books for helping me further refine this book and bring it to the larger public. I also wish to thank the many readers who have shared their stories and the details of their dreams and journeys with me.

Finally, I thank my husband, Larry Barns, and my children for their interest, support, and total faith in my work.

Author's Workshops and Web Site

For more information and a schedule of the How Much Joy Can You Stand? workshops and lectures, as well as *The Joy Letter*, a free, inspirational newsletter by Suzanne Falter-Barns, please visit our Web site at www.howmuchjoy.com.

Index

© LARRY BARNES

ABOUT THE AUTHOR

SUZANNE FALTER-BARNS is a novelist *(Doin' the Box Step)* and writer of inspirational books. Her articles and essays have appeared in *Self*, *New Woman*, *Fitness*, *Parents*, *Writer's Digest*, and the *New York Times* Op-Ed page. She also lectures and leads workshops on inspiration and creativity and has taught creative writing at New York University School for Continuing Education. She is a graduate of Wellesley College.

A LONG SHADOW

Retreat of the Confederate Government

Map by George Taylor

A LONG SHADOW

*Jefferson Davis
and the Final Days of the
Confederacy*

Michael B. Ballard

University Press of Mississippi
JACKSON & LONDON

Copyright © by the **University Press of Mississippi**
All rights reserved
Manufactured in the United States of America

Library of Congress Cataloging-in-Publication Data

Ballard, Michael B.
   A long shadow.

   Bibliography: p.
   Includes index.
   1. Richmond (Va.)—History—Siege, 1864–1865.
2. Davis, Jefferson, 1808–1889.   3. Confederate
States of America—Politics and government.   I. Title.
E477.61.B35   1986   973.7'38   86-5650
         ISBN 0-87805-295-X

Designed by John Langston

Contents

Preface

Most historians of the Civil War South have ignored the final days of the Confederate States of America, including the government's April–May 1865 retreat from Richmond. The only previous scholarly account, Alfred Jackson Hanna's *Flight into Oblivion*, was published in Richmond in 1938. Hanna focused on the fortunes of President Jefferson Davis's cabinet during the retreat. Indeed, half of his book details the escape of cabinet members after the government had been dissolved and Davis captured. Journalist James C. Clark uses the same format in his slim popular work, *Last Train South: The Flight of the Confederate Government from Richmond* (Jefferson, N.C., 1984). Burke Davis's *The Long Surrender* (New York, 1985) goes beyond Hanna and Clark to include a survey of the activities of the retreat's main characters during the postwar years. None of these accounts successfully investigates the historical significance of the crucial final hours.

My book is an attempt to present a thorough, interpretive account of the retreat and to demonstrate its influence on later Southern and American history. The major portion is devoted to the period from 2 April, the day the government evacuated Richmond, to 10 May, when Jefferson Davis was arrested in Georgia. I have tried to place the story of the retreat in perspective as the final chapter of the Confederacy by showing the mood of Southerners facing defeat; describing the personalities, roles and interrelationships of Confederate government and military leaders during the last days; and analyzing the various controversies born during the flight and continuing into the postbellum era.

As the title suggests, my emphasis is on Jefferson Davis rather than on his cabinet. None of the many Davis biographers have given enough attention to the effect of the Confederacy's final days on Davis's presidency and his image in the postwar years. As Southerners began to sense the inevitability of defeat during the winter months of 1864–1865,

Davis became the target of increasing criticism. However, during his final three months in Richmond, the determined president skillfully handled several major issues, some of which threatened the very existence of his presidency. As a result, Davis's image just prior to the loss of Richmond was not as negative as many historians have suggested. Much of the protest against his leadership came from those who had long been his political enemies. The Confederate president's actions and experiences during the retreat reinforced his status as the last, beleaguered defender of the cause and provided the foundation for martyrdom that came with his imprisonment. In large part because of the events of the last days, Davis emerged as a central figure in the postwar Lost Cause movement in the South. The final days of the Confederacy and of Davis's presidency reveal the nature of a dying nation during its waning months and give glimpses of the South that was to evolve from the ruins of war.

Many people made the writing of this book possible. I am especially indebted to John F. Marszalek of Mississippi State University for his invaluable advice and timely encouragement and for his guidance and friendship during my graduate school years. William E. Parrish of Mississippi State University, Emory M. Thomas of the University of Georgia, and Paul D. Escott of the University of North Carolina at Charlotte read early drafts of the manuscript and made significant suggestions that enhanced the final version.

Many archivists and librarians provided expert assistance, and I am grateful to them all. Those who deserve special mention include Allen Stokes, University of South Carolina; Bill Meneray, Tulane University; Cathy Carlson, Museum of the Confederacy at Richmond, Virginia; and Martha Irby, Mississippi State University.

Others who made vital contributions to the cause were Norman Simons, Pensacola, Florida, Historical Society; T. S. Kennedy, Jr., a descendant of Stephen Mallory, who generously permitted me to consult the Mallory diaries; Linda McCurdy, Chapel Hill, North Carolina, who helped obtain research material from the University of North Carolina's

Southern Historical Collection and from Duke University; and Peggy Bonner, who typed all drafts, from the first to the final.

The University Press of Mississippi has been most supportive. I especially thank Executive Editor Seetha Srinivasan for her cooperation, encouragement, and efficiency.

Finally, I would be remiss in not mentioning Jim Shoalmire and Charles Lewis, two Mississippi State University professors who passed away tragically in the prime of their lives. They contributed nothing to this volume, but they contributed more than they ever realized to the development of a history student. I think they would be proud; I know I am proud and fortunate to have known them.

A LONG SHADOW

ONE

The Old Story of the Sick Lion

"AT THE COMMENCEMENT OF 1865," wrote Confederate Assistant Secretary of War John Archibald Campbell, "there was no connection between the government in Richmond and the Trans-Mississippi Department; the defeat of the Army [of Tennessee] at Nashville had opened the West and the South-west to invasion in every part; Sherman's army had devastated Georgia and all the railroad communication in the South and South-west. The war was on the part of the Confederates limited to the defense of Richmond and its dependencies."[1] Campbell's postwar assessment paints a justifiably bleak picture. Though Confederate forces still controlled sections of Virginia and the Carolinas, the port city of Mobile, Alabama, and considerable portions of the Trans-Mississippi, this dominance meant little. Union forces were concentrating for decisive onslaughts against rebel armies in all theaters.

The Confederate war machine against which the Union offensives were to be launched faced serious logistical and manpower problems. In January 1865 Confederate Commissary General Lucius B. Northrop reported to Adjutant General Samuel Cooper: "The feeding 'from hand to mouth' is our permanent condition with a ravaged country, broken-down teams, and R. Rd. transportation not sufficient for bringing

3

forward current supplies, and indebtedness rapidly increasing with a credit impaired." Northrop doubted that the situation would improve.[2]

When Major General John C. Breckinridge replaced James A. Seddon as secretary of war in February 1865, he asked his bureau chiefs for status reports and received a collection of pessimistic appraisals. Echoing problems Northrop had cited the previous month, the chiefs also complained of poor administrative coordination and the lack of manufacturing materials. Breckinridge took immediate action to try to improve the situation. He persuaded Confederate President Jefferson Davis to remove the unpopular Northrop and worked to get much-needed operational funds from the Treasury Department. Unfortunately, despite Breckinridge's efforts, the disastrously inflationary Confederate economy and the continuing transportation problems proved insurmountable.[3]

Keeping the ranks filled with men to supply posed an even larger and more immediate problem. Casualties and disease had taken a heavy toll, and many disheartened men had simply decided to go home. "By 1865," as Ella Lonn noted, "[the Confederate] army was visibly melting away." By then, the wife of one veteran recalled, "The common soldier perceived that the cause was lost. He could read its doom in the famine around him, in the faces of his officers, in tidings from abroad. His wife and children were suffering. His duty was now to them; so he stole away in the darkness, and in infinite danger and difficulty, found his way back to his own fireside. He deserted but not to the enemy." Another contemporary commented: "March [1865] came in gloomy and melancholy, and brought with it a dreadful certainty of disaster and defeat. One thing that almost quenched the last hope in me, was seeing the men coming home; every day they passed, in squads, in couples or singly, all leaving the army." An amnesty proclamation appealing to patriotism of deserters brought little result other than a temporary ebbing of the tide.[4]

The deteriorating military situation weighed heavily upon President Jefferson Davis. At a January wedding party in Richmond, the fifty-six-year-old Davis impressed one observer as "thin and careworn. Naturally refined in his appearance, his hair and beard were bleaching rapidly; and his bloodless cheeks and slender nose . . . gave him almost the appearance of emaciation."[5]

The Mississippian had not found his pioneer presidency to be an easy task. His personality traits had compounded the awesome challenge of at once creating a new nation and leading it in a war for its existence. Once he formed opinions of individuals, whether positive or negative, Davis seldom altered his judgments. Thus, he had supported generals who failed to perform while opposing others who had proved capable, and he found it difficult to deal diplomatically with politicians he did not like. Davis was a proud man who did not take criticism well, and it was for this reason, Varina Howell Davis wrote in later years, that she opposed his acceptance of the presidency. He "was abnormally sensitive to disapprobation; even a child's disapproval discomposed him. He felt how much he was misunderstood, and the sense of mortification and injustice gave him a repellent manner. It was because of his supersensitive temperament and the acute suffering it caused him to be misunderstood, I had deprecated his assuming the civil administration."[6]

As military setbacks blurred Southern visions of independence, criticism of Davis naturally increased. Yet, no one could question what was perhaps his most important attribute as president—his unshakable devotion to the success of the Southern cause. Despite the reverses, Davis remained as defiant as he had been throughout the war. In his November 1864 message to the Confederate Congress, Davis had declared, "not the fall of Richmond, nor Wilmington, nor Charleston, nor Savannah, nor Mobile, nor of all combined, can save the enemy from the constant drain of blood and treasure which must continue until he shall discover that no peace is attainable unless based on the recognition of our indefeasible rights."[7]

During the first three months of 1865, Jefferson Davis had to face several crises that threatened the credibility of his bold words. His most pressing problem was the lack of an adequate force to stop the threatened advance of Union Major General William T. Sherman from Georgia through North and South Carolina. To assemble the necessary numbers, President Davis needed the cooperation of state officials. As in the past, however, Southern governors were preoccupied with the safety of their own states. The governors' obstructionism throughout the war has perhaps been overstated, but certainly in the Confederacy's most critical hour there was no hint of a united front with the president. The military crisis, though it no doubt worried them, did not change their attitudes. Indeed, some of Davis's generals now seemed to have developed the same sentiments.[8]

The president first looked to the Trans-Mississippi area for relief. He urged Major General Edmund Kirby Smith either to create a diversion by marching into Missouri or to cross the Mississippi River and reinforce the Army of Tennessee. Smith responded that high water and logistical problems made both movements impossible. In truth, the general probably had a more personal motive. Since the fall of Vicksburg in 1863, the Trans-Mississippi region, comprising Louisiana, Texas, and Arkansas, had been cut off from effective contact with Richmond. With the consent of appropriate state and central government authorities, Kirby Smith had assumed "the functions . . . of the president and cabinet and attempted to carry on the government." He had developed a strong sense of responsibility for the area and thus felt an obligation to stay on the western side of the Mississippi.[9]

Davis next looked to the Army of Tennessee, decimated during the Nashville campaign of November–December 1864. Early in 1865, General Richard Taylor, former head of the Department of Alabama and Mississippi, had replaced John Bell Hood as its commander. Taylor reported to the president that any attempt to move the crippled army eastward "would complete its destruction." Appeals for replacements to governors in Taylor's old district brought little result. Both Taylor and Major General P. G. T. Beauregard, commander of the Military Division of the West, opposed dividing the army and leaving Alabama and Mississippi defenseless against Union raids and bands of outlaws.[10] President Davis had to continue his search for more manpower elsewhere.

Georgia seemed a logical source. Its lengthy border with

South Carolina minimized the logistical problems of getting additional men from one state to the other. In Georgia, however, Jefferson Davis faced a most formidable states' rights advocate. Davis had feuded with Governor Joseph E. Brown for most of the war over whether states' rights should take priority over national concerns. Brown had become increasingly furious at Davis's handling of the war and in November 1864 had advocated a convention of Confederate states "to formulate a peace program and force Davis to accept it." The proposal attracted little support, and to avoid being branded a deserter of the Southern cause, Brown had abandoned the idea, but he had not changed his attitude toward Davis.[11]

Aware of the governor's feelings, the president decided that a direct appeal for more troops would be fruitless. Instead, he wired General William J. Hardee to intervene: "If your relations to Governor Brown enable you to influence him that is the means to be employed." The ploy partially succeeded, for Brown did send a few state troops to Hardee in South Carolina. Meanwhile, Davis decided that the emergency situation dictated a personal appeal to Brown. In a letter to the governor, Davis reviewed Hardee's needs and the status of the Army of Tennessee. "We must look forward," he argued, "and leave discussions of the past to a more convenient season." The message moved Brown to call out his reserve militia and state patrol forces "to arrest and send forward deserters and stragglers."[12] Nevertheless, his minimal response did little to alleviate the manpower shortage.

While Davis was working to gather troops to keep Sherman out of South Carolina, that state's governor was contriving to break up the Confederacy. In November 1864 South Carolinians had chosen a chief executive who placed the state's interests first. The election of A. G. Magrath, concludes one historian, "may be regarded as the culmination of the anti-Davis, state rights reaction in South Carolina."[13]

In January 1865 Magrath clearly stated his position in letters to Governors Brown of Georgia and Zebulon Vance of North Carolina. He proposed "the pooling of state militia forces when necessary to defend one of the states" and suggested that the three state governments protest central government policies. Neither Brown nor Vance responded positively. Brown did not wish to take the political risk involved. Vance had frequently opposed Davis, but he had no taste for Magrath's scheme. Not yet ready to abandon the Southern cause, Vance turned his back on political intrigue, worked to round up deserters, and attempted unsuccessfully to persuade the state legislature to fill depleted ranks with state militia and older draftees.[14]

In a letter to Jefferson Davis, Governor Magrath insisted that his doomed plan had been conceived only with the best interests of South Carolina in mind. He warned Davis that hope and confidence in the cause was rapidly disappearing in his state. "To restore these and rally the people here and elsewhere," he continued, "there must be a stand point to which all should look as the place where the purposes and strength of our Government are exhibited. Circumstances have plainly made Charleston . . . that place."[15]

The continuing decline in Confederate military fortunes overshadowed whatever anger the president might have felt toward Magrath. Despite all his efforts, Davis had been unable to reinforce Hardee's small army adequately. In early February, General Beauregard wrote Richmond that Hardee had 13,700 effectives; he could anticipate reinforcements from Taylor of only about 10,000. Beauregard urged Davis to send additional men from Virginia and North Carolina.[16]

North Carolina was having its own problems. Fort Fisher, the last major supply port under Confederate control, fell on 15 February. This disaster and severe desertion problems in the state made it an unlikely source of reinforcements for Hardee. In Virginia matters were even more serious. Robert E. Lee's heavily outnumbered Army of Northern Virginia was in a life-and-death struggle with Lieutenant General U. S. Grant's Army of the Potomac in the trenches of Petersburg. Lee believed that sending any of his men to South Carolina would only invite disaster for both Confederate armies. He eventually sent southward a brigade of infantry and a division of cavalry, the loss of which hurt his army and did little to help Hardee.[17]

President Davis clearly had failed to concentr
forces to defend the Carolinas. He commented t
that the result was "more discouraging than
pated," but he refused to lose hope. He sugg.
general request auxiliary forces from Brown and Magɪaᴜ.
and urge the two governors "to use all available means to
restore absentees to the service."[18]

The philosophy of states' rights played a key role in Jefferson Davis's futile efforts to meet the military challenge of
1865. Despite the crisis, the president did not demand help
from the states. Instead, he appealed to the patriotism of state
officials by emphasizing the desperate needs of the Confederate armies and the danger to the Southern cause. His
persuasive approach to the problem sharply contrasted with
the antagonistic tactics of Governors Brown and Magrath,
and even the belligerent Brown responded positively, if reluctantly and ineffectively, to the overtures. Certainly, however,
Davis's firm adherence to states' rights principles produced
poor results. At the same time, his recognition of political
realities may have slowed the Confederacy's disintegration.

Failure to fill the ranks of his armies brought President
Davis face-to-face with an issue much more sensitive than
states' rights: whether to use slaves as soldiers. In his November 1864 message to Congress, he had reasoned that "should
the alternative ever be presented of subjugation or of the
employment of the slave as a soldier, there seems no reason to
doubt what should then be our decision." He had called for a
policy that would free slaves who had been working as la-
borers in the army.[19] By implication, slaves who took up arms
for the South would also be freed. These words and related
developments created a heated debate during the early weeks
of 1865.

Actually, the idea of arming Southern slaves predated the
Civil War. South Carolina had allowed slaves to carry guns
during emergencies as early as 1703, and in 1783 Virginia
adopted a similar policy to meet the exigencies of the American Revolution. In 1861 the concept had experienced a rebirth in the Confederate South. Most proposals involved
arming free blacks only, but citizens in Virginia and Arkansas

had asked the Confederate government to arm the slaves. At the time, the War Department had decided that arming any blacks would be impolitic and had rejected the idea.

The proposal to arm the slaves reemerged in 1863 after the South's military reverses at Vicksburg and Gettysburg. In the spring of that year, the Confederate Congress passed an impressment law to fill the noncombat ranks of the army with slave workers. Arming slaves was again rejected. In January 1864 General Pat Cleburne of the Army of Tennessee responded to the increasingly dismal outlook of the war effort by recommending not only the arming of slaves but also their emancipation. A stormy exchange of letters among Cleburne's fellow officers then ensued, and several disavowed the proposal. Secretary of War James Seddon issued an edict on behalf of President Davis to stop the debate, but the issue refused to die. At an October 1864 conference in Augusta, Georgia, several Southern governors recommended government use of slaves for "public service as may be required." Davis then endorsed the idea in his November message.[20]

During the ensuing weeks, the president decided that arming the slaves had become a necessity. In February 1865 he wrote frankly to Mobile editor John Forsyth: "It is now becoming daily more evident to all reflecting persons that we are now reduced to choosing whether the negroes shall fight for us or against us, and that all arguments as to the positive advantages or disadvantages of employing them are beside the question, which is, simply one of relative advantage between having their fighting element in our ranks or in those of the enemy." During a speech in Richmond the same month, Secretary of State Judah P. Benjamin expanded upon the president's sentiments to the roar of an approving crowd: "Let us say to every negro who wishes to go into the ranks on condition of being made free—'Go and fight; you are free'!" The Davis administration had unmistakably declared itself in favor of immediately arming slaves and granting them freedom as compensation.[21]

Davis began trying to line up support for his policy. He felt confident that the popular general Robert E. Lee could sell the idea to the army and the public, and he knew Lee favored the plan. The general had already responded in January to an inquiry from a Virginia state senator, Andrew Hunter, about the issue. He had said then that the Confederacy either had to use slaves in the army or had to lose them. They would make good soldiers, he believed, and should be freed in return for fighting. He had called for the immediate implementation of the plan. Hunter did not make Lee's reply public, but he did spread the word. Thus, Davis knew the general's feelings before enlisting his support.

Secretary Benjamin asked Lee to encourage his soliders to endorse arming slaves and resolutions of acceptance by various army units soon began to appear in Southern newspapers. Lee went even further and wrote a public letter to a member of the Confederate Congress, in which he argued that bringing slaves into the army was "not only expedient but necessary" and repeated his belief that slaves would make good soldiers.[22]

The president also decided to test reaction to the slave-soldier proposal in the diplomatic arena. He sent Louisiana Congressman Duncan Kenner to Great Britain and France to warn the governments of both countries that their failure to intervene in the war on the side of the Confederacy would eventually lose them the opportunity to take advantage of a divided America. As an inducement, he promised that the Confederacy would take steps toward the emancipation of slaves. This tactic, characterized by one historian as little more than "a last-minute bid to avoid . . . humiliation" of reunion on Northern terms, failed largely because Britain and France had already decided the Confederacy was doomed.[23]

Yet, diplomatic considerations provided some impetus for the slave-soldier policy. Slave owner F. G. Johnston wrote fellow Mississippian Jefferson Davis that to secure foreign intervention on behalf of the Confederacy, "ninety nine out of every hundred . . . slave holders would generally agree to the gradual emancipation of their slaves." Despite such an exaggerated reassurance, Davis concluded in March that the emancipation proposal would not bring positive foreign action. Furthermore, he refused to make any unilateral decision that "would interfere with State institutions."[24]

As time passed, the attitude of the public began to swing toward the Davis administration's position. The desperate military situation changed the editorial slant of some initially hostile Southern newspapers. A letter from Alabama assured Davis that many in that state supported the plan. A Georgian declared, "We should away with the pride of opinion . . . and take hold of all the means that God has placed within our reach to help us through this struggle." The wife of a Georgia congressman wrote her husband that since slavery appeared to be doomed anyway, it would be a good strategy to place slave-soldiers on the front lines, for "some of them will be killed," she reasoned, thus reducing the number of blacks in the South.[25]

One of the more significant letters of support for Davis came from Dr. John Henry Stringfellow, a Virginian who had lived in Missouri and Kansas during the 1850s. In Kansas he had been active in the proslavery movement, had established a newspaper, and had been elected speaker of the first Kansas legislature. During the Civil War, he had lived both in his native Virginia and in his adopted Kansas. In a February 1865 letter to the president, Stringfellow called for "the prompt abolition of slavery." "If we emancipate," he elaborated, "our independence is secured, the white man only will have any political rights, retain all his real and personal property, exclusive of his property in the slave; make the laws to control the freed negro, who having no land, must labor for the landowner on terms about as economical as those owned by him."[26] Stringfellow's anticipation of postbellum jim crow laws and tenant farming, together with his other arguments in support of the slave-soldier policy, indicate that many Southerners had accepted the inevitability of emancipation and were groping for ways to adapt to the change.

Despite such favorable trends in public opinion, strong opposition remained, and Davis had difficulty getting the necessary legislation passed. Pro-Davis Senator W. S. Oldham of Texas and Representative Ethelbert Barksdale of Mississippi introduced the administration's bills in the two houses of Congress on 10 February. After extensive and bitter debates, the House bill passed on 20 February by forty votes to thirty-seven. The Senate did not follow suit until 8 March, when the administration won by one vote, nine to eight. But the bill that became law five days later was less than Davis wanted. The final version provided emancipation only "by the consent of the owners and of the States in which they may preside." Subsequent War Department regulations bypassed the bill by providing an emancipated status for slaves who fought.[27]

In his 13 March message to Congress, the president strongly criticized the delay in passing the bill, noting that "much benefit is anticipated from this measure, though far less than would have resulted from its adoption at an earlier date." He would have agreed with a former congressman's assessment of his colleagues that many are "'die in the last ditch men,' until they come to the ditch." In fact, the law had come much too late to provide any reinforcements to the beleaguered Confederate armies. On 22 March a few companies of black troops paraded in Richmond, one witness calling the event "rather a ridiculous affair." As late as 27 March, Robert E. Lee still had no implementation orders from the War Department. On 1 April, Jefferson Davis wrote the frustrated general, "I have been laboring without much progress to advance the raising of negro troops." A more fitting obituary to the slave-solider issue could not have been written.[28]

Dismal results aside, Davis had handled the controversial affair well. By demonstrating his willingness to do whatever was necessary to secure victory, he had made a favorable impression on public opinion. The deteriorating military situation and his readiness to take a radical step to meet it combined to give Davis a victory in the reluctant Congress. Though the legislation proved meaningless, the president had scored a personal political triumph.

Nevertheless, hostility toward the Davis administration remained strong throughout the early months of 1865, as continuing Confederate retreats and defeats kept public confidence in his leadership abilities low. By contrast, there was widespread belief in the invincibility of Robert E. Lee, and Southerners began to call for his promotion to the position of commander in chief of all Confederate armies. The day after Christmas 1864 Brigadier General William N. Pendleton diplomatically suggested in a letter to Davis the creation of a position to be called "Field Commander in Chief to be filled by Genl. Lee." Pendleton argued that such a move would enhance the president in the public eye. About the same time, War Department clerk J. B. Jones confided some Richmond rumors to his diary: "There is supposed to be a conspiracy on foot to transfer some of the powers of the Executive to Gen. Lee. It can only be done by revolution, and the overthrow of the Constitution. Nevertheless, it is believed many executive officers, some high in position, favor the scheme." Such rumors exaggerated the threat to Davis's presidency. A few days earlier, Jones had written closer to the mark: "It is said Gen. Lee is to be invested with dictatorial powers, so far as our armies are concerned."[29]

On 9 January 1865 the Confederate Senate began deliberating a bill "to provide for the appointment of a directing general of the armies of the Confederate States." Most of the debate took place in secret sessions where Davis supporters attempted to modify the language of the bill. They succeeded in adding an amendment recommending that Lee become "directing general" while retaining his personal command of the Army of Northern Virginia; that Beauregard assume command of forces in South Carolina, Georgia, and Florida; and that Joseph E. Johnston return to command the Army of Tennessee. The amendment advised rather than required Davis to accept the suggestions. The senate passed the watered-down statement by a fourteen-to-two vote, and the final version of the bill passed on 16 January by an even greater margin, twenty to two. The Senate did not recommend any individuals for the various command positions, but it did pass a separate resolution calling for General Johnston's reinstatement. The House of Representatives approved a similar Johnston resolution. On 23 January, President Davis signed the legislation that eventually made Robert E. Lee

commander in chief of Confederate military forces. In effect
the president had "emerged . . . unscathed," according to the
historian of the Confederate Congress. What might have been
a prelude to a more serious challenge to presidential authority had been settled with Davis's constitutional prerogatives intact.[30]

Regardless of the outcome, the strong public pressure to
promote Lee did rankle the proud president. Davis's irritation
was evident in his response to a Virginia State Assembly
resolution calling for Lee's promotion. He pointed out that
Lee had in fact been commander of all Confederate armies
since he assumed command of the Army of Northern Virginia.
It was Lee himself who had insisted on having one command,
wrote Davis, and he had therefore placed the general at the
head of the Virginia army only. Lee's original position remained intact, concluded Davis, and if he changed his mind,
he would certainly be placed in overall command.[31]

Jefferson Davis, a strong believer in his own military
prowess, would normally have fiercely resisted such an attempt to challenge his authority. Given the current military
situation and Lee's personal popularity, however, the president swallowed his pride. Yet, Davis resented what he believed to be Lee's personal involvement in the affair. After
responding to the Virginia resolution, Davis reported to Lee
Richmond rumors that he had changed his mind about not
taking command of all the armies. If the reports were accurate, Davis continued, Lee could have his wish. Lee promptly
replied that he had not changed his mind, noting that present
circumstances would make such a move impossible. "If I had
the ability," he said, "I would not have the time." Undoubtedly, the president welcomed these words, which erased
whatever apprehension he might have felt in signing the
bill.[32]

Once again, Jefferson Davis had demonstrated good political judgment, and like the states' rights and slave-soldier
decisions, his handling of the promotion issue won public
approval. Davis's enemies had hoped to use Lee to fragment
the president's power, but Lee clearly had no designs on the
presidency. Davis and Lee had always consulted on military

uld continue to do so. In any event, the Con-
ary affairs had deteriorated to the point that
tle to formulate a national strategy. Still, his
ted the morale of soliders and civilians alike.
e's promotion, Davis had benefited his admin-

The proposed reinstatement of Joseph E. Johnston called
for a more difficult decision. The Johnston-Davis feud had
been long and bitter, escalating over the conduct of the
Vicksburg campaign. The two had temporarily put their differences aside when Johnston had received command of the
Army of Tennessee at the beginning of the Atlanta campaign
in 1864. Davis's removal of Johnston near the conclusion of
that campaign ultimately placed the onus of the loss of Atlanta on Johnston's successor, John Bell Hood, and on Davis
himself.

This ironic turn of events helped inspire the public outcry
for Johnston's reinstatement in 1865. No army under his immediate command had ever suffered a great defeat, and his
cautious defensive tactics had kept casualty figures relatively
low, making him especially popular with soldiers and their
families. His friends in high places lobbied on his behalf.
Georgia Congressman Warren Akin sarcastically informed his
wife: "It is believed that General Johnson [sic] will soon be
placed in command of the Army of Tenn. His friends are
clamorous for this. I am rather inclined to think it ought to be
done. I have not much confidence in that army, and think it
will have to continue to retreat, or, in military parlance, 'fall
back,' and I think Johnson the best man we have for that sort
of work." One Southern diarist noted that "Johnston seemed
generally desired," and another wrote that the rumor of his
reinstatement "gives general satisfaction." A Georgia newspaper summed up press views: "We hope . . . that President
Davis will not persist in outraging the wishes and hopes of the
public by refusing to restore Gen. Joseph E. Johnston to . . .
command." Davis's supporters urged him to comply with
public opinion.[34]

The president wisely did so, but he chose a face-saving
method. On 22 February, thirteen days after assuming his

new role, Lee assigned Johnston to a departmental command. On 25 February Johnston resumed command of the Army of Tennessee.[35] The public and the politicians had what they wanted, but Lee, not the president, had made the decision. Once more, Davis had emerged from an uncomfortable situation unscathed.

Another manifestation of anti-Davis feeling, in the guise of a peace movement, presented a more serious challenge to the president than the Lee-Johnston episode. There had been such movements in the South practically since the birth of the Confederacy. Their motives varied. Some Southerners had had unionist sentiments from the beginning of the war. Others politically opposed Jefferson Davis. Still others truly believed that a peace based on Confederate independence could be achieved, if Davis would make a sincere effort. North Carolina was in the forefront of peace activities, but by 1864 they were on the decline. The state's most vocal peace advocate, Raleigh editor William W. Holden, lost the 1864 gubernatorial election. Thereafter, peace resolutions failed by narrow margins in the state legislature. By 1865 the peace movement had been so weakened that its adherents contented themselves with awaiting the inevitable defeat of the Confederacy and forced reunion with the North.[36]

Among the other states, the strongest agitation for peace emerged in 1864 in Georgia. A coalition of Governor Joseph E. Brown, Confederate Vice-President Alexander H. Stephens, and the latter's half brother Linton hoped to oust Davis by forcing a peaceful settlement of the war. From their coalition emerged Brown's convention proposal. Whatever their true incentives—and there is evidence that the trio had patriotic motives—they gave an impression of treasonous activity. No doubt their many anti-Davis, anti-administration public utterances, together with Sherman's military blows, broke the fighting spirit of some fellow Georgians, but political opposition within Georgia doomed their efforts. The Georgia legislature soundly defeated convention legislation in February 1865.[37]

Peace sentiments had existed in the Confederate Congress in varying degrees for most of the war. In 1862 a proposal in the House to send peace commissioners to Washington had failed by a wide margin. As the war drifted on and victories became rarer, attitudes began to change. Decisive military defeats in 1863, conscription, impressment, suspension of the writ of habeas corpus, localism, perceptions of an increasingly centralized government in Richmond, and war weariness—all contributed to increased peace activity among lawmakers. Peace advocates faced a major problem, however. How were they to achieve an honorable peace? The First Confederate Congress generally soft-pedaled the issue. Suggestions that the Confederacy appeal to Northern peace Democrats during the Union's 1864 elections failed to gain significant support. But even Abraham Lincoln's reelection did not dampen congressional optimism that peace based on Southern independence could be negotiated. Several peace proposals were introduced when the Second Congress convened in November 1864. One called for Congress, not Davis, to make peace. Another proposed postwar reconstruction based on equality of all states. On 12 January, by a vote of forty-two to thirty-eight, the House narrowly postponed debate on a bill that called for the formation of a peace commission.[38]

Congressional peace activities convinced Jefferson Davis that he had to act. On the day of the narrow House vote, he arranged for a meeting in Richmond with Francis P. Blair, Sr., an old Jacksonian whose sons served the Union on the battlefield and in Lincoln's cabinet. Blair acted as an unofficial intermediary in setting up the Hampton Roads peace conference of 3 February.[39]

To placate the peace activists, President Davis appointed three peace men to represent him: Vice-President Stephens, Assistant Secretary of War John A. Campbell, and Virginia Senator R.M.T. Hunter. Davis believed the negotiations would fail and probably hoped the peace advocates' connection with the failure would cripple their movement. As an enticement to Abraham Lincoln, the Confederate president followed Blair's counsel and congressional advice and instructed the commissioners to propose joining forces with the North to drive French troops out of occupied Mexico. The three Confederate representatives personally opposed the idea and presented it in negative terms to Lincoln. The proposition would not have succeeded in any event, because Davis's further instructions made any meaningful negotiations impossible. He told the commissioners that they could "make any treaty, but one that involved reconstruction of the Federal Union."[40]

A curious aspect of the negotiations concerned a proposal Lincoln made during the talks. Stephens later wrote that the Union president favored a fair indemnity for Southern slave owners as part of a reconstruction settlement. Hunter corroborated Stephens's account, but the two agreed that Lincoln insisted he could make no promises regarding such a plan. Apparently Campbell did not take discussion of the matter too seriously, since one of his intimate associates wrote after the war that in all their conversations about the conference Campbell never mentioned any such proposal. Three days after the meeting, Lincoln's cabinet rejected the idea on political grounds. Given the condition of the Confederacy at the time, he certainly did not have to make such an offer. Perhaps he only intended to emphasize his deep desire for peace or to force a quicker end to the fighting. A more fascinating theory is that Lincoln hoped to lay the groundwork for a postwar political coalition between his supporters and Southern Democrats to control radical elements in the Republican party.[41]

If Jefferson Davis intended to undercut the Southern peace movement, he succeeded admirably. When the results of the meeting reached the public, sentiment swung away from further negotiations. The language of the three commissioners' report rekindled the Southern fighting spirit. In part it stated that no armistice could be arranged except by "complete restoration of the United States" and that "whatever consequence may follow the reestablishment of that authority must be accepted." Davis reportedly asked the three to make the report even more inflammatory by adding that "Lincoln and [William H.] Seward insisted on abolition and submission." They refused, but Campbell noted that the report had an electric effect in Richmond, nevertheless. Residents of the city first greeted it with surprise, "then . . . indignation, disdain, denunciation, defiance."[42]

Why had Davis so adamantly refused to accept peace based on reunion? The sovereignty of states was almost a religious ideal for the Confederate president. He was not willing to trust the safety of this principle in the hands of Lincoln, who had already proclaimed the freedom of slaves and who seemed determined to work his will on the South if or when it returned to the Union. When Lincoln took the position that "whatever consequence may follow . . . must be accepted," he confirmed to Davis and to many Southerners the legitimacy of their separatist position.

The Hampton Roads conference thus proved something of a political master stroke for the harried Confederate president. Some of his most vehement press critics praised him for his efforts to attain peace. Taking advantage of the public mood after the conference, the administration organized a day of public oratory in Richmond. On 9 February in "the African Church, in the theatre, and in a large hall in the capitol, speakers' stands were erected and occupied . . .; business was suspended; and a long procession, in which walked some of the cabinet officers . . ., designated as orators of the day, passed through the streets." Davis did not speak that day, but other distinguished officials filled the air with patriotic addresses.[43]

The president had already spoken at the African Church, a favorite site for white political rhetoric, during a public meeting on the evening of 6 February. He had received impressive reviews. The Richmond *Examiner's* Edward Pollard, normally a bitter Davis critic, recalled: "Many who had heard this Master of Oratory in his most brilliant displays in the Senate and on the hustings, said they never before saw Mr. Davis so majestic!" Alexander H. Stephens found it, "in all its circumstances, the most splendid and dramatic oration he had ever made." Pollard noted that Davis, despite ill health, "held the audience" while scorning the "insolent officials" of the North. The president commemorated the fallen and talked of surrender only in terms of the disgrace it would bring. A Richmond paper reported, "Never before has the war spirit burned so fiercely and steadily."[44]

The abatement of peace talk in the public sector did not

extend to the military. In late February, during a routine conference at Petersburg regarding bartering between the opposing armies, Union Major General E. O. C. Ord and Confederate Lieutenant General James Longstreet discussed current military and political affairs. Ord suggested a suspension of hostilities so that Grant and Lee could meet and talk over possible peace terms. Longstreet reported Ord's idea to Lee, and the two Confederates contacted Davis and Secretary of War Breckinridge. The administration decided to pursue the matter, but Lee quickly concluded that further communications would be unproductive. Grant refused to discuss peace terms, pointing out that Lincoln alone had that authority. Even before he had learned Grant's position, Lee had written Davis, "I am not sanguine. My belief is that he will consent to no terms, unless coupled with the condition of our return to the Union. Whether this will be acceptable to our people yet awhile I cannot say."[45]

The continual downward spiral of Confederate affairs soon had propeace politicians on the offensive again. William C. Rives, an influential Virginian, formerly United States senator and diplomat and, most recently, member of the Confederate House of Representatives, emerged as a central figure in the rebirth of the peace movement. No longer a member of the House, Rives was one of a small group of peace advocates to whom Confederate congressmen turned for advice in March. Sometime during the weekend of 4–5 March, Rives discussed the military situation with Robert E. Lee, who was in Richmond to consult with Davis. Lee's grim assessment convinced Rives that it was time to act.[46]

After the meeting, Rives wrote a peace resolution in which he summarized the hopelessness of further resistance. The resolution called on Davis "to propose to the enemy . . . an armistice preliminary to the re-establishment of peace & union, and for the special purpose of settling whether the seceded states, on their return, will be secured in their rights & privileges as states under the Constitution of the United States." After much discussion among themselves, the Senate peace men decided that Rives's resolution would accomplish nothing even if enough votes could be mustered to pass it.

Following congressional adjournment, peace advocate Senator William A. Graham of North Carolina returned the official copy of the unintroduced resolution to its author.[47] Hoping to keep the new peace fires burning, former commissioner John A. Campbell wrote to Breckinridge on Sunday, 5 March. He reviewed the disastrous military circumstances and the fractured political condition of most of the Confederate states and argued that the time had come for states to act. He urged Breckinridge to ask Lee's views and to recommend that the president seek congressional advice on meeting the crisis. "There is anarchy in the opinions of men here," Campbell concluded, "and few are willing to give counsel. Still fewer are willing to incur the responsibility of taking or advising action."[48]

On 8 March Breckinridge wrote Lee along the lines suggested by Campbell. "It is my purpose," he explained "to submit your views (with my own remarks upon them) to the President, to be communicated to the Congress, if he shall think such a course proper."[49] Lee replied the next day: "It must be apparent to every one that it [the military condition] is full of peril and requires prompt action." He described the army's difficulties and the lack of evident solutions. The general then concluded with a pointed analysis:

> While the military situation is not favorable, it is not worse than the superior numbers and resources of the enemy justified us in expecting from the beginning. Indeed, the legitimate military consequences of that superiority have been postponed longer than we had reason to anticipate.
>
> Everything in my opinion has depended on and still depends upon the disposition and feelings of the people. Their representatives can best decide how they will bear the difficulties and sufferings . . . and how they will respond to the demands which the public safety requires.[50]

There is a theory that Lee, Breckinridge, and Rives collaborated to use Rives's resolution to undercut Davis's position. The only supporting evidence is a memo Rives wrote after his conference with Lee. According to Rives, Lee "thought true policy required us to close the war on the best terms we could." He also claimed that Lee suggested future cooperation with states in the middle and far West and the necessity of preparing to take advantage of possible hostilities between the United States and Europe. Rives's account is the only report of the meeting. If accurate, it only indicates that Lee, like the peace politicians, wanted to avoid unconditional surrender. Furthermore, there is no evidence to indicate that Breckinridge ever spoke with Rives. Lee's response to Breckinridge's 8 March letter shows that although he had little further hope for the Confederacy, he had no intention of rebelling against the Davis administration. Rives noted in his memo that Lee vowed to fight on "to the last extremity" as long as the war continued. Jefferson Davis had no reason to fear a conspiracy from Lee or Breckinridge. These two military men wanted responsible action based on an honest assessment of the condition of the Confederacy. They would not, however, defy the president.[51]

The ultimate failure of the various peace movements probably left Davis feeling somewhat vindicated. To the last, a few Southerners wished to openly challenge his position that any peace be based on the independence of the South. However, developments on the battlefield were rapidly destroying the prerogatives of the Davis administration. The president's victories in this area, like other recent ones, would be short-lived.

By March 1865 the western Confederacy between the Carolinas and Mississippi River had almost ceased to exist. Kirby Smith's continuing hesitation to bring reinforcements across the river left most of the area vulnerable to Union activity. On 25 March Union Major General E. R. S. Canby laid siege to the port city of Mobile. About the same time, Brigadier General James H. Wilson led a strong force of Federal cavalry on a destructive raid diagonally across Alabama from the northwest to the southeast.[52]

Confederate attempts to check General Sherman's advance through South Carolina also failed miserably. By the end of February, Charleston and Columbia had fallen. Joe Johnston could do little more than try to rally the retreating Confederate units in North Carolina. Unfortunately for the Confederacy, he had no enthusiasm for the task. Reportedly he told his wife that he had only been given his former command "so that he would be the one to surrender." Later, Johnston admitted he had assumed command "with a full consciousness on my part . . . that we could have no other object, in continuing the war, than to obtain fair terms for peace."[53]

Eventually, Johnston would reveal his sentiments to President Davis. For the moment, however, the defensive-minded general decided to attack. On 19 March Johnston sent his heavily outnumbered army against Sherman's left wing at Bentonville, North Carolina. When the attack failed, the Confederates withdrew and encamped at Smithfield. Johnston expected to hear from Lee regarding possible combined operations by the two rebel armies, but Lee had decided that such strategy would be fruitless.[54]

In Virginia, Lee faced a dilemma. U.S. Grant's ever-lengthening siege lines threatened the Army of Northern Virginia's flanks. If Sherman continued northward unimpeded, Lee and his men would be caught between the two Federal armies. Lee decided to attack Fort Stedman, a seemingly vulnerable spot in Grant's lines east of Petersburg. Success would reduce the length of the front and give Lee more flexibility in dealing with the Sherman threat. The attack on 25 March proved unsuccessful, and the failure was compounded when Grant received reinforcements and proceeded to extend the front Lee had hoped to reduce. A week later, on 1 April, Union forces smashed the Confederate right flank at the Battle of Five Forks. The next morning Grant launched a general assault that forced Lee to abandon Petersburg. Richmond stood unprotected.[55]

The possibility of Richmond's loss had been contemplated for some time. As early as May 1864 J. B. Jones had confided to his diary, "It is said . . . that preparations have been made for the flight of the President, his cabinet, etc. up the Danville Road, in the event of the fall of the city." The Congress had authorized removal of the capital to another location and had approved emergency measures providing for the safety of government archives. By 1865 fears had increased, and in

February, John C. Breckinridge gave War Department bureau chiefs evacuation directives. Nonessential materials were to be sent to Danville. On 27 February Ordnance Bureau chief Josiah Gorgas recorded, "An order has been given to remove all cotton and tobacco preparatory to burning it. All the departments have been ordered to move." Breckinridge also worked with Richmond city officials to save certain records and property and destroy others. In early March supplies and a few boxes of archives were shipped to Lynchburg. A clerical worker in the War Department captured the mood of the times in her 10 March diary entry: "Fearful orders have been given in the offices to keep the papers packed, except such as we are working on. The packed boxes remain in the front room, as if uncertainty still existed about moving them. As we walk in every morning, all eyes are turned to the boxes to see if any have been removed, and we breathe more freely when we find them still there."[56]

Natives of the city also prepared to leave their homes. In late March, red flags lined one residential street, signifying "sales of furniture and renting of houses to the highest bidder." Evacuees included the prominent. On 29 March, Jefferson Davis sent his wife and family southward to Charlotte, North Carolina, where a rented, furnished home awaited. Davis told his wife, Varina, that "for the future his headquarters must be in the field, and that [his family's] presence would only embarrass and grieve, instead of comforting him." Many of the Davis household goods were sold, "but in the hurry of departure," the check for the amount of the sale was never cashed. Varina left the executive residence as it was, "taking only our clothing" and her four children (Maggie, nine; Jefferson, Jr., seven; Billy, three; and Winnie, nine months), her younger sister, and Jim Limber. Limber, a free black orphan about six years old, had been rescued from the Richmond streets by Varina and virtually adopted by the Davis family. Burton N. Harrison, a Yale graduate and the president's trusted private secretary, served as escort and bodyguard. Completing the entourage were Treasury Secretary George A. Trenholm's four daughters. Before she left,

Varina received lessons from her husband on the art of loading and firing a small pistol. Even the chief executive's family participated in preparations for the worst.[57]

The first three months of 1865 had rushed to an uncertain, frantic conclusion. During these eventful weeks, most Southerners tried to come to grips with the crisis of their failing nation. There had been desperate calls for Robert E. Lee and Joe Johnston to work military miracles. If all else failed, many people had been willing to end slavery and adopt alternative methods of controlling the freed blacks. Peace politicians, who acknowledged that the war had been lost, sought to gain some measure of political victory from the impending military defeat. They convinced themselves that negotiated peace terms would result in the retention of some, if not most, of the South's political institutions. In the weeks ahead, they would continue their efforts. The Confederate government's attempts to gather military reinforcements had shown that the very course of the war had guaranteed the reinforced survival of the philosophy of states' rights, a philosophy that would be more in evidence in the coming weeks. Taken all together, these manifestations of a dying nation planted seeds of a transition in attitudes. Perhaps the essence of the South, as Southerners perceived it, could be saved even if the Confederacy could not.

Beyond anti-Davis political ramifications, the unrealistic expectation that Lee and Johnston could somehow stem the tide of military reverses indicated the larger-than-life image many Southerners had of their generals. In their sometimes real, sometimes imagined heroic imagery of Confederate military leaders, the people of the South seemed to be trying to salvage something worthwhile from a movement that now appeared doomed. Perhaps heroes could give some meaning to the thousands of Confederate graves. Such rationalizations would become more evident in the development of the postwar Lost Cause movement.

Much had happened during these first three months of 1865 that would also affect the status of Jefferson Davis in the Lost Cause mythology. He had been a shrewd politician for most of the period, perhaps more acute than at any other time during his presidency. Yet, as president, Davis found himself constantly exposed to criticism. As the Confederacy irrevocably fell apart, Southerners became depressed over the future. They blamed their president and government and became more vocal in their condemnation. Diarists noted that "March came in gloomy and melancholy," that "people are almost in a state of desperation," and that "God's hand has been laid heavily upon our unhappy land." The government offered little comfort or reassurance. President Davis and the Congress fought bitterly over delays in legislation and the impending congressional adjournment.[58]

This disarray made the president seem weak, giving significance to the words of a Richmond resident earlier in the year: "He is in a sea of trouble, and has no time or thought for anything except the safety of the country. I fear the Congress is turning madly against him. It is the old story of the sick lion whom even the jackass can kick without fear. It is a very struggle for life with him."[59] Perhaps this was an accurate assessment of the Confederacy at the time, but the analogy does not fit the president's case. Davis's skillful handling of the major issues he had faced since the first of the year had not destroyed his stature. More important, his performance boded well for his future image in the South. The methods he had used in searching for reinforcements had maintained the preeminence of states' rights in the Confederacy. Davis had consented to Robert E. Lee's promotion and had refrained from interfering with Johnston's reinstatement, refusing to let pride or personal animosity pit him against the public will. Davis's call for the use of slaves as soldiers and for the freeing of those slaves who did bear arms proved to fellow Southerners that he would make any sacrifice necessary to save the Confederacy. In meeting the challenge of the peace movements, Davis also stood firmly for Confederate independence. His actions did little to salve the wounds of Southerners mourning the imminent passing of their nation. However, the actual lost cause would eventually become the remembered Lost Cause. Most Southerners would recall Jefferson Davis more for his resolute position on the issues than for the failure of his policies.

As April 1865 dawned in the South, Davis's presidency still had not run its course, but it had become more symbolic than real. The same military events that had increasingly isolated the states from Richmond had limited the operations of the Confederate government. Collapse of local governments and local resistance and the devastation wrought by military campaigns had severely crippled the collection of taxes from the states. Rigorous tax acts passed in March had not and would not result in any funds for the central government. Most military districts outside Virginia and North Carolina were on their own. Beyond occasional telegraphic communication with commanders in Georgia, Alabama, Mississippi, and Florida, the Confederate government's spheres of actual influence were rapidly closing in on the city limits of Richmond.[60]

Jefferson Davis nevertheless maintained his stubborn belief in the ultimate success of the Confederacy. During his March visit to Richmond, Lee had been impressed by Davis's "Remarkable faith" in the cause and his "unconquerable will power." The general also thought the president was "pertinacious in opinion and purpose." In a letter to his old friend Major General Braxton Bragg, Davis revealed that Lee had missed the point. "We both entered into this war at the beginning of it; we both staked everything on the issue, and have lost all which either public or private enemies could take away."[61] Davis thus admitted to Bragg that the cause seemed hopeless while making clear that he would not let such thoughts dominate him. He felt he had risked all and now faced the prospect of losing all. He certainly found no enticement in peace terms that confirmed defeat by effecting reunion. He had to work to save the Confederacy, as much to justify his own beliefs and the role he had played as to preserve the cause. In his view, this was the only option available.

As he penned his thoughts to Bragg, Davis did not know that Lee's disastrous situation at Petersburg would soon force the evacuation of Richmond. His government would soon be a fugitive one traveling a desperate trail southward. The pertinacity of Jefferson Davis faced a severe test in the coming weeks, beginning on Sunday, 2 April.

1. John A. Campbell, *Reminiscences and Documents Related to the Civil War during the Year 1865* (Baltimore, 1887), 20.

2. Willard E. Wight, ed., "Some Letters of Lucius Bellinger Northrop, 1860–1865," *Virginia Magazine of History and Biography* 68 (Oct. 1964): 745.

3. Edward Younger, ed., *Inside the Confederate Government: The Diary of Robert Garlick Hill Kean, Head of the Bureau of War* (New York, 1957), 199; Rembert W. Patrick, *Jefferson Davis and His Cabinet* (Baton Rouge, 1944), 151–52; "Resources of the Confederacy in 1865," *Southern Historical Society Papers*, 2 (July 1876): 58 (Aug.): 86, 88–89 (Sept.): 113, 124–25; William C. Davis, *Breckinridge: Statesman, Soldier, Symbol* (Baton Rouge, 1974), 480, 486–87; *War of the Rebellion: A Compilation of the Official Records of the Union and Confederate Armies*, 128 vols. (Washington, D.C., 1880–1901), ser. 4, vol. 3, p. 1094, hereinafter cited as *O.R.*

4. Ella Lonn, *Desertion during the Civil War* (Gloucester, Mass. 1928), 226; Mrs. Roger A. Pryor, *Reminiscences of Peace and War* (New York, 1904), 321; Cornelia McDonald, *A Diary, with Reminiscences of the War and Refugee Life in the Shenandoah Valley, 1860–1865* (Nashville, 1934), 248; *OR*, ser. 1, vol. 46, pt. 2, pp. 1229–30, 1265.

5. John S. Wise, *The End of an Era* (Boston, 1900). 400.

6. Varina Davis, *Jefferson Davis, Ex-President of the Confederate States of America: A Memoir by His Wife*, 2 vols. (New York, 1890), 2:163; Stephen Russell Mallory Diaries, 2 vols. Stephen R. Mallory Papers, Southern Historical Collection, University of North Carolina at Chapel Hill, vol. 2.

7. James D. Richardson, ed., *The Messages and Papers of Jefferson Davis and the Confederacy, Including Diplomatic Correspondence, 1861–1865*, 2 vols. (New York, 1966), 1:482–85.

8. In 1925 Frank Lawrence Owsley made his famous statement: "If a monument is ever erected as a symbolical gravestone over the 'lost cause' it should have engraved upon it these words: 'Died of State Rights.'" Owsley, *State Rights in the Confederacy* (Chicago, 1925), 1. Debate over the extent of the effect of states' rights on the fate of the Confederacy has continued through the years. For recent opposing view points, see Paul D. Escott, *After Secession: Jefferson Davis and the Failure of Confederate Nationalism* (Baton Rouge, 1978); Emory M. Thomas, *The Confederacy as a Revolutionary Experience* (Englewood Cliffs, N.J. 1971).

9. *OR*, ser. 1, vol. 45, pt. 2, p. 636; Florence Elizabeth Holladay, "The Powers of the Commander of the Confederate Trans-Mississippi Department," *Southwestern Historical Quarterly* 21 (Jan. 1918): 279, 281-98 (April): 359; John H. Reagan, *Memoirs, with Special Reference to Secession and the Civil War* (Austin, 1968), 157; Joseph Howard Parks, *General Edmund Kirby Smith, C.S.A.* (Baton Rouge, 1954), 444.

10. *OR*, ser. 1, vol. 45, pt. 2, pp. 683, 784–85, 789, 791, 794; T. Harry Williams, *P. G. T. Beauregard: Napoleon in Gray* (Baton Rouge, 1955), 249; John K. Bettersworth, *Confederate Mississippi: The People and Policies of a Cotton State in Wartime* (Baton Rouge, 1943), 88–89.

11. T. Conn Bryan, *Confederate Georgia* (Athens, 1953), 97–100; Joseph H. Parks, *Joseph E. Brown of Georgia* (Baton Rouge, 1977), 316, 322–23. According to Parks, Brown "advocated a type of confederacy in which each state retained complete sovereignty."

12. Parks, *Joseph E. Brown*, 314, 316; *OR*, ser. 1, vol. 47, pt. 2, pp. 1003, 1015–16, 1038, ser. 4, vol. 3, p. 1049.

13. Charles Edward Cauthen, *South Carolina Goes to War, 1860–1865* (Chapel Hill, 1950), 222.

14. Cauthen, *South Carolina Goes to War*, 226–27; *OR*, ser. 1, vol. 47, pt. 2, p. 1035; Richard E. Yates, *The Confederacy and Zeb Vance* (Tuscaloosa, 1958), 108–9. As a Confederate judge earlier in the war, Magrath had rejected states' rights arguments in upholding the conscription law. Cauthen, 165.

15. A. G. Magrath to Jefferson Davis, 22 Jan. 1865, Jefferson Davis Papers, Special Collections Department, Robert W. Woodruff Library, Emory University.

16. *OR*, ser. 1, vol. 47, pt. 2, pt. 1083.

17. Glenn Tucker, *Zeb Vance: Champion of Personal Freedom* (Indianapolis, 1965), 383; Virgil Carrington Jones, *The Civil War at Sea*, 3 vols. (New York, 1960–62), 3:364; Clifford Dowdy and Louis H. Manarin, eds., *The Wartime Papers of R. E. Lee* (Boston, 1961), 885; Douglas Southall Freeman, *Lee's Lieutenants: A Study in Command*, 3 vols. (New York, 1942–44), 3:638–39.

18. *OR*, ser. 1, vol. 47, pt. 2, p. 1090.

19. Richardson, *Messages and Papers of Davis*, 1:494–95.

20. Bill G. Reid, "Confederate Opponents of Arming the Slaves, 1861–1865," *Journal of Mississippi History* 22 (Oct. 1960): 249–68; Robert F. Durden, *The Gray and the Black: The Confederate Debate on Emancipation* (Baton Rouge, 1972), 99–100.

21. Dunbar Rowland, ed., *Jefferson Davis, Constitutionalist: His Letters, Papers, and Speeches*, 10 vols. (Jackson, Miss. 1923), 6:482; Richmond *Dispatch*, 10 Feb. 1865, quoted in Durden, *The Gray and the Black*, 194.

22. *OR*, ser. 1, vol. 46, pt. 2, p. 1229, ser. 4, vol. 3, pp. 1008, 1012–13; Durden, *The Gray and the Black*, 205–7, 209–15.

23. D. P. Crook, *The North, the South, and the Powers, 1861–1865* (New York, 1974), 356; Durden, *The Gray and the Black*, 147–51.

24. F. G. Johnston to Jefferson Davis, 8 Feb. 1865, Jefferson Davis Papers, Special Collections Department, Howard-Tilton Memorial Library, Tulane University; Rowland, *Jefferson Davis*, 6:519.

25. Farmer to Jefferson Davis, 4 Jan. 1865, Davis Papers, Tulane; *OR*, ser. 4, vol. 3, p. 1010; Bell Irvin Wiley, ed., *Letters of Warren Akin, Confederate Congressman* (Athens, 1959), 117. See also *OR*, ser. 1, vol. 45, pt. 2, p. 784. For examples of newspaper reaction, see Durden, *The Gray and the Black*, passim, and Bettersworth, *Confederate Mississippi*, 171.

26. "Dr. Stringfellow Dead," Atchison *Daily Globe*, 24 July 1905, Kansas Scrapbook, Biography, vol. 162; "Atchison's Father," Atchison *Daily Globe* Clippings, 16 July 1894, Kansas State Historical Society, Topeka; *OR*, ser. 4, vol. 3, p. 1068. There were many attempts to control blacks in 1865 after the war had ended. See William C. Harris, "Formulation of the First Mississippi Plan: The Black Code of 1865," *Journal of Mississippi History* 29 (May 1967): 181–201; Roger A. Fischer, *The Segregation Struggle in Louisiana, 1862–1867* (Urbana, 1974), 31–32; Alan Conway, *The Reconstruction of Georgia* (Minneapolis, 1966), 47–48; W. McKee Evans, *Ballots and Fence Rails: Reconstruction on the Lower Cape Fear* (Chapel Hill, 1966–67), 69–74; Francis B. Simpkins and Robert Woody, *South Carolina during Reconstruction* (Chapel Hill, 1932), 41, 48–51.

27. *Journal of the Congress of the Confederate States of America, 1861–1865*, 7 vols. (Washington, D.C., 1904–5), 4:543, 550, 7:562, 582, 612; Charles W. Ramsdell, ed., *Laws and Joint Resolutions of the Last Session of the Confederate*

Congress (November 7, 1864–March 18, 1865), Together with the Secret Acts of Previous Congresses (Durham, 1941), 118–19; *OR,* ser. 4, vol. 3, pp. 1161–62.

28. Richardson, *Messages and Papers of Davis,* 1:547; J. B. Jones, *A Rebel War Clerk's Diary at the Confederate States Capital,* ed. Howard Swiggett, 2 vols. (New York, 1935), 2:457; Robert E. Lee to John C. Breckinridge, 27 March 1865, Davis Papers, Tulane; Rowland, *Jefferson Davis,* 6:526, 8:214.

29. William N. Pendleton to Jefferson Davis, 26 Dec. 1864, Davis Papers, Emory; J. B. Jones, *Rebel War Clerk's Diary,* 2:368, 370–71.

30. *Journal of the CSA Congress,* 4:432, 453–54, 457–58, 477–78, 482, 486, 7:462–64, 476, 479, 495; Wilfred Buck Yearns, *The Confederate Congress* (Athens, 1960), 227–28.

31. *OR,* ser. 1, vol. 46, pt. 2, pp. 1084, 1092. See also Rowland, *Jefferson Davis,* 6:453–54.

32. Rowland, *Jefferson Davis,* 6:452–53; Dowdy and Manarin, *Papers of Lee,* 884–85.

33. Lynchburg *Daily Virginian,* 25 Jan. 1865; Greensboro (N.C.) *Patriot,* 9 Feb. 1865. See also Mobile *Register and Advertiser,* 2 Feb. 1865.

34. Wiley, *Letters of Akin,* 84; John F. Marszalek, ed., *The Diary of Miss Emma Holmes, 1861–1866* (Baton Rouge, 1979), 395; John Q. Anderson, ed., *Brokenburn: The Journal of Kate Stone, 1861–1868* (Baton Rouge, 1955), 312–13; Macon *Southern Confederacy,* 22 Jan. 1865; Mobile *Register and Advertiser,* 2 Feb. 1865.

35. E. B. Long, *The Civil War Day by Day: An Almanac, 1861–1865* (Garden City, N.Y., 1971), 636, 642–43.

36. Wilfred B. Yearns, "The Peace Movement in the Confederate Congress," *Georgia Historical Quarterly* 41 (March 1957): 1, 6; Horace W. Raper, "William W. Holden and the Peace Movement in North Carolina," *North Carolina Historical Review* 31 (Oct. 1954): 515–16. See also Larry E. Nelson, *Bullets, Ballots, and Rhetoric: Confederate Policy for the United States Presidential Contest of 1864* (University, Ala. 1980).

37. John E. Talmadge, "Peace-Movement Activities in Civil War Georgia," *Georgia Review* 7 (Summer 1953): 190–203; John R. Brumgardt, "Alexander H. Stephens and the State Convention Movement in Georgia: A Reappraisal," *Georgia Historical Quarterly* 59 (Spring 1975): 38–49. Brumgardt argues that in 1865 Stephens turned his back on the state convention proposal.

38. This discussion of congressional peace activities is based on Yearns, "Peace Movement in the Confederate Congress," 2–15.

39. See Rowland, *Jefferson Davis,* 6:465–478.

40. Yearns, *Confederate Congress,* 180–81; Paul J. Zingg, "John Archibald Campbell and the Hampton Roads Conference: Quixotic Diplomacy, 1865," *Alabama Historical Quarterly* 36 (Spring 1974): 24, 28; Alexander H. Stephens, *A Constitutional View of the Late War between the States,* 2 vols. (Philadephia, 1870), 2:608; Campbell, *Reminiscences and Documents,* 4. Hunter alleged that Judah Benjamin tried to persuade Davis to eliminate the demand for continued separation. Benjamin rejoined that he had only suggested that Davis offer vague terms, thereby forcing Lincoln to propose specifics. R. M. T. Hunter, "The Peace Commission of 1865," *Southern Historical Society Papers* 3 (April 1877): 170; Judah P. Benjamin to Jefferson Davis, 17 May 1877, Samuel Richey Collection, Walter Havighurst Special Collections, Miami University, Oxford, Ohio.

41. Stephens, *Constitutional View of the War,* 2:617; Hunter, "Peace Com-

mission," 174; B. R. Wellford, "Mr. Goode Sustained as to the Historic Hampton Roads Conference," Richmond *Dispatch*, 18 May 1902; Gideon Welles, *Diary of Gideon Welles*, 2 vols. (Boston, 1911), 2:237; Ludwell H. Johnson, "Lincoln's Solution to the Problem of Peace Terms, 1864–1865," *Journal of Southern History* 34 (Nov. 1968), 576–86.

42. Rowland, *Jefferson Davis*, 6:466–67; Younger, *Inside the Confederate Government*, 202; Campbell, *Reminiscences and Documents*, 19. Similar reactions occurred elsewhere in the Confederacy. See Wilfred Buck Yearns and John G. Barrett, eds., *North Carolina: Civil War Documentary* (Chapel Hill, 1980), 305–6; Randy J. Sparks, "John P. Osterhaut: Yankee, Rebel, Republican," forthcoming publication in the *Southwestern Historical Quarterly*, 19 (page number refers to original typescript in possession of Randy J. Sparks).

43. Richmond *Whig*, 30 Jan. 1865; Macon *Southern Confederacy*, 7 Feb. 1865; Mobile *Register and Advertiser*, 29 Jan. 1865; Edward A. Pollard, *Life of Jefferson Davis, with a Secret History of the Confederacy* (Philadelphia, 1869), 471–72. See the Richmond *Sentinel*, 10 Feb. 1865, reprinted in the New York *Times*, 13 Feb. 1865, for texts of the speeches delivered at the 9 Feb. rally.

44. Stephens, *Constitutional View of the War*, 2:623–24; Pollard, *Life of Jefferson Davis*, 470–73; Richmond *Dispatch*, 7 Feb. 1865, quoted in the New York *Times*, 10 Feb. 1865. In his *Life of Jefferson Davis*, Pollard gives the location of Davis's speech as Metropolitan Hall, Franklin Street, in Richmond. However, the *Dispatch* names the African Church as the site, as does Stephens, *Constitutional View of the War*, 2:623.

45. James Longstreet, *From Manassas to Appomattox: Memoirs of the Civil War in America*, ed. James I. Robertson, Jr. (Bloomington, Ind., 1960), 583–87; *OR*, ser. 1, vol. 46, pt. 2, p. 1264; Dowdy and Manarin, *Papers of Lee*, 911–12.

46. John Hammond Moore, "The Rives Peace Resolution, March 1865," *West Virginia History* 26 (April 1965): 155–56. Other members of the peace advisory group were William A. Graham, James C. Orr (South Carolina senator), R. M. T. Hunter, and John Campbell.

47. Moore, "Rives Peace Resolution," 156–57, 159–60.

48. *OR*, ser. 1, vol. 51, pt 2, p. 1064–67.

49. Ibid., vol. 46, pt. 2, pp. 1292.

50. Dowdy and Manarin, *Papers of Lee*, 912–13. Lee's public comments were an elaboration of his private thoughts mentioned to a friend in Nov. 1864 that the "cause had to fail." Rowland, *Jefferson Davis*, 8:30–31.

51. Moore, "Rives Peace Resolution," 157–59.

52. E. B. Long, *Civil War Day by Day*, 657; James Pickett Jones, *Yankee Blitzkrieg: Wilson's Raid through Alabama and Georgia* (Athens, 1976), 13.

53. C. Vann Woodward, ed., *Mary Chesnut's Civil War* (New Haven, 1981), 729; Joseph E. Johnston, *Narrative of Military Operations Directed during the Late War between the States* (New York, 1874), 372.

54. Thomas Lawrence Connelly, *Autumn of Glory: The Army of Tennessee, 1862–1865* (Baton Rouge, 1971), 522–30; Dowdy and Manarin, *Papers of Lee*, 915, 917.

55. Freeman, *Lee's Lieutenants*, 3:638, 645–54, 662–74, 680.

56. J. B. Jones, *Rebel War Clerk's Diary*, 2:207, 440–42; William C. Davis, *Breckinridge*, 493–94, 499; *Journal of the CSA Congress*, 4:702, 7:740; Frank E. Vandiver, ed., *The Civil War Diary of General Josiah Gorgas* (University, Ala., 1947), 171; Judith W. McGuire, *Diary of a Southern Refugee during the War* (New York, 1972), 334.

57. J. B. Jones, *Rebel War Clerk's Diary*, 2:455, 461; Varina Davis, *Jefferson Davis*, 2:575–77; Peggy Robbins, "Jim Limber and the Davises," *Civil War Times Illustrated* 17 (Nov. 1978): 23–24.

58. McDonald, *Diary*, 248; Vandiver, *Diary of Josiah Gorgas*, 172; Daniel E. Huger Smith et al., eds., *Mason Smith Family Letters, 1860–1868* (Columbia, S.C., 1950), 171; Richardson, *Messages and Papers of Davis*, 1:544–51; *Journal of the CSA Congress*, 4:726–31; Rowland, *Jefferson Davis*, 6:525. For an analysis of Davis's relationship with the congress see Mallory Diaries, vol. 2.

59. [Virginia Clay], *A Belle of the Fifties: Memoirs of Mrs. Clay of Alabama, Covering Social and Political Life in Washington and the South, 1853–1866* (New York, 1905), 239.

60. John E. Johns, *Florida during the Civil War* (Gainesville, 1963), 80–81; Bryan, *Confederate Georgia*, 64–65; Richard Cecil Todd, *Confederate Finance* (Athens, 1954), 153–54. See also Bettersworth, *Confederate Mississippi*, 124–25. For an overview of communications between Richmond and the military departments, see *OR*, ser. 1, vol. 46, pt. 3, vol. 47, pt. 3, and vol. 49, pt. 2.

61. John B. Gordon, *Reminiscences of the Civil War* (New York, 1903), 393; Jefferson Davis to Braxton Bragg, 1 April 1865, Davis Papers, Tulane.

TWO

The Scream and Rumble of the Cars

CONFEDERATE ADMIRAL RAPHAEL SEMMES remembered the first April Sunday of 1865 as a bright, sunny day. Nature had begun "to put on her spring attire," birds glided above Richmond earth "green with early grass," and plowed fields awaited the planting of corn. Richmond resident Mary Johnston recalled "fruit trees in bloom, white butterflies above the dandelions, the air all sheen and fragrance." Sallie Ann Brock noted "a soft haze rested over the city," but above, the sun glistened brightly in a cloudless sky. It seemed impossible that sounds of war could disturb such a day, when only "the subdued murmur" of the James River and "the cheerful music of the church bells" interrupted the quiet of the morning. This Sunday began predictably enough. At the War Department and post office, early risers hoped to hear news from the Petersburg front. Others set out to visit relatives or perhaps to see the sick and convalescents, who ventured outside to enjoy the weather. Pleasant Sundays often meant full churches, and today would be no exception. As the hour of morning worship approached, the streets became crowded with churchgoers.[1]

The congregations appeared as relaxed and easy as the weather. Rumors of impending disaster to Robert E. Lee's army and the possible evacuation of Richmond faded into the background on this beautiful Sabbath, Communion day for many of the churches. Charles Minnigerode, pastor of Saint Paul's Episcopal Church, was one of the few who recorded uneasiness. The day brought memories of another time; this was a Sunday "like that of the first Manassas, and the air seemed full of something like a foreboding of good or bad."[2] About half an hour before church services began, a telegraph key gave credence to Minnigerode's foreboding. A message from Robert E. Lee addressed to General J. C. Breckinridge reached Richmond at 10:40 A.M. The news proved to be the direct opposite of the good tidings received from the Manassas plains nearly four years before. In concise detail, Lee outlined his dismal situation at Petersburg:

> I see no prospect of doing more than holding our position here till night. I am not certain that I can do that. If I can I shall withdraw to-night north of the Appomattox, and, if possible, it will be better to withdraw the whole line to-night from James River. The brigades on Hatcher's Run are cut off from us; enemy have broken through our lines and intercepted between us and them, and there is no bridge over which they can cross the Appomattox this side of Goode's or Beaver's which are not very far from the Danville railroad. Our only chance, then, of concentrating our forces, is to do so near Danville railroad, which I shall endeavor to do at once. I advise that all preparation be made for leaving Richmond to-night. I will advise you later, according to circumstance.[3]

In the traditional story Davis first learned of Lee's situation while sitting in his special pew at Saint Paul's Church, but in fact, he evidently knew of the telegram beforehand. According to War Bureau chief Robert Kean's diary, both Postmaster General John Reagan and Davis aide Francis R. Lubbock witnessed receipt of the wire at the War Department. Reagan claims to have gone immediately to inform Davis of the message. He says he met both Davis and Lubbock on their way to church and told them of the situation at Petersburg. Navy Department clerk C. E. L. Stuart wrote of the morning's events: "Mr. Davis went, as usual, to St. Paul's Episcopal Church. . . . He looked careworn, yet contrived to tinge his concern with a briskness which warded off suspicion. A certain ominous telegram that he received in the early part of the morning was, however, a tormenting demon, manifestly too much for the perfect quiet which would be needed in the house of prayer and praise." Thus, Davis evidently knew of Lee's message, which arrived twenty minutes before the beginning of eleven o'clock services, before he entered Saint Paul's.[4]

Meanwhile, another message from Lee, this one addressed to President Davis, arrived in Richmond. More pointed than the earlier wire to Breckinridge, it informed Davis that retreat was "absolutely necessary." A courier hurried to Saint Paul's with the telegram.[5]

The president sat in his usual pew that morning, "seemingly as placid and confident as others" in attendance. The German-born Minnigerode, speaking with a slight accent, was delivering, as one worshiper later recalled, "one of his stirring and fervid" Communion Sunday sermons. As he spoke, Minnigerode "saw the sexton go to Mr. Davis's pew and hand him what proved to be a telegram. I could not but see it. Mr. Davis took it quietly, not to disturb the congregation, put on his overcoat and walked out." Davis later admitted that his leaving undoubtedly attracted attention, but since he often received messages in church, he believed there was no great disturbance this time. Accounts to the contrary "were the creations of fertile imaginations."[6]

Many other versions of the incident contradict Davis. They note that the sexton made additional trips down the aisles, and several more people, "all connected with the government and military service," left the church. Sensing the import of these interruptions, Minnigerode nevertheless tried to continue the service. "Of course the congregation became very restless," he recalled, "and I tried to finish my address as soon as I could, without adding to the threatening panic." Finally, the pastor himself had to leave the pulpit for a conference in the church vestry with the city provost-marshal. He returned to the service and "found the congregation streaming out of the church." Most worshippers returned when he called them back, and Minnigerode told them of Lee's plans to retreat from Petersburg and that the home guard had orders to form at three o'clock in Capitol Square. Perhaps three hundred stayed until the end of the service, but it seemed "as if they were kneeling there with the halter around their necks. The panic was so great."[7]

Other eyewitnesses had similar recollections of disturbances. C. E. L. Stuart concluded, "Had an unseen hand written the coming doom on the wall in letters of fire, the effect could not have been more appalling or more instantaneous." A military officer's wife felt the "ominous fear" that quickly spread through the church. Others could not forget the "uneasy whisper" and the "universal tremor of alarm" that raced through the congregation.[8]

Perhaps Davis played down the reaction to his departure to convey the impression that people in Richmond generally and those at Saint Paul's in particular had accepted the bad news with dignity and calm. Perhaps because he left the church first, he actually saw no evidence of panic. Whatever the case, his view of the situation has no foundation in fact.

The president apparently remained calm. Richmond resident Mary Johnston saw Davis rise from his seat "with a still face" and go "softly down the aisle, erect and quiet." A soldier nearby was struck by Davis's "calm expression," and a youngster who witnessed the scene remembered that Davis's "self-control was perfect." One witness wrote to a friend a few days later that the president left immediately, "his face set so we could read nothing."[9]

Others denied that Davis was so stoic. The future wife of Burton Harrison, Davis's secretary, recalled, "I happened to sit in the rear of the President's pew, so near that I plainly saw the sort of gray pallor that came upon his face as he read a scrap of paper thrust into his hand." Sallie Brock similarly recounted that Davis "was noticed to walk rather unsteadily out of the church."[10]

If events at Petersburg momentarily unnerved Davis, he quickly regained his composure. Hurrying to his office in the former United States Customhouse, he called the cabinet into session. The able men who assembled that morning had varied backgrounds and perhaps held divergent views on proper government policy during the current crisis, but their loyalty to President Davis remained firm. They would support his decisions as long as possible.[11]

Secretary of War John C. Breckinridge had had a long, illustrious political career. Beginning in 1851, he had successively been a United States representative, vice-president of the United States under James Buchanan, and at the outbreak of the war a United States senator. The forty-four-year-old Kentuckian had attended law school at Princeton, had practiced law in Iowa and Kentucky, and had fought in the Mexican War. Before accepting the job as head of the War Department, Breckinridge had been a brigadier and major general in the army, where he had shown good leadership qualities. Breckinridge was tall, humorous, and frank, and he sported a long, curvy moustache that had become his trademark. He had no illusions about prospects for continuing the war. A few weeks earlier, he had remarked during an informal meeting with a group of congressmen that he hoped the Confederacy would surrender as a country and not "disband like banditti."[12] In the days ahead, Breckinridge would be a key adviser to the president and would become a central figure in the retreat of the government.

Judah P. Benjamin, the only cabinet member who had not been at church services that morning, was probably the first to arrive at the meeting, for he was already in his office, only a few feet from Davis's, when the president arrived. He had spent most of the previous evening packing documents to be shipped south in case of emergency. Adjutant General Samuel Cooper, who considered the threat to Richmond no matter for levity, had been outraged to find Benjamin singing and whistling to entertain those who worked with him. The secretary of state had an irrepressible sense of humor and a keen mind. Now fifty-three, he had had a successful legal and political career in Louisiana before the war and was the first professing Jew to be elected to the United States Senate. Benjamin had served the Confederacy as attorney general and secretary of war before becoming secretary of state in 1862, and his actions had often been controversial. Yet there was probably no one in the government that Jefferson Davis trusted more. Benjamin was short, swarthy, and stocky. He had been well educated at private preparatory schools and Yale, and his philosophy "was to live in and for the present," a view that allowed him to take the current situation in stride.[13]

Like Benjamin, Stephen R. Mallory was born in the West Indies. He grew up in Florida, where he had enjoyed a successful legal and political career, including ten years in the United States Senate, and he was nearly fifty when the war began. Head of the Navy Department since the beginning of the war, Mallory had performed well, despite lack of funds and material. He had not been a staunch advocate of secession, and although loyal to the president, he had never developed a particularly close relationship with Davis. Now, as chief of a naval force near extinction, Mallory would have few duties to perform in the days ahead. He would, however, produce a valuable written account of the government's retreat.

One of the South's most successful businessmen, Secretary of the Treasury George A. Trenholm had not gained his current post until July 1864. Before entering the cabinet, Trenholm had been a financier of Confederate shipping and a financial advisor to the government. A distinguished-looking man, he made friends easily, thus helping the public image of the administration. Trenholm vigorously attacked the problems of the economy, but the task proved impossible. Chronic neuralgia plagued the fifty-eight-year-old South Carolinian, and the coming weeks would be especially trying for him.

Forty-six-year-old Postmaster General John H. Reagan had risen from somewhat humble beginnings in Tennessee to a successful legal and political career in Texas. When war broke out in 1861, Reagan resigned the seat he had held in the United States House of Representatives for four years. After the formation of the Confederate government, he accepted the cabinet post he still held in 1865. A good administrator, Reagan had met the awesome challenge of establishing a postal system, but his determination could not overcome scarce means and the interference of military operations. A strong Davis loyalist, Reagan would play a prominent role in the weeks ahead.

Attorney General George Davis had not attended his usual

church the morning of 2 April. Messengers thus had trouble locating him, and he arrived late for the cabinet meeting.[14] He was a North Carolinian, not related to the president, and had initially been a foe of secession. He had changed his mind after attending the 1861 peace conference in Washington, where he became convinced that the South could not coexist with an antislavery Republican government. A graduate of the University of North Carolina, the forty-five-year-old Davis had practiced law before the war. Unlike his fellow cabinet members, he had held no political office before Fort Sumter. However, he had served two years in the Confederate Senate before losing his seat to the prounion peace advocate William A. Graham. The congenial Davis had become the Confederacy's fourth attorney general in January 1864. Since then, he had developed a relationship of mutual respect and confidence with the president.

Jefferson Davis called the emergency meeting to order. Those assembled in addition to the cabinet included Richmond Mayor Joseph Mayo, Virginia Governor William Smith, and former governor John Letcher. They listened while the president calmly reviewed the developments at Petersburg. Mallory observed that none of his colleagues "betrayed . . . evidence of the emotions which filled their breasts." Benjamin he compared with "the last man outside the ark, who assured Noah of his belief that 'it would not be such a hell of a shower after all.'" Jefferson Davis and Mallory both claimed later that the events of 2 April had long been expected and the government was prepared. Yet, as Davis would later write, "The event had come before Lee had expected it, and the announcement was received by us in Richmond with sorrow and surprise; for, though it had been foreseen as a coming event which might possibly, though not probably, be averted, and such preparation as was practicable had been made to meet the contingency when it should occur, it was not believed to be so near at hand." His words offer a clue as to why Davis went to church after learning of Lee's first message. The president simply could not accept the reality at Petersburg. One of his biographers concluded that Davis believed Lee would wire him directly on a matter of such magnitude.[15]

After being informed of the 10:40 message, Davis had tele-graphed Lee that evacuation by nightfall would result in "the loss of many valuables, both for want of time to pack and of transportation."[16] Obviously, Davis still did not appreciate the severity of the crisis. It took Lee's later message delivered to him at Saint Paul's to move the president to act.

The cabinet meeting ended with what seemed to be no more sense of urgency than Davis had exhibited earlier when he had decided to go ahead with his plans to attend church. Each member left to take care of his various duties. One of the most immediate problems involved the disposition of government archives.

The president's staff immediately set to work sorting and packing executive papers. Davis was fortunate in having competent and loyal aides: John Taylor Wood, William Preston Johnston, Francis R. Lubbock, and Micajah H. Clark. Wood, grandson of Zachary Taylor and nephew of Jefferson Davis by Davis's first marriage to Sarah Knox Taylor, had served before the war in the United States Navy and had been a professor at the Naval Academy. He had also served in the Confederate Navy until early 1865 when he had joined Davis's staff. Johnston at thirty-four was the same age as Wood. He was the son of Major General Albert Sidney Johnston, martyred at Shiloh. Before the war, he attended several colleges, including Yale. In 1861 he enlisted in the First Kentucky Infantry and served until May 1862, when he became aide-de-camp to President Davis. Lubbock, a successful Texas politician, had been governor of his state from 1861 to 1863. Afterward, he had served in the army as a lieutenant colonel before joining the presidential staff in 1864. Clark, a native of Richmond and member of an old and respected Virginia family, was chief clerk in the executive office and a valuable and hard worker.[17]

The staff supervising the removal of office papers to the executive mansion for packing found departed secretary Burton Harrison's trunk convenient for their purposes, since Harrison's papers had already been packed before his departure with the president's family. Documents deemed valuable enough to save included the personal items of Davis and his staff and some official correspondence, including some of

Lee's dispatches to Davis. The overall responsibility for evacuating the papers from Richmond apparently fell to Clark, who arranged to have them transported to the railroad station. In spite of Wood's later insistence that all of the president's personal papers made it out of the city, a number of letters addressed to Davis turned up in private hands after the war. Fire also consumed a large portion of executive records considered either insignificant or too bulky for transfer.[18]

Other departments frantically packed their files. The most important records of the Post Office Department had been sent away earlier in the care of Henry Offut, chief of the Contract Bureau. Perhaps he had taken records of the Congress as well, for these records were found with postal documents in South Carolina after the war.[19]

War Department archives met a variety of fates. Officials sent significant general records to the railroad depot. Files from several departments, including most quartermaster records, had been sent westward to Lynchburg a few weeks earlier. Other departmental records simply disappeared in the confusion. Lack of transportation prevented the removal of some files; others were judged unimportant; and many Navy Department and other files undoubtedly burned in the fire that swept through the city during the evening of the evacuation. However, a few must have survived, since an observer claimed to have seen navy files being destroyed later at the navy yard in Charlotte, North Carolina.[20]

In spite of his nonchalant demeanor, Judah Benjamin was one of the few officials who had taken the dangerous situation seriously. On 28 March, William J. Brownell, a trusted Benjamin assistant, had left Richmond with several boxes of State Department records for storage at Charlotte. On the way, Brownell had stopped in Danville, Virginia, to collect more records that had been stored in buildings of the Danville Female College. During the evacuation, Benjamin himself burned records of the secret service. The fate of the bulk of diplomatic files remains uncertain. One account traces them to an unspecified barn in Virginia, another to a barn near Charlotte. Since Brownell took so many records there, Charlotte seems the most logical site.[21]

While clerks in the Treasury Department prepared papers and money for shipment, Stephen Mallory sent instructions to navy Captain William H. Parker to have a corps of midshipmen at the depot by six o'clock. Parker gave the order and then hurried to the Navy Department to see Mallory. There he and his men learned that they would be responsible for guarding the train carrying the Treasury funds and personnel out of Richmond.[22]

The extent and content of government records destroyed, misplaced, or stolen on 2 April is incalculable. Untold numbers of items to be printed by the office of the public printer burned in their storage areas. Haste and the lack of transportation forced the destruction of many documents. The government's advance preparation for this day, though minimal, undoubtedly saved many records but, unfortunately, not all. The story of the government archives illustrates Davis's later admission that Confederate leaders did not seriously expect the end to come so soon, if ever. The trail of records already sent out of Richmond to the three separate locations of Lynchburg, Danville, and Charlotte also demonstrates lack of coordinated planning for a post-evacuation period. The government had decided to let events dictate its future rather than carefully calculate a strategy.[23]

Other developments in Richmond also showed the turmoil resulting from lack of preparation. Those who remained for the conclusion of services at Saint Paul's drifted onto the porch of the church and noticed the streets rapidly filling with people. Across the street from the church stood a government office building in the process of being emptied of its records. A large pile of papers flamed in the street between the two structures. Young Dallas Tucker was impressed by the dumbfounding effect of the fire on the citizenry: "I think these burning papers were the first intelligent intimation the people had of what was occurring." Others noticed "little discussion of events" among the crowd, which seemed "too full of forebodings and anguish to express the surprise and despair which possessed every mind."[24] The populace, unprepared for what was happening, appeared dazed. "So great was the general gloom, arising from the overwhelming conviction that the Confederacy was lost, that consideration of personal safety or peril failed to arouse attention," wrote Mallory. Demoralization blanketed the city, and beneath excitement born of uncertainty lingered "quiet" and "solemnity." The effect undoubtedly arose from the suddenness of it all. The government had done no more to prepare the people for this moment than it had done to prepare itself. One resident later wrote to a relative: "You will no doubt wonder at our having remained here, but it all came upon us so suddenly & unexpectedly, that we had no time for any preparations."[25]

As the first numbing shock subsided, confusion ensued. The streets filled with feverish activity. Many residents decided to try to flee rather than live under Yankee rule. John Reagan noticed that "everything was hustle and bustle and preparation, for never before had Richmond felt that the doom of capture was in store for her." Chaotic scenes became commonplace, as "bundles, trunks and boxes were brought out of houses for transportation from the city or to be conveyed to places within it which were fancied to be more secure."[26]

The desire of many to leave and the needs of government agencies created an insatiable demand for every means of transportation available. Heavy government wagons clogged the streets in a seemingly incessant trek to and from departmental offices and the railroad depot. "Vehicles of all kinds," including "carts, drays, and ambulances," further congested streets with a stream of personal possessions. Sallie Brock recalled that as more and more people determined to leave, "vehicles commanded any price in currency possessed by the individual desiring to escape from the doomed capital."[27]

Responsibility for arranging government transportation out of Richmond rested with Secretary of War Breckinridge. The immediate destination was Danville, where Davis and other officials hoped to be safe from Grant's army at least for a while. Acting on Breckinridge's orders, soldiers sealed the depot entrance against everyone not carrying a pass. Eight trains had been reserved for an emergency evacuation, but Breckinridge and his staff faced a difficult task in getting them ready. Peter Helms Mayo, a private in the governor's

Mounted Guard and an experienced railroad worker, had been busy with other workers for several days trying to keep the Richmond to Petersburg line open. Mayo noted in his memoirs that railroaders also had to keep the Danville line open, because it provided the most logical escape route to the southwest. The two lines posed a major problem for railroad officials because they had different gauges and no connecting tracks. Scattered crews, given Sunday off despite the situation at Petersburg, had left "with no expectation or intimation of any emergency call" and were not summoned back until that afternoon when a warning whistle sounded across the city. The assembled crews had much work to do. Rolling stock had not been concentrated, "for want of due notice." It was not until six o'clock that the special train Mayo had been ordered to have ready for the president and cabinet sat waiting. Meanwhile, workers hurried to assemble additional trains for other government officials.[28]

Late in the afternoon, Breckinridge received welcome word from Lee that the route to Danville would remain safe until morning. The war secretary informed Davis and the rest of the cabinet that their train would be ready to depart by eight o'clock. The president spent the afternoon desperately trying to get his personal affairs in order. He gave his housekeeper a paper authorizing her to pack and store mansion furniture at her discretion, and on the paper, he asked the Richmond mayor to aid and protect her. Alabama Senator Clement C. Clay stopped by to see Davis and found him "hastily packing a valise, his clothing and papers scattered in little heaps about." Despite his haste, Davis took time to reassure several acquaintances that he still hoped Lee could be reinforced and saved if Hardee came north in time. After the war, *Examiner* Editor Edward Pollard criticized Davis for not saying a few words of "noble farewell" to the residents of Richmond. Under the circumstances, however, it would have been ridiculous for Davis to have attempted such a speech. Neither he nor the citizenry had time for orations.[29]

On the way to the depot, Davis and his cabinet saw the deterioration of order firsthand. Streets "blocked by panting fugitives, or by groups of wonder-gapers" greeted the departing officials. Breckinridge met his colleagues at the depot and consulted with Davis. With so many duties left to perform, Breckinridge would have to remain behind and try to reach Danville later as best he could.[30]

While Davis and Breckinridge conferred at the train station, confusion between Lee's headquarters and the War Department portended further trouble for the Army of Northern Virginia. Lee asked that supplies for his army be sent to Amelia Courthouse, but the orders never reached the proper Richmond authorities. Lee's preparations for retreat and pandemonium in Richmond disrupted communications. Lack of preparedness had again complicated matters on this April Sunday.[31]

At the depot, a series of delays kept the Davis train immobile long after the expected departure time had passed. Davis and Breckinridge consulted with railroad president Lewis E. Harvie on possible routes wagon supply trains could take out of the city. They also hoped to get further news from Lee over the railroad telegraph. William Parker arrived at the depot at six o'clock to find the Treasury train already loaded. He noticed that Breckinridge and Davis seemed calm, and other officials "had the air . . . of wishing to be off." Parker also observed that like the Treasury train, the presidential cars were packed "not only inside, but on top, on the platforms, on the engine,—*everywhere*, in fact, where standing-room could be found."[32]

Around eleven o'clock Davis finally returned to his seat, and the train slowly pulled out of the station. Members of the presidential party adjusted their spurs and checked sidearms as the cars rattled forward. In case of trouble down the line, they had arranged to continue on horseback. One of the cars carried the emergency equine transportation for the fleeing government. In Davis's car, "many and sad were the commentaries . . . made upon the Confederate cause." Postmaster Reagan still shuddered years afterward at "the terrible tenseness of that one night."[33]

Military personnel left behind in Richmond to take care of last-minute details also experienced anxious moments. About four o'clock Raphael Semmes had received orders to contact

Lee, then burn all Confederate ships and outfit his men for future duty with Lee. Semmes waited until dark to begin the destruction of navy vessels. The preparations were so extensive that it was not until the early morning hours of 3 April that explosives could be ignited. The exploding gunboats seemed to be a "signal for an all day carnival of thundering noise and flames." Semmes led his men on a desperate search for an escape route from the city, while other fires began springing up. Finally, these seamen-turned-infantry confiscated a train that had been left on a sidetrack and made good their escape.[34]

The exploding ships seemed a fitting climax to the frenzy in the Richmond streets. Early that Sunday afternoon, government officials had opened supply depots all over town to prevent their capture by Grant's forces. Phoebe Yates Pember, matron of Chimborazo Hospital, saw "thousands of the half-starved and half-clad people of Richmond" clamor to the storehouses. Banks opened and depositors poured in to collect specie; meanwhile, bank officials destroyed millions in worthless paper money. In an attempt to reduce disorder, city officials directed that stores of liquor be poured into the gutters. "Men, women, and boys rushed with buckets, pails, pitchers, and in the lower streets, hats and boots, to be filled." In the atmosphere of anarchy that emerged "scoundrels who had been restrained by authority" began looting the city.[35]

As the afternoon became night, conditions worsened. General Richard S. Ewell carried out his order to destroy cotton, tobacco, and other supplies that could not be moved in case of quick evacuation. As he had feared, the firing of warehouses further compounded the chaos of the evening. While flames spread from the warehouses, mobs began to set other fires indiscriminately. Convicts broke out of the state prison and infiltrated the crowds. Destruction of artillery shells and the explosion of the main powder magazine intensified the din. Wounded soldiers, trying to escape the city, added to the congestion in the streets. Pember, remembering the exit of wounded from the hospital, wrote afterward, "The miracles of the New Testament had been re-enacted." A group of fleeing naval cadets found dead men in the streets, "shot down in the attempt to rob," and blacks fighting over supplies rescued from burning warehouses. As he left the railroad depot about one o'clock in the morning, Peter Mayo saw supplies at the station engulfed by the mob. Liquor poured into street gutters caught fire, and the flames spread along the ditches in all directions. "Madness ruled the hour," one observer recalled, providing an appropriate commentary on the havoc wrought by the miscalculations of government officials.[36]

Jefferson Davis left the dying capital with his dignity relatively intact. Contemporary descriptions of the president during this day reflect almost unanimous admiration. Most agree he kept control of his emotions as he left Saint Paul's. Accounts generally support the conclusion that he conducted himself calmly and presidentially for the remainder of the day and at the depot that evening. Those who recorded their observations, whether their memoirs were written soon or years after the event, wanted the world to know that President Davis did not leave Richmond a beaten man, a leader in disgrace. Like the cause he would come to represent, he could be described in none but approving terms.

The events of 2 April indicated that such a portrait of Davis was not totally inaccurate. He had never seemed to accept the possibility that Richmond could fall, and he had no intention of conceding the war to the enemy. His close friend and confidant, Judah Benjamin, if more realistic, shared the president's optimism. To a French diplomat, the secretary of state emotionally remarked that the evacuation was "simply a measure of prudence. I hope that we will return in a few weeks." Davis certainly hoped to return, too. But it was not to be. The sounds from the depot the night of 2 April sounded taps for Confederate Richmond. As one resident recalled, "The scream and rumble of the cars never ceased all that weary night, and was perhaps the most painful sound to those left behind."[37]

During the preceding weeks, the president of the Confederacy had shown that the survival of his nation had become an end in itself. As his special train left for Danville, Davis did not know where or how the retreat would end. He had been shaken, but his pertinacity had emerged intact from the Richmond rubble. Reality for Davis was what he determined it to be, and he still had faith that somehow Lee would save the day. As he had indicated in his letter to General Bragg, Jefferson Davis had channeled his whole being into the fight for Southern independence. The collapse of the capital had not diminished his resolve to keep the Confederate banner waving as long as there were soliders left to fight for it.

1. Raphael Semmes, *Memoirs of Service Afloat, during the War between the States* (Baltimore, 1869), 810; Elizabeth Wright Weddell, *St. Paul's Church, Richmond, Virginia: Its Historic Years and Memorials*, 2 vols. (Richmond, 1931), 1:245; Katharine M. Jones, ed., *Ladies of Richmond, Confederate Capital* (Indianapolis, 1962), 271, 276, 293; John Leyburn, "The Fall of Richmond," *Harper's New Monthly Magazine* 33 (June 1866): 92.

2. McGuire, *Diary of a Southern Refugee*, 343; Dallas Tucker, "The Fall of Richmond," *Southern Historical Society Papers* 29 (1901: 153; *Life and Reminiscences of Jefferson Davis by Distinguished Men of His Time* (Baltimore, 1890), 233.

3. *OR*, ser. 1, vol. 46, pt. 3, p. 1378.

4. Younger, *Inside the Confederate Government*, 205; Reagan, *Memoirs*, 196; [C.E.L. Stuart], "Davis' Flight," New York *Hearld* 4 July 1865. In his memoirs, Lubbock does not mention meeting Reagan or going to church with Davis.

5. *OR*, ser. 1, vol. 46, pt. 3, p. 1378.

6. Tucker, "Fall of Richmond," 153, 155; *Life and Reminiscences of Davis*, 234; Jefferson Davis, *The Rise and Fall of the Confederate Government*, 2 vols. (New York, 1881), 2:667.

7. *Life and Reminiscences of Davis*, 234–35.

8. [Stuart], "Davis' Flight"; Katharine M. Jones, *Ladies of Richmond*, 270–71; Mrs. Burton Harrison, *Recollections Grave and Gay* (New York, 1911), 207.

9. Weddell, *St. Paul's Church*, 1:246; William LeRoy Brown, "The Red Artillery: Confederate Ordnance during the War," *Southern Historical Society Papers* 26 (1898): 375; Tucker, "Fall of Richmond," 156; Pryor, *Reminiscences*, 354.

10. Mrs. Burton Harrison, *Recollections*, 207; Katharine M. Jones, *Ladies of Richmond*, 271.

11. Jefferson Davis, *Rise and Fall*, 2:667. Except where otherwise noted, the following discussion of individual cabinet members is based on entries in Jon L. Wakelyn, *Biographical Dictionary of the Confederacy* (Westport, Conn. 1977), and information in Patrick, *Davis and His Cabinet, passim*.

12. William C. Davis, *Breckinridge*, 496–97.

13. Robert Douthat Meade, *Judah P. Benjamin: Confederate Statesman* (New York, 1943), 244, 312; W. H. Swallow, "Retreat of the Confederate Government from Richmond to the Gulf," *Magazine of American History* 15 (June 1886): 596–97; Quotation from Patrick, *Davis and His Cabinet*, 157.

14. W. T. Walthall, ed., "The True Story of the Capture of Jefferson Davis," *Southern Historical Society Papers* 5 (March 1878): 124.

15. Rembert W. Patrick, *The Fall of Richmond* (Baton Rouge, 1960), 19; Stephen R. Mallory, "Last Days of the Confederate Government," *McClure's Magazine* 16 (December 1900): 100–102; Jefferson Davis, *Rise and Fall*, 2:656; Hudson Strode, *Jefferson Davis: Tragic Hero, 1864–1889* (New York, 1964), 166.

16. *OR*, ser. 1, vol. 46, pt. 3, p. 1378.

17. Wakelyn, *Biographical Directory*, 261–62, 291, 446; Micajah H. Clark, "Retreat of the Cabinet," *Southern Historical Society Papers* 26 (1898): 96–97.

18. Rowland, *Jefferson Davis*, 7:548–53; Walthall, "True Story of Capture," 100; Micajah H. Clark, "The Last Days of the Confederate Treasury and What Became of Its Specie," *Southern Historical Society Papers* 9 (Dec. 1881): 542–43; J. Morton Callahan, "The Confederate Diplomatic Archives—The 'Picket Papers,'" *South Atlantic Quarterly* 2 (Jan. 1903): 2; Dallas D. Irvine, "The Fate of Confederate Archives," *American Historical Review* 44 (July 1939): 823; Reagan, *Memoirs*, 197.

19. Irvine, "Fate of Archives," 837–38; Reagan, *Memoirs*, 197.

20. Irvine, "Fate of Archives," 828–30, 832–33; Colonel Frank Potts to Brother, April [?], 1865, Manuscript Collections of the Museum of the Confederacy, Richmond, Virginia.

21. Meade, *Benjmain*, 311; Walter A. Montgomery, "What Became of Seal of Confederate States of America," Richmond *Times-Dispatch*, 15 October 1911; Callahan, "Diplomatic Archives," 2; Irvine, "Fate of Archives," 826–27.

22. Robert Gilliam, "Last of the Confederate Treasury Department," *Confederate Veteran* 37 (Nov. 1929): 423; William Harwar Parker, *Recollections of a Naval Officer 1841–1865* (New York, 1883), 350.

23. Rowland, *Jefferson Davis*, 8:208.

24. Weddell, *St. Paul's Church*, 1:246; Tucker, "Fall of Richmond," 156; Mrs. Burton Harrison, *Recollections*, 207–8.

25. Mallory, "Last Days," 102; Leeland Hathaway Recollections, 9 vols., Southern Historical Collection, University of North Carolina at Chapel Hill, vol. 7; Parker, *Recollections*, 351; M. K. Ellis to Powhatan Ellis, Jr., 1 May 1865, Munford-Ellis Family papers, Manuscript Department, William R. Perkins Library, Duke University.

26. Reagan, *Memoirs*, 197; McHenry Howard, *Recollections of a Maryland Confederate Soldier and Staff Officer under Johnston, Jackson, and Lee* (Dayton, Ohio, 1975), 363.

27. McGuire, *Diary of a Southern Refugee*, 344; Katharine M. Jones, *Ladies of Richmond*, 272; Emmie Sublett to Emily Anderson, 29 April 1865, Manuscript Collections of the Museum of the Confederacy, Richmond, Virginia.

28. William C. Davis, *Breckinridge*, 502–3; Mallory, "Last Days," 102; J. B. Jones, *Rebel War Clerk's Diary*, 2:466; Leyburn, "Fall of Richmond," 92; Peter Helms Mayo, "Episodes of a Busy Life," Typescript, Peter Helms Mayo Recollections, Southern Historical Collection, University of North Carolina at Chapel Hill, 44–45; Potts to Brother, April [?], 1865, Museum of the Confederacy.

29. Dowdy and Manarin, *Papers of Lee*, 925; William C. Davis, *Breckinridge*, 503–5; J. B. Jones, *Rebel War Clerk's Diary*, 2:466; Pollard, *Life of Jefferson Davis*, 491; Katharine M. Jones, *Ladies of Richmond*, 293–94; Jefferson Davis to Mary Omelia, 23 April 1865, Jefferson Davis Papers, Manuscript

Collections of the Museum of the Confederacy, Richmond, Virginia; [Clay], *Belle of the Fifties*, 245; Strode, *Davis: Tragic Hero*, 167–69.

30. [Stuart], "Davis' Flight"; Walthall, "True Story of Capture," 100; William C. Davis, *Breckinridge*, 504–5.

31. William C. Davis, *Breckinridge*, 503; Freeman, *Lee's Lieutenants*, 3:689–690; Mayo, "Episodes of a Busy Life," 48–49; Walthall, "True Story of Capture," 101.

32. [Stuart], "Davis' Flight"; William C. Davis, *Breckingridge*, 504–5; Parker, *Recollections*, 351–52.

33. [Stuart], "Davis' Flight"; Mallory, "Last Days," 102; Reagan, *Memoirs*, 198.

34. Semmes, *Memoirs*, 809–16; Mrs. Burton Harrison, *Recollections*, 211; Katharine M. Jones, *Ladies of Richmond*, 288.

35. Phoebe Yates Pember, *A Southern Woman's Story: Life in Confederate Richmond*, ed. Bell Irvin Wiley (Jackson, Tenn. 1959), 130; Katharine M. Jones, *Ladies of Richmond*, 272, 287; Hathaway Recollections, vol. 7.

36. R. S. Ewell, "Evacuation of Richmond," *Southern Historical Society Papers* 13 (1885):247–49; William C. Davis, *Breckinridge*, 503, 505; Brown, "Red Artillery," 376; John W. Harris, "The Gold of the Confederate States Treasury," *Southern Historical Society Papers* 32 (1904): 159; Mayo, "Episodes of a Busy Life," 47; Potts to Brother, April [?], 1865, Museum of the Confederacy; Pember, *Southern Woman's Story*, 131, 137; Patrick, *Fall of Richmond*, 52.

37. A. A. Hoeling and Mary Hoeling, *The Day Richmond Died* (San Diego, 1981), 120–21; Smith, *Smith Family Letters*, 199; Pember, *Southern Woman's Story*, 130.

THREE

We'll Fight It Out to the Mississippi River

IN THE PRESIDENTIAL CAR "silence reigned over the fugitives" as the train carrying the Confederate government crawled slowly toward Danville. Stephen Mallory described his colleagues. John Reagan was "silent and somber, his eyes as bright and glistening as beads, but evidently seeing nothing around them." He "sat chewing and ruminating in evident perplexity" as he whittled on a stick. George Trenholm, suffering from neuralgia, worried over the Treasury, "a very troublesome elephant," while his wife tried to comfort him. The irrepressible Judah Benjamin interrupted the quiet with hopeful talk of "other great national causes which had been redeemed from far gloomier circumstances." President Davis's staff members John Taylor Wood and William Preston Johnston sat silent, but Francis Lubbock recounted an endless supply of Texas stories in "a style earnest and demonstrative." Mallory himself reflected on his naval vessels, already in flames on the James River.[1]

Jefferson Davis displayed a mixture of emotions. Crowds waited at all the stops, and everyone wanted to see, speak to, and shake hands with the president. He maintained a "bold front" and spoke encouragingly to seas of anxious faces. At one stop during the morning hours of 3 April a waiting crowd saw Davis sitting next to a window of his car. Cheers rang out. "He smiled and acknowledged their compliment, but his expression showed physical and mental exhaustion." During another halt, Davis left his seat to step outside briefly, but because of "his unsightly spectacles," he went momentarily unnoticed. When spectators finally recognized him, they offered what amounted to condolences. Even the derailing of two advance trains and the resulting deaths of five convalescing Alabama soldiers evoked no visible emotion from the president. He "said not a word, sighed, and leaned back to peer vacantly at dim distance."[2]

Dawn and food and drink provided by the Trenholms temporarily dissipated the somber mood of the presidential party. Prophetic weather followed daylight, however, and by midmorning, dark clouds accompanied the fleeing government to its new home. The poor condition of the railroad kept progress at ten to fifteen miles per hour. About three o'clock in the afternoon the lead engine of the caravan steamed into Danville. The Davis train arrived two hours later to a warm welcome from another large gathering. President and cabinet removed their spurs, and Davis pocketed his glasses before leaving the car. The usual applause greeted him, but according to Mallory, "there was that in the cheers which told as much of sorrow as of joy."[3]

Danville Mayor James M. Walker led the official reception delegation forward to greet the city's guests. Carriages and other vehicles waited to transport them to their new quarters, some of Danville's finest homes. The president, his staff, Trenholm, and Mallory would temporarily stay with wealthy William T. Sutherlin, retired major and quartermaster, whose mansion stood atop a hill in the western edge of the city. Benjamin and Reagan also found quarters in houses of wealthy Danvillians. Many lower-level officials roomed in other private residences, and clerks filled the town's two hotels.[4]

Confederate officials had chosen Danville as their surrogate capital for a number of reasons. It lay between Lee's and Johnston's armies, appeared to be militarily defensible, and had a well-stocked quartermaster department, a railroad repair shop, and ordnance machinery sent over the past few weeks from Richmond. It also had rail connections for any possible retreat farther south. Moreover, keeping the capital in Virginia was psychologically important. This consideration carried the most weight in discussions on the train from Richmond. Officials had discussed alternatives to Danville, which, with its population of only about six thousand, appeared to some to be too small, even for a provisional capital. Davis had settled the matter by proclaiming "that he would not leave Virginia until Lee was whipped out of it," and he repeated this point often during the next several days. Thus, when he arrived in Danville, Davis had no immediate plans beyond establishing the government there and hoping that Lee could somehow manage a miracle.[5]

The selection of their town must have seemed ironic to Danvillians who remembered local reluctance for secession in 1861. Fort Sumter had changed that attitude, however, and the citizens thereafter had enthusiastically supported the war effort. The town had seen a great deal of military activity over the intervening years, but in 1863 the atmosphere had turned "gruesome" when Union prisoners began to arrive from overcrowded Richmond prisons. Six former tobacco factories had quickly become crammed, disease-filled centers of incarceration. By April 1865 exchanges and deaths had dramatically reduced the prison population from over seven thousand in 1864 to a few hundred. Meanwhile, the threats of prison breaks and disease, food shortages, and depressing war news had wearied the people of Danville. Nevertheless, they now cooperated fully with the government's attempts to reorganize in their town.[6]

En route from Richmond, a basic plan of action for setting up government departments had been formed. An observer noted:

> The course finally determined on was this: the War and Navy Departments were to remain intact. . . . As the State Department had nobody but Mr. Benjamin, and his assistant . . . , there was no trouble about that. As the Department of Justice had only Mr. George Davis himself, there was

no trouble about that. The War Department had General Cooper and a host of clerks; that was the only trouble left. By sending all the Quartermaster's and Commissary General's clerks on to Charlotte, the difficulty was brought to a practical bearing.

For the moment, then, officials viewed Charlotte only as an immediate means of alleviating problems at Danville. They did not want to think about being forced that far south themselves.[7]

As the skeleton government began to take shape, navy personnel had to assume unfamiliar duties. The detachment of midshipmen commanded by Colonel William Parker guarded the train that contained Treasury funds. Raphael Semmes arrived with his sailors on Tuesday, 4 April, and received orders to operate as an artillery brigade in the city's defenses. Secretary Mallory described these men as "fish out of water" who searched constantly for ways to relieve the boredom. Their morale at times sank quite low, and many became "generally grave and silent."[8]

The Treasury Department operated to the extent of depositing part of the funds from the train in local banks to take care of operating expenses. Clerks also sold specie at 70:1 for currency to pay the armies.[9]

In Secretary of War Breckinridge's absence, Samuel Cooper and R. G. H. Kean set up the War Department, and a small staff of five began opening mail brought on the train from Richmond. Josiah Gorgas made a "spasmodic effort" to get the Ordnance Bureau in operation. Workers found ordnance machinery previously shipped to Danville as a precautionary measure lying scattered around the depot.[10]

The Benedict House, a two-story brick building originally established as a girls' school, served as government headquarters. The Executive, the War Department, and several other agencies were established in the building. At the insistence of the Sutherlins, Davis maintained his personal headquarters in their home. Reagan set up the Post Office Department in the Masonic Hall. George Davis and Benjamin did little more than mark time, since "law and foreign affairs were in abeyance." The uncertain military situation made thorough organization impractical, but most departments soon were conducting routine business.[11]

Under the circumstances, it had been a rather successful relocation, but President Davis and his cabinet needed to do something to ameliorate the depressing events of the past two days. Their first meeting in Danville was on the drizzly Tuesday morning of 4 April. Discussions focused on the military situation, affairs seeming more hopeless with every minute that passed without news from Lee. The desperate atmosphere produced plans for the issuance of a proclamation to the people of the Confederacy.[12]

Immediately following adjournment, President Davis went to the Sutherlins' library, sat down at a small, curved-legged table with a top "of mottled Egyptian marble," and began to write. The 4 April message, Davis later claimed, sought neither "to diminish the magnitude of our disaster nor to excite illusory expectations." Yet, "viewed by the light of subsequent events," he admitted, "it may fairly be said it was over-sanguine." Beginning with a review of Lee's retreat and the loss of Richmond, the president issued a challenge: "It is for us, my countrymen, to show by our bearing under reverses how wretched has been the self-deception of those who have believed us less able to endure misfortune with fortitude than to encounter danger with courage." The war had now entered a "new phase," and the South must therefore adopt a new strategy:

> Relieved from the necessity of guarding cities and particular points, important but not vital to our defense with our army free to move from point to point, and strike in detail the detachments and garrisons of the enemy; operating in the interior of our own country, where supplies are more accessible, and where the foe will be far removed from his own base, and cut off from all succor in case of reverse, nothing is now needed to render our triumph certain, but the exhibition of our own unquenchable resolve. Let us but will it, and we are free.

Davis pledged "that it is my purpose to maintain your cause with my whole heart and soul; that I will never consent to abandon to the enemy one foot of the soil of any one of the States of the Confederacy." If forced to withdraw temporarily from any state, "again and again will we return, until the baffled and exhausted enemy shall abandon in despair his endless and impossible task of making slaves of a people resolved to be free."[13]

The desperate president was proposing a war of persistent guerrilla-type harassment and was personally pledging never to give up. The message was an obvious attempt to rekindle public confidence. Under the circumstances, however, it reached only a very limited number of Southerners. The Danville *Register* published the proclamation on 5 April, but other Southern papers would not print it until its words had become even more meaningless. Handbills containing the message were distributed around the city to local citizens and refugees, hardly a sufficient audience for a significant resurgence of Southern morale.[14]

While Jefferson Davis struggled to keep the government alive in Danville, John A. Campbell tried to revive the political strategy of the peace movement in Richmond. When Abraham Lincoln visited the ruins of the evacuated capital, Campbell negotiated with him "to secure for the citizens of Richmond, and the inhabitants of the State of Virginia . . . as much gentleness and forbearance as possible." Campbell proposed calling into session the same Virginia assembly that had served during the war. Once convened it would formally withdraw Virginia troops from the war and discontinue all other state activities in support of the Confederacy. In return, Lincoln would give back certain confiscated property. At least that is how Lincoln interpreted Campbell's suggestion, and the president authorized Major General Godfrey Weitzel, commander of Union occupation forces in Richmond, to facilitate the plan. However, on 12 April Lincoln angrily withdrew his permission upon learning that Campbell believed he had agreed to allow the restoration of the state body "as the rightful Legislature of the State, to settle all differences with the United States." The Union president declared that Lee's surrender eliminated the need for any session of the old legislature.[15]

In a letter to New York *Tribune* editor Horace Greeley, Campbell indicated he had hoped to coordinate his efforts with those of former North Carolina governor David Swain, presecession unionist and now president of the University of North Carolina, and William Graham, former Confederate senator and Hampton Roads delegate. In correspondence carried on while Davis was in Danville, the two North Carolinians deliberated how to use the state government "for the purpose of effecting an adjustment of the quarrel with the United States." Graham confided to Swain that he was convinced Davis would make no peace "so long as he shall be supplied with the resources of war." The two agreed to work for a meeting of state officials with General Sherman "on the subject of peace." Other states would be invited "to unite in the movement." Graham considered the proposal consistent with Davis's stated position that as president he could not negotiate a settlement on any conditions other than the independence of the Confederacy. The states, then, could and would have to act on their own. As a courtesy, Davis would be kept informed of their talks with Sherman.[16]

Though the results of the North Carolina intrigue remained to be seen, Campbell's actions constituted a direct threat to Jefferson Davis. Campbell considered the Confederate government and its president politically dead and attempted to restore Virginia's state assembly to power with Lincoln's blessing. For Lincoln to have agreed to such a plan would have been the height of political folly. Yet, if Lincoln had agreed, Campbell and those who supported his efforts in Virginia might have emerged as heroic peacemakers who had saved their state from further destruction. Success would have undercut Davis's efforts to keep the war going. Indeed, the old peace movement strategy of condemning Davis for unnecessarily protracting the war would have been much more effective. Thus, Lincoln's stand, even though he had no alternative, served to protect Davis's position. Union military personnel continued to rule Richmond for the present, while Davis held the Confederate banner high in Danville. The contrast would not soon be forgotten by the people of the South.

Cut off from any communications with Richmond, Davis

knew nothing of Campbell's activities, and knowledge would only have compounded his frustrations. Understandably, the president was quite pessimistic during most of his stay in Danville. No proclamation could obscure the reality of exile. Writing to Varina on 5 April, Davis interrupted the flow of the letter with, "I weary of this sad recital and have nothing pleasant to tell." These private words contrasted sharply with the optimism of the proclamation published the same day. His hosts, the Sutherlins, were concerned about their guest, who seemed so "careworn" and "anxious."[17]

During extensive conversations with Major Sutherlin, Davis exhibited a curious mixture of hope and resignation. He continued to express his faith that Lee could escape from Grant. However, in answer to his host's query about the course of the war, the president replied morosely, "I think under all circumstances we have done the best we could." Despite "a great attachment for the Union," he had, after assenting to the secession of his home state of Mississippi, devoted himself to seeing "the Southern people united and happy under a government of their own choice." Now he reaffirmed his belief in the preeminence of states' rights over Union. Davis's "whole heart and soul seemed to be absorbed in his feeling for the people of the South," Sutherlin commented, "and I believe he would have cheerfully laid down his life at any time if it would have saved them from defeat." Davis further impressed his listener by asserting that he could not take young boys into the army, for it would be "too much like grinding seedcorn." Yet there remained a conflict between his concern for the people of the South and his desire to continue fighting for the cause. When Mrs. Sutherlin asked if Lee's surrender might end the war, Davis quickly responded, "By no means. We'll fight it out to the Mississippi River."[18]

In Danville such bravado was not contagious. In most minds, all depended on the fate of the Army of Northern Virginia. Uncertainty over the military situation, especially the status of Lee's army, haunted Confederate officials. Mallory remembered that anxiety was "intense." Raphael Semmes characterized the days as "anxious" and "weary."

Benjamin's "no news is good news" attitude was shared by few others. In Mallory's opinion, there could be no permanent reestablishment of the government, since a stable regime would depend on "the protection of an army, a protection that seemed very uncertain." Still, endless rumors of a victory by Lee filled the town. Such stories helped justify the continued silence of the telegraph lines. The fighting had to be so heavy that Lee had no time to bother with messages to the government. Charging troops had probably destroyed all in their path, including the silent wires. So the stories went, constantly fueled by the steady flow of refugees. Such "pleasing fictions" did not fool many, though; one witness noted that "apprehension laid hold of every one, and some misfortune was expected."[19]

On 4 and 5 April, Davis wired Generals Beauregard and Johnston in North Carolina that he had received no word from or about Lee, except "rumors of hard fighting." For several days the anxious president poured message after message over the wire to Clover Station south of Richmond. Finally on 6 April, Lee telegraphed Davis that he was at Farmville and that communication would have to be carried on by courier and telegraph. Davis would not receive that telegram until three days later.[20]

Although the fate of the Confederacy hinged on developments in North Carolina and Virginia, President Davis tried to keep an eye on other parts of the South as well. He was especially concerned about Alabama and Georgia, perhaps because he admitted to himself that he might ultimately have to continue his retreat in that direction. Bad news came from Alabama, where, on 2 April, James Wilson's raiders had driven Nathan Bedford Forrest's outmanned defenders from Selma. In a letter to her husband on 7 April, Varina Davis compared the loss of Richmond to "the 'abomination of desolation,' the loss of Selma like the 'blackness thereof.'" Selma did contain important ordnance works, but the Southern manpower shortage made the effect of the loss more symbolic than real.[21]

Communications with the lower Southern states did not imply any significant government influence there. Davis sent wires advising authorities in Alabama and Georgia to cooperate against Wilson, but that was all the president could do. A message from Columbus, Mississippi, which arrived in Danville on 8 April (it had been sent five days earlier), indicated that many blacks were volunteering for service, but no recruiting guidelines had been received from the War Department.[22] These situations confirmed what had become apparent by the time Richmond had been evacuated. The actual powers of Jefferson Davis and the Confederate government extended no further than the periphery maintained by Lee's and Johnston's armies. And the communications blackout with Lee fed fears that a reduction of executive prerogatives might be imminent.

Perhaps to relieve tension and to make the most of being in the field close to the military life he preferred, Davis took an active interest in the defense of Danville. He personally inspected fortifications around the city, found them ineffective, and gave orders to improve them. By 6 April, Semmes's artillery brigade was placing guns in position and constructing magazines in trenches north of the Dan River.[23]

Brigadier General Henry Harrison Walker, whose command was guarding the Richmond and Danville Railroad at the time of the Richmond evacuation, had wired Beauregard on 3 April that Danville was being prepared for possible attacks. At his Greensboro headquarters, Beauregard worried that George Stoneman might lead his Federal cavalry from North Carolina, where he was in the midst of a successful raid, toward Danville. Lack of Confederate cavalry and insufficient transportation hindered Beauregard's efforts to ensure the safety of the government. On 4 April, Beauregard wrote Davis that some troops were on the way and more could be sent "if absolutely needed." If Davis read between the lines, he probably could see a thinly veiled hint that Johnston's Army of Tennessee required all available forces. Johnston, indeed, argued against Beauregard's decision to send Joseph Wheeler's Confederate cavalry to Danville. On 4 April, Wheeler received conflicting orders from the two generals, and Beauregard finally assented to Johnston's position. Johnston feared that pressure on Lee in Virginia would "make

Sherman move" to threaten Lee's rear, and he wanted to concentrate all his forces to stop or at least slow Sherman's march. The episode demonstrated the tangled links in the chain of command in North Carolina.[24]

Perhaps in reaction to an unfounded concern that Stoneman might be screening an advance on Danville by Union General George H. Thomas's army from the west, Beauregard continued to keep Walker abreast of scouting reports. Reinforcements kept filtering into the city, and on 6 April, Walker received orders to consolidate all his forces in Danville. By 9 April about three thousand infantry- and artillerymen manned the Danville defenses. On that date Davis wired Greensboro that Walker needed Beauregard's assistance in organizing the men and placing them properly in the trenches. Later that evening, Beauregard, now in Raleigh, replied that he would leave for Danville as "soon as practicable."[25]

Joseph E. Johnston felt just as isolated in North Carolina as Confederate authorities did in Danville. On 5 April he wired Beckinridge from his headquarters near Smithfield, "It is important that I should know the state of affairs in Virginia. Please give me all the information you can of General Lee." Obviously, Johnston was not aware that Breckinridge was not in Danville with the rest of the government. In fact, Johnston had not been kept properly informed at all. He later elaborated:

> The press dispatches, received in the morning of April 5th, announced that Richmond was evacuated by the Administration in the night of the 2d. I inferred from this that General Lee was about to abandon the defense of Richmond, to unite our forces. Supposing the Secretary of War to be with the President at Danville, I asked him, in a telegram directed to that place, to give me full information of the movements of the Army of Northern Virginia. This dispatch was acknowledged on the same day by the President, who was unable to give me the information asked for.

Davis's reply admitted that no word had been received from Lee and concluded lamely, "Your knowledge of General Lee's plans will enable you to infer movements and his wishes in regard to your forces."[26] The confusion of getting the government established in Danville can be blamed for Johnston's never having received an official report on why Richmond had been evacuated. Nevertheless, the oversight is incredible, and the fact that he was still uninformed on 5 April is inexcusable. Perhaps everyone assumed someone else had taken care of the matter.

Johnston received other messages indicating that the situation in Virginia remained favorable, but on 9 April word came from Breckinridge that all was not well. Johnston still did not know the truth about Lee's situation. He wrote of all the messages, "There was nothing in any one of [them] to suggest the idea that General Lee had been *driven* from the position held many months with so much skill and resolution."

Joe Johnston's rival, William T. Sherman, knew on 6 April, of the situation at Richmond and Petersburg. He had resolved to move against Johnston on 10 April and to apply pressure as long as necessary to bring the Carolina campaign to a conclusion. Johnston knew nothing of Sherman's plans until scouting reports reached him on 9 April, indicating that Union forces were about to advance. Johnston's lack of information not only left him in the dark about Lee but also made him more vulnerable to a better-informed enemy. Fortunately for the immediate future of the Confederate government, Sherman would be pushing northeastward toward Raleigh, rather than toward the piedmont of North Carolina where he could have cut off any retreat from Danville.[27]

Meantime, having taken care of last-minute details in flaming Richmond, John C. Breckinridge had ridden off to rejoin his colleagues in Danville, but first he determined to try to find Lee. What he saw as he rode southward convinced him that the military situation was critical. He found Lee even as the general was sending his 6 April message to Davis. The two talked for several hours. In a follow-up report to Davis, the secretary wrote, "The straggling has been great, and the situation is not favorable." Despite his pessimism, Breckinridge determined to remain in the struggle and headed with his escort toward Danville. A soldier who saw the party ride by was impressed by the "calm, buoyant manner" of the man he had last seen presiding over the United States Senate.[28]

The day Lee attempted to contact his government proved a fateful one. On 6 April, during his last major battle against Grant, Lee lost about a third of his force at Sayler's Creek. This debacle, together with the earlier communications problems that had prevented the shipment of supplies to Amelia Courthouse, drove the final nails in the coffin of the Army of Northern Virginia.[29]

Shortly after Sayler's Creek, Lieutenant John Wise made his way to Lee's headquarters. Lee quietly explained that Wise was to take a personal message to the president in Danville. Fearing capture of a written communication, Lee instructed Wise, "You seem capable of bearing a verbal response. You may say to Mr. Davis that, as he knows, my original purpose was to adhere to the line of the Danville Road. I have been unable to do so, and am now endeavoring to hold the Southside Road as I retire in the direction of Lynchburg." Wise then asked if the general had an objective point in mind. Lee replied that he could only be governed by each day's developments and added, "A few more Sailor's [sic] Creeks and it will all be over—ended—just as I have expected it would end from the first."[30]

Saturday night, 8 April, an exhausted Lieutenant Wise arrived in Danville and asked directions to the president's headquarters. He found the Sutherlin house "brilliantly illuminated" and Davis and the cabinet inside in the midst of a meeting. Wise delivered Lee's message and then answered a multitude of anxious questions. He overestimated Lee's strength at thirty thousand, but even that figure brought expressions "of sad incredulity" to the faces around the table. A perceptible and collective shudder greeted Wise's opinion that surrender seemed certain. After the meeting, Davis asked the young officer more questions in private and requested that he report back early the next morning for orders. At eight o'clock, Sunday, 9 April, Wise met Davis, who handed him several dispatches to take back to Lee.[31]

The president attended the local Episcopal church that

Sunday and finally received the 6 April message from Lee. In a lengthy response, he reviewed the military situation at Danville and complained of the "embarrassing" absence of Breckinridge and other War Department officials who had not arrived from Richmond. He further implored: "You will realize the reluctance I feel to leave the soil of Virginia, and appreciate my anxiety to win success North of the Roanoke."[32] Apparently Davis had concluded that young Wise was overly pessimistic and that all was not yet lost. If Lee ever received the message, it did not matter. Several miles away, at Appomattox Courthouse, he was attending to the details of surrendering his army to Grant.

Word of Lee's surrender came to President Davis and the cabinet at midafternoon, 10 April. They had gathered earlier at the Benedict House and had decided to remain there for a meeting after a thunderstorm made returning to the Sutherlin home impractical. Captain W. P. Graves brought the calamitous news. On 7 April, General Walker had sent Graves to try and establish contact with Lee. He and his detachment never reached the general, but they did learn from authoritative sources of the surrender. Graves handed a note to Davis who sent it around the room. As the paper went from hand to hand "a great silence prevailed for a moment." Mallory wrote that the news "fell upon the ears of all like a fire-bell in the night." Forty-five years earlier, Thomas Jefferson had used the same simile to describe his reaction to the controversy over the extension of slavery to the Missouri Territory, which he had considered the "knell of the Union." Perhaps the second ringing would mean rebirth.[33]

Despite their shock, Davis and the cabinet managed to finish the evening meal they had begun just before Graves arrived. Benjamin ate his fill and then walked back to his quarters. There he found fellow Richmond refugee and Presbyterian minister, Dr. Moses Hoge, in conversation with a group of ladies. He motioned Hoge to follow him upstairs where he shared the news. Benjamin said he feared the cause was lost, but vowed not to be taken alive. For now, he would follow Davis and other cabinet members southward to Greensboro.[34]

Conversations during the last meal at the Benedict House

centered on plans for the immediate evacuation of Danville. Fears that Union cavalry might now more diligently attempt to prevent the government's escape prompted quick action. Davis wired Johnston of the surrender and informed him that troops and officials were leaving immediately for Greensboro. Johnston should contact him there for further orders. With Lee out of the picture, Johnston would no longer have poor communications with the government. Beauregard learned of the surrender as he was leaving Raleigh for Danville. His trip would now end at Greensboro.[35]

In a farewell message to Danville Mayor J. M. Walker, Jefferson Davis noted the necessity to continue the retreat, while asking for a vote of confidence:

> Permit me to return . . . my sincere thanks for your kindness shown to me when I came among you, under the pressure of adversity which is more apt to cause the loss of friends than to be occasion for forming new ones.
>
> I had hoped to have been able to maintain the Confederate Government on the soil of Virginia. . . . I had hoped to have contributed somewhat to the safety of your city; the desire . . . was rendered more than a mere sense of public duty by your generous reception of myself and the Executive officers who accompanied me. The shadows of misfortune . . . have become darker, and I trust you accord to me now as then your good wishes and confidence in the zeal . . . with which I have sought to discharge the high trust . . . conferred upon me.[36]

The departure from Danville provoked just as much chaos as the evacuation of Richmond eight days earlier. Belief in Lee's invincibility again had led to inadequate planning, and bad weather compounded the situation. One participant recorded, "Gloom the densest was abroad, and in harmony with its horrors the sky poured out its torrents, making Danville the most miserable and muddy place I ever tried to drag my feet through."[37]

Burton Harrison, Davis's secretary, had returned to Danville after delivering Varina Davis safely to Charlotte. He oversaw the preparation of the escape train. He probably also assumed responsibility for preparing executive papers for shipment. On the previous Saturday, John Taylor Wood had traveled to Greensboro to check on the welfare of his family and was about to return when he heard of the evacuation of Danville. Thus, a valuable Davis aide was not available.[38]

Stephen Mallory rode the streets of Danville, "issuing orders and doing hard work, to secure the transportation of all that was most valuable belonging to the navy." One problem Mallory did not have to deal with was the Treasury. A few days earlier, Parker and his men had departed with about $327,000 in coin to be deposited in the mint at Charlotte.[39]

The passive attitude of other cabinet members contributed to the lack of organization and the "great confusion" of evacuation efforts at the Danville railroad depot. George Trenholm could be excused because of his illness. He was transported part of the way to the station in a dilapidated cart and finished the trip in an ambulance. His wife, Anna, confided to her diary that at the depot "there were no cars to be seen, no body knew anything, we could not find out whether the President had gone or if any train was going." She finally found room for her husband in one of the boxcars brought to the station. The exhausted treasury secretary practically collapsed onto a bed of blankets and shawls. At the depot, Postmaster General Reagan "sat moodily on a trunk," while Benjamin and George Davis perched respectively on "soft luggage" and a valise.[40]

As workers hurriedly connected a train of freight and passenger cars, it became obvious that capacity would not meet demand. The twelve cars collected proved too heavy a load for the engine, which had to be replaced after breaking down a few miles outside Danville. Some refugees and government officials were forced to find other transportation. A few, including War Bureau chief R. G. H. Kean, decided to delay their departure until the next day.[41]

Several contemporaries described President Davis's mood during these hectic hours as agitated. He wasted part of the day consulting with railroad authorities over either changing the gauge of the Piedmont line or building fortifications to save equipment on the Richmond and Danville tracks. The threat of Federal cavalry left no time to carry out such plans. Virginia Governor William Smith, in exile at Lynchburg since

2 April, came to Danville to meet with Davis and found the president "walking to and fro in his yard, evidently in great excitement." Josiah Gorgas noted that Davis "was evidently overwhelmed by this astounding misfortune." Mallory perceived the key to the president's behavior when he observed that Davis was "wholly unprepared for Lee's capitulation."[42]

Bureaucratic confusion, baggage problems, unauthorized personnel trying to get on board, and rumors of Yankee raiders delayed the train's scheduled 8 P.M. departure until 11. Around 10 P.M., the cabinet and other officials, all carefully guarding their individual baggage, gathered near the train in darkness "lighted only by Mr. Benjamin's inextinguishable cigar." Davis waited to board until shortly before the train was ready to leave. He found himself sharing a seat with an officer's daughter, a young women "of a loquacity irrepressible." While others, including the president, sat mournfully waiting for the trip to begin, the lady "prattled on in a voice everybody heard." Unabashedly inquisitive, she asked Davis many questions and intermittently discussed the weather and a variety of other subjects. Finally the train jerked forward into a cloudy night of misty rain.[43]

The government that departed for Greensboro that night was considerably smaller than the one that had been driven from Richmond. The train left behind many workers, as well as other Richmond refugees who had decided to go home. One of those who remained pondered the sequence of events that led others to abandon the cause. First came the "paralyzing shock" of Lee's surrender. "Then came the breaking of some of the bonds which held the government together, and some who had followed to this point, seeing that they could be of no real service, and might be an encumbrance, sought the president to express their great grief, and seek his advice for their own actions. These he received with profound dignity . . . and set them free to private life."[44]

The fleeing president and government left behind another city in pandemonium. Refugees, both soldiers and civilians, were passing through Danville on their way to a variety of possible destinations, including Greensboro, Johnston's army, homes farther south, or the Trans-Mississippi. A Confederate soldier recalled scenes of the night of 10 April, "the rumbling of wagon trains, the scattering of the crowd gathering in the little town, emptying into every direction . . . , the throwing open of the large stores collected here." At the railroad depot the soldier observed a scene of poignant symbolism. "Two feeble old men, with white hair, Commodores in Naval Service," stood looking southward at empty tracks. They had made their retreat in a buggy driven all the way from Richmond, but they had arrived too late to catch the train to Greensboro.[45]

The next day matters worsened in the city. Another soldier provided a vivid description: "As we approach Danville the roads become thronged with stragglers of all descriptions, wagon loads of people and their effects, moving into Danville, and crowds moving from the town. No one appears to have any settled conviction of what they are going to do or what the government is going to do. All is confusion and panic." Crowds from the surrounding countryside, including stragglers from the Appomattox campaign, gathered around warehouses. These people were more concerned about the necessities of life than the southern cause. A leader emerged from the throng, a "tall woman," who cried out, "Our children and we'uns are starving; the Confederacy is gone up; let us help ourselves." Rioters overwhelmed the passive guards and the "plundering began." The streets cleared, however, when Confederate ordnance stored near the warehouses was accidentally ignited. Several victims of the explosion lay mangled, and "fragments of [human] limbs were scattered in all directions." The mob thought Yankee soldiers were attacking and scattered to the winds.[46]

Thus, destruction and disorder continued to follow in the wake of the government's retreat. Moreover, the problems of Davis and his cabinet now extended beyond the fragmenting of the social order and the resulting destruction of nationalist sentiments. Lee's surrender had precipitated the loss of both government personnel and other supporters who had followed their leaders from Richmond. In the minds of many, the Confederacy's only hope had vanished at Appomattox. Despite brave remarks to the contrary, Jefferson Davis believed this himself; yet he continued, as he had so often promised. In doing so, he perpetuated his image as the symbol of Confederate determination. His persistence would be a significant factor in his future. For while the Confederate nation was dying, its successor was being born. The nature of that successor, still unclear, was gradually coming into focus.

The transformation of the war from battlefield to symbolic images in the Southern mind had become more evident during the trip to Danville. The reverent crowds that waited at each train stop demonstrated both their devotion to the cause and its president and their sorrow over the current state of affairs. Citizens of Danville had similar sentiments. It was just a beginning, little more than an impression, but more and more it appeared that while Confederate armies were being battered into submission, the idea of the Confederacy was advancing beyond the range of Union guns.

For the moment, this was a development of little consequence to Jefferson Davis, who faced a future more uncertain than when he left Richmond. He had resolved to fight on all the way to the Mississippi. But with the Army of Northern Virginia now a memory, Davis's train continued the retreat of a government that had lost its major fighting tool.

1. Mallory, "Last Days," 104–5.
2. H. W. Bruce, "Some Reminiscences of the Second of April 1865," *Southern Historical Society Papers* 9 (May 1881): 209; Wise, *End of an Era*, 415; [Stuart], "Davis' Flight."
3. Mallory, "Last Days," 105; John H. Brubaker III, *The Last Capital: Danville, Virginia, and the Final Days of the Confederacy* (Danville, 1979), 3; Danville *Register*, 3 April 1965; [Stuart], "Davis' Flight."
4. Bruce, "Reminiscences," 209; Edward Pollock, *Illustrated Sketchbook of Danville, Virginia* (Danville, 1885), 51; Brubaker, *Last Capital*, 19; John Taylor Wood Diary, 3 April 1865, John Taylor Wood Papers, Southern Historical Collection, University of North Carolina at Chapel Hill.
5. Brubaker, *Last Capital*, 5; Danville *Register*, 2 April 1965; [Stuart], "Davis' Flight"; Jefferson Davis, *Rise and Fall*, 2:676; Hudson Strode, ed., *Jefferson Davis: Private Letters, 1823–1889* (New York, 1966), 149, 151; Rowland, *Jefferson Davis*, 6:543; Reagan, *Memoirs*, 198.

6. Brubaker, *Last Capital*, 11, 12, 14, 17–18; Jefferson Davis, *Rise and Fall*, 2:676.

7. [Stuart], "Davis' Flight."

8. William H. Parker, "The Gold and Silver in the Confederate States Treasury," *Southern Historical Society Papers* 21 (1893): 306; W. Stanley Hoole, ed., "Admiral on Horseback: The Diary of Brigadier General Raphael Semmes, February–May 1865," *Alabama Review* 28 (April 1975): 138; Mallory, "Last Days," 106.

9. Clark, "Last Days of the Confederate Treasury," 545.

10. Younger, *Inside the Confederate Government*, 206; [Stuart], "Davis' Flight"; B. R. Wellford Diary, 1865, in White, Wellford, Taliaferro, and Marshall Family Papers, Southern Historical Collection, University of North Carolina at Chapel Hill; Mallory, "Last Days," 105; Joseph R. Haw, "The Last of C.S. Ordnance Department," *Confederate Veteran* 34 (Dec. 1926): 450.

11. Brubaker, *Last Capital*, 27; [Stuart], "Davis' Flight"; Mallory, "Last Days," 105; Wood Diary, 6 April 1865; Micajah H. Clark, "Retreat of Cabinet from Richmond," *Confederate Veteran* 6 (July 1898): 293; J. William Jones, *The Davis Memorial Volume; or, Our Dead President, Jefferson Davis, and the World's Tribute to His Memory* (Atlanta, 1890), 395.

12. Brubaker, *Last Capital*, 25, 27; Meade, *Benjamin*, 313; B. Boisseau Bobbitt, "Our Last Capital: Danville's Part in the Closing Hours of the Confederacy," *Southern Historical Society Papers* 31 (1903): 338; [Stuart], "Davis' Flight."

13. Jefferson Davis, *Rise and Fall*, 2:676–77; Rowland, *Jefferson Davis*, 6:529–31; Bobbitt, "Our Last Capital," 338. After the war, a controversy arose over who actually wrote the proclamation. A printer's apprentice in the office of the Danville *Register* claimed that Judah Benjamin was the author. The evidence indicates, however, that Benjamin rewrote the rough draft Davis had composed at the Sutherlins'. See James Elliott Walmsley, "The Last Meeting of the Confederate Cabinet," *Mississippi Valley Historical Review* 6 (Dec. 1919): 338; Meade, *Benjamin*, 313; Brubaker, *Last Capital*, 32.

14. Edward Pollock, "President Davis' Stay in Danville," Danville *Register* 17 May 1914; Pollock, *Sketchbook of Danville*, 55; Brubaker, *Last Capital*, 32. Despite what some historians have written, Davis's words do not indicate an advocacy of guerrilla warfare per se. The South still had enough men in the army in April 1865 to wage an effective guerrilla war. A recent study has concluded, however, that "the Confederate military establishment would have found guerilla warfare uncongenial to its view of war." See Herman Hattaway and Archer Jones, *How the North Won: A Military History of the Civil War* (Urbana, 1983), 701–2.

15. John A. Campbell, "Evacuation Echoes," *Southern Historical Society Papers* 24 (1896), 351–53; Roy P. Basler, ed., *The Collected Works of Abraham Lincoln*, 8 vols. (New Brunswick, N.J., 1959), 8:386–87, 389, 406–7.

16. J. A. Campbell to Horace Greeley, 26 April 1865, Campbell and Colston Family Papers, Southern Historical Collection, University of North Carolina at Chapel Hill; Max R. Williams and J. G. de Roulhac Hamilton, eds., *The Papers of William Alexander Graham*, 7 vols. (Raleigh, 1957–85), 6:292–97.

17. Strode, *Davis: Private Letters*, 149; *Memorials of the Life, Public Services, and Character of William T. Sutherlin* (Danville, Va., 1894), 13; J. William Jones, *Davis Memorial Volume*, 395.

18. *Memorials of William Sutherlin*, 13–17; J. William Jones, *Davis Memorial Volume*, 396.

19. Mallory, "Last Days," 105; Semmes, *Memoirs*, 819; [Stuart], "Davis' Flight."

20. Rowland, *Jefferson Davis*, 6:529, 532; Wise, *End of an Era*, 417; Dowdy and Manarin, *Papers of Lee*, 931.

21. Rowland, *Jefferson Davis*, 6:535–36, 538, 540; *OR*, ser. 1, vol. 49, pt. 2, pp. 1212–13, 1220.

22. *OR*, ser. 1, vol. 49, pt. 2, pp. 1193, 1199, 1208, 1212, 1220. The Bureau of Conscription had been abolished in March 1865. Commanders of state troops were put in charge of recruiting. They reported to the War Department, which continued to issue recruiting directives.

23. Jefferson Davis, *Rise and Fall*, 2:676; Bobbitt, "Our Last Capital," 337; Brubaker, *Last Capital*, 33–34; Semmes, *Memoirs*, 817–19; Hoole, "Semmes Diary," 139; Burton N. Harrison, "The Capture of Jefferson Davis," *Century Magazine* 27 (Nov. 1883): 131. See also A. S. Rives to Jefferson Davis, 10 April 1865, Jefferson Davis Papers, Manuscript Department, William R. Perkins Library, Duke University.

24. Ezra J. Warner, *Generals in Gray: Lives of the Confederate Commanders* (Baton Rouge, 1959), 318; H. H. Walker to P.G.T. Beauregard, 3 April 1865, Pierre Gustave Toutant Beauregard Papers, Manuscript Department, William R. Perkins Library, Duke University; *OR*, ser. 1, vol. 46, pt. 3, pp. 746, 750–55.

25. *OR*, ser. 1, vol. 46, pt. 3, pp. 757, 760–61, 774, 1390; Williams, *Beauregard*, 254.

26. *OR*, ser. 1, vol. 46, pt. 3, pp. 755; Johnston, *Narrative*, 395.

27. Johnston, *Narrative*, 395–96; John G. Barrett, *The Civil War in North Carolina* (Chapel Hill, 1963), 369–70.

28. William C. Davis, *Breckinridge*, 505–8; *OR*, ser. 1, vol. 46, pt. 3, p. 1389; Joseph Packard, "Ordnance Matters at the Close," *Confederate Veteran* 16 (May 1908): 229.

29. Freeman, *Lee's Lieutenants*, 3:687–725.

30. Wise, *End of an Era*, 429, 435.

31. Ibid., 444–46, 448.

32. Brubaker, *Last Capital*, 50; Rowland, *Jefferson Davis*, 6:541.

33. Mallory, "Last Days," 107; Brubaker, *Last Capital*, 55; Pollock, "Davis' Stay in Danville"; Albert Ellery Bergh, ed., *The Writings of Thomas Jefferson*, 20 vols. in 10 (Washington, D.C., 1907), 15:249.

34. Pollock, "Davis' Stay in Danville"; Meade, *Benjamin*, 313–14; Brubaker, *Last Capital*, 55.

35. Mallory, "Last Days," 107; Rowland, *Jefferson Davis*, 6:542–43; Williams, *Beauregard*, 254.

36. Rowland, *Jefferson Davis*, 6:543.

37. [Stuart], "Davis' Flight."

38. Burton N. Harrison, "Capture of Davis," 131; Wood Diary, 8–9, 10 April 1865.

39. [Stuart], "Davis' Flight"; Parker, "Gold and Silver," 306; Clark, "Last Days of the Confederate Treasury," 545.

40. [Stuart], "Davis' Flight"; Anna Trenholm Diary, George Alfred Trenholm Papers, South Caroliniana Library, University of South Carolina; Younger, *Inside the Confederate Government*, 205.

41. W. H. Swallow, "Retreat of the Confederate Government," 599; Younger, *Inside the Confederate Government*, 205; Wellford Diary; J. H. Averill,

"Richmond, Virginia: The Evacuation of the City and the Days Preceding It," *Southern Historical Society Papers* 25 (1897): 269.

42. Robert C. Black III, *The Railroads of the Confederacy* (Chapel Hill, 1952), 286; *OR*, ser. 1, vol. 46, pt. 3, pp. 1391–92; Pollock, *Sketchbook of Danville*, 63–64; Vandiver, *Diary of Josiah Gorgas*, 180; Mallory, "Last Days," 105.

43. Mallory, "Last Days," 107; Burton N. Harrison, "Capture of Davis," 132.

44. [Stuart], "Davis' Flight"; Clark, "Retreat of Cabinet from Richmond," 293.

45. Danville *Register*, 10 April 1965; Reagan, *Memoirs*, 198.

46. Joseph T. Durkin, ed., *John Dooley, Confederate Soldier: His War Journal* (Washington, D.C., 1945), 179–80; Averill, "Richmond, Virginia," 270–71.

FOUR

Much Depended on These Generals

ANOTHER CITY HAD BEEN EVACUATED, and again silence soon enveloped members of the exiled government as their train crept out of Virginia into North Carolina. Most of them probably reflected on the Confederacy's future without Robert E. Lee and his army. Jefferson Davis may have pondered the irony that he must now place his hopes in the hands of his old enemy, Joseph E. Johnston. Davis and his colleagues probably wished for a faster, less public trip. The slow train carried with it the news of Appomattox, which adversely affected citizen morale along the route. The hours passed uneventfully until, a few miles outside Greensboro, the train passed over a trestle only minutes before the bridge was destroyed by Federal cavalry. Finally, in midafternoon of Tuesday, 11 April, the cars screeched to a halt at the Greensboro depot.[1]

As in Danville, unionist sentiment in this central North Carolina town had been strong before the outbreak of civil war. In February 1861 the citizens of Guilford County had voted overwhelmingly against secession. After North Carolina joined the Southern exodus from the Union in May, however, "unionist Greensboro [had] turned secessionist with great enthusiasm."[2]

By 1864 this ardor for the Confederate cause had turned

74

sour. In February a large so-called unionist rally had been held in the city, with citizens voicing many complaints against the Davis administration. General Sherman's 1865 march into North Carolina had not brought him to Greensboro, but the invasion's effects were being felt in the city. During February 1865 frightened refugees from Charlotte had poured into town. Trains brought supplies from all over the state in such large quantities that some homes had been pressed into use as commissaries. Incoming wounded from the Virginia front compounded a growing housing shortage.[3] In the words of a local resident, "Greensboro was no longer the beautiful quiet, delightful place of yore. The streets were swimming in mud, and the houses looked as if they sympathized with their deplorable condition." Infantry and horses constantly stirred the mud to the tune of "drum and fife and bugle." Cannon rumbled through the streets, "the jingling of spurs and clashing sabres, the shrill whistle of the coming engines . . . the excitement of war and fear, the rushing to and fro of citizens and soldiers . . . , all presented a scene and sound and aspect never before witnessed or heard in the wild woods of this inland town."[4]

Unsavory elements, seemingly always on the fringes of war, began drifting into the city. One of Lee's soldiers, hoping to join Johnston, remembered his first impression of the town: "What attracted our attention most was the various gambling games in progress everywhere." Lee's veterans, most of them anxious to find a way home, streamed through Greensboro. The disastrous condition of railroads to the south forced these paroled soldiers to search desperately for horses, and "few had any scruples as to how to get one." The presence of the large store of military supplies created other problems, as drifters, citizens, and soldiers constantly threatened to raid the depots.[5]

Detraining at the railroad station, Confederate officials quickly realized that the mood in their new home differed drastically from that in Danville. No great crowds awaited their arrival here. Indifference seemed to be the prevailing attitude. Stephen Mallory saw that "there were many commodious and well-furnished residences in and about" the town, "but their doors were closed . . . against the members of a retreating government." One government refugee complained that local citizens were constantly asking, "How long are you going to stay?" Mallory concluded that among other Southerners, known for their hospitality, any prediction of this kind of reception "would have encountered universal disbelief." Burton Harrison soon discovered the rationale for the coldness: "It was rarely that anybody asked one of us to his house; and but few of them had the grace even to explain their fear that, if they entertained us, their houses would be burned by the enemy, when his cavalry got there."[6]

Fear of retaliation by George Stoneman's cavalry and the nearness of Sherman's army undoubtedly contributed to the "cold unconcern" of Greensboro. Joe Johnston had refused to set up his headquarters in town, in part no doubt "from a motive of delicacy . . . , fearing he might compromise those who would thus be indicated as his friends." For the same reason, President Davis reportedly turned down a few invitations to lodge with local citizens.[7]

Nevertheless, in Harrison's opinion, the "people in that part of North Carolina had not been zealous supporters of the Confederate Government; and, so long as we remained in the State, we observed their indifference to what should become of us." A Confederate soldier expressed his feelings more bluntly by regretting that the government had established itself "in this little Union hole of Greensboro."[8]

Writing in the local newspaper soon after the war, a Greensboro citizen felt compelled to defend his city's reputation. He did not deny that most of his fellow townsmen had not supported Jefferson Davis and his administration. But his words illustrate how Davis's refusal to give up the fight bolstered his postwar image:

> When [Davis] . . . became the head of the Confederacy and leader of the South in the great struggle, they followed him and gave their whole support to the government. They rejoiced at his success . . . and sorrowed over his failures. . . . When victory turned against us and hope fled from our borders and our chief left his capital a defeated and sorrowing old man, we sorrowed with him and for him, and our respect

and admiration . . . increased when we saw how noble his bearing was under the accumulation of misfortune such as has rarely been borne by mortal man.[9]

Many Southerners were not convinced by any attempt to justify the city's actions. An old Davis enemy, Richmond *Examiner* editor Edward A. Pollard, demonstrated the lingering effect of Greensboro's behavior in his otherwise critical 1869 biography of the president. Pollard called the retaliation excuse "cowardly" and the lack of hospitality a "stigma of shame."

> There were many in the South who dissented from the government of Mr. Davis, who were hostile to his administration, who gave him no confidence and bore him no affection, as a ruler; yet even among these, the truly noble and sincere could have respected the misfortunes of the President, when they found him a distressed fugitive. They would have obeyed the promptings of but an ordinary human generosity . . . , to tender some hospitality, or to offer an honorable condolence. But even such manifestations of humanity did a North Carolina town . . . refuse to show to the man who, but a few weeks before, had been their supreme magistrate and chief, who was yet such under the unexpired forms of the Confederacy, and who now came among them a broken, aged fugitive, making a feeble flight from the enemy.

Greensboro's "stigma of shame" refuses to die. Davis's most recent biographer denounced the "city that disgracefully refused hospitality to the little band."[10]

The "little band" of government refugees ignored Greensboro's slight and settled in for an indefinite stay in their new home. With two exceptions, the presidential party set up government headquarters in a "dilapidated leaky passenger car," where they "ate, slept, and lived." John Taylor Wood provided Jefferson Davis with a bed in the small, second-floor apartment he had earlier rented for his family. The president had been slightly ill since leaving Danville, probably suffering from the pressures of the past two days and exposure to the rainy weather in Virginia. Treasury Secretary Trenholm, still ailing with his own more severe neuralgia, found quarters in the mansion of former North Carolina governor John

M. Morehead. Cynical members of the government suspected Morehead of wanting to influence the secretary into swapping securities for specie. Morehead reportedly also offered Davis a room, but the president refused, supposedly because he feared Union reprisals against the governor's family.[11]

"It would have been ludicrous," wrote a Davis aide, "if it were less provocative of painful reflections, to think that the whole rebel government was cooped in those miserable cars." Occupants of the "cabinet car" remembered the days in Greensboro as uncomfortable. Visitors to the headquarters, nevertheless, received a jovial welcome, "seasoned by a flow of good spirits, which [threw] a charm around the wretched shelter and made the situation seem rather a matter of choice than of necessity."[12]

The consumption of plentiful rations from the well-stocked commissaries helped pass otherwise idle hours. In his notes, Mallory painted a humorous portrait of his cabinet colleagues' culinary activities. George Davis sampled "middling" meat and hoecake, "his face beaming unmistakable evidence of the condition of the bacon." Benjamin showed a revitalized spirit as he sat happily munching stewed apples and hard-boiled eggs. Postmaster General Reagan put his Bowie knife to work on a ham, "as if it were the chief business of life." Mallory gulped down scalding coffee so that the ill-humored Adjutant General Samuel Cooper would not have to wait too long for the only available cup.[13]

The higher priority of food replaced questions of state sovereignty, secession, foreign recognition, and finances. The government brain trust also diligently tackled the vexing problem of how "a man of six feet [could] sleep upon a car seat four feet long." Beneath the devil-may-care facade, however, lurked the harsh reality of the crumbling Confederacy. As Mallory wryly recalled, "The times were 'sadly out of joint' just then, and so was the Confederate Government."[14]

Jefferson Davis would admit to no such sentiments. His fighting spirit had returned. It was apparent to P. G. T. Beauregard, whose train from Raleigh arrived in Greensboro shortly after the president's, that Davis was not a beaten man. After setting up his headquarters in boxcars on sidetracks near the depot, Beauregard walked over to the government cars. Cabinet members heartily welcomed the general and bombarded him with questions about the military situation in North Carolina, but Beauregard "was struck by the helpless appearance of the gentlemen there." Davis soon arrived and guided Beauregard to one side of the car for a private conversation. The president heard a pessimistic analysis of Johnston's situation, as well as the bad news of Federal cavalry successes in Alabama and Georgia. The general further reported word from Richard Taylor that Mobile appeared doomed and Mississippi was threatened by increased Union military activity. As he spoke, Beauregard observed that Davis seemed completely unshaken by all the bad news. Indeed, Davis argued that by making good use of all its resources, the Confederacy could survive, even if forced across the Mississippi River to join Kirby Smith. The brief meeting ended, and Beauregard departed, "amazed at this evidence of visionary hope on the part of the President."[15]

His correspondence gave further evidence of Davis's positive attitude. An 11 April message from North Carolina Governor Zebulon Vance pleaded, "Please tell me what of General Lee. Much depends here [in Raleigh] on a correct knowledge of the situation. Answer to-night." Davis calmly replied that he had received no official report from Lee, but information from reliable scouts left no doubt of the surrender. He would be glad to meet with Vance in Greensboro or anywhere else that might be convenient. Meanwhile, Davis continued, "we must redouble our efforts to meet present disasters. An army holding its position with determination to fight on, and manifest ability to maintain the struggle, will attract all the scattered soldiers and daily and rapidly gather strength. Moral influence is wanting, and I am sure you can do much to revive the spirit and hope of the people."[16]

On the same day, Davis wired General Johnston that he expected Secretary of War Breckinridge to arrive that afternoon. He suggested that the three of them confer as soon as possible, either at Johnston's headquarters or, preferably, in Greensboro, where it would be more convenient for Beauregard to attend. As in his note to Vance, Davis acknowledged the lack of official word from Lee, but continued: "The important question first to be solved is at what point shall concentration be made in view of the present position of the two columns of the enemy, and the routes which they may adopt to engage your forces before a prompt junction with General Walker and others. Your more intimate knowledge of the data for the solution of the problem deters me from making a specific suggestion on that point." However, the president immediately sent a follow-up telegram proposing a concentration of forces based on statements made by Beauregard during their earlier discussion. When Breckinridge had not yet arrived later in the afternoon Davis dispatched still another telegram, canceling his earlier messages. Johnston should come on to Greensboro, he wrote, "to save time and have all information."[17]

General Johnston's train steamed into the depot the following morning. Beauregard met his colleague and gave Johnston office space in his boxcar quarters. The two generals consulted through the morning hours until nearly noon, when President Davis summoned them to the government cars. Cabinet members Benjamin, Mallory, Reagan, and George Davis also attended the meeting in Davis's makeshift office.[18]

Generals Johnston and Beauregard came to the conference assuming they would be briefing Davis on the military situation. They soon realized, however, that "the President's object seemed to be to give, not to obtain information." He insisted that by gathering conscripts and deserters the Confederacy could quickly field an army large enough to continue the war. Johnston and Beauregard pointed out that men who had deserted during less desperate times were not likely to return now. Furthermore, they saw little hope that conscripts would now volunteer. Davis refused to be swayed and announced that the discussion would continue the following day. By then, he hoped Breckinridge would be on hand with more information for their consideration.[19]

The long-absent secretary of war had left Danville early on 12 April and arrived in Greensboro late that evening. He hurried to Davis's quarters and gave his report, confirming Lee's surrender. The news surely came as no surprise. Yet, not everyone wanted to believe it. In a message sent to Varina Davis in Charlotte, one of Davis's personal aides had earlier reflected the president's tendency to expect miracles. "The disaster to General Lee's army is extreme," William Preston Johnston had written, "but our latest advices lead to the hope that he and the leaders of the army may have escaped with a remnant of the command."[20]

After hearing Breckinridge's report, Beauregard and Johnston again consulted privately and "agreed in the opinion that the Southern Confederacy was overthrown." In their view, the only option Davis had was to initiate negotiations with General Sherman. Johnston discussed the matter with Breckinridge, who promised to give the general an opportunity to air his views at the meeting next morning. Stephen Mallory also felt it was time to negotiate, and he urged Johnston to suggest this course to the president. The general hedged, preferring that one of Davis's "constitutional advisers" introduce the subject. Mallory received Johnston's assurance, however, that he would state his opinions and that "you will not find me reticent upon them."[21]

The next morning, Thursday, 13 April, the president and his cabinet, less the incapacitated Trenholm, met in John Taylor Wood's cramped apartment. Jefferson Davis later wrote that when he attended this meeting, despite "the gravity of our position. . . , I did not think we should despair." After reviewing current matters with his government officers, Davis asked the two generals to come in. In his mind, the conference with Beauregard and Johnston "was not to learn their opinion as to what might be done by negotiation with the United States government, but to derive from them information in regard to the army under their command, and what it was feasible and advisable to do as a military problem." In short, Davis wanted to hear no talk of surrender.[22]

John Reagan remembered the meeting that morning as "one of the most solemnly funereal I ever attended." Yet, President Davis proceeded in his usual manner by talking on a variety of unrelated subjects before finally getting to the issue at hand. According to Mallory, Davis stated the purpose of the meeting and then remarked: "Of course we all feel the magnitude of the moment. Our late disasters are terrible; but I do not think we should regard them as fatal. I think we can whip the enemy yet, if our people will turn out. We must look at matters calmly, however, and see what is left for us to do. Whatever can be done must be done at once. We have not a day to lose."[23]

A pause followed Davis's words, and the president thought Johnston to be reserved and "far less than sanguine." Indeed, neither Johnston nor Beauregard offered any hope of carrying on the war. They estimated Confederate effective strength at 25,000 men and guessed that Sherman and Grant together had close to 300,000. Johnston reported his opinion that the Southern people were weary of war and "will not fight." Under the present circumstances of overwhelming odds, increasing desertions, depleted supplies, and low morale, he continued, "it would be the greatest of human crimes for us to attempt to continue the war." He concluded with a strong assertion that Davis as president should initiate negotiations for peace. Mallory sensed a bitterness in the general's remarks, a manifestation of the old feud perhaps, and noted, "The tone and manner, almost spiteful, in which General Johnston jerked out brief decisive sentences, pausing at every period, left no doubt as to his own convictions."[24]

A silence of some two or three minutes followed Johnston's speech. Davis had sat listening, folding, unfolding, and refolding a piece of paper "without a change of position or expression." Finally, the president shifted his gaze to Beauregard and asked his opinion. The Louisianian quietly indicated his agreement with Johnston's position. Polling his cabinet, Davis found all but Benjamin in support of the generals.[25]

Obviously annoyed, Davis argued that the United States government would not recognize his authority to negotiate. Johnston suggested that, under such circumstances, opposing military commanders could act as intermediaries in conducting peace talks. John Reagan then proposed the terms Johnston should present to Sherman. They included disbanding the forces of the Confederacy, recognition by the South of the United States government and Constitution, preservation and continuity of present state governments, preservation of individual political rights of former rebels, freedom from prosecution for participation in the war for all but Davis and the cabinet, allowing Confederate soldiers to return to their home states to surrender, and a truce pending settlement of all issues. By eliminating the Confederate president and his cabinet from the terms, the conferees hoped to persuade Sherman to accept the other items, which, in effect, ignored the fact that the Confederacy had lost the war. At Johnston's suggestion, Davis dictated a letter to Mallory. Johnston then signed it and assumed the responsibility for getting it to Sherman.[26]

Davis's message did not mention the word *surrender* but said only:

> The results of the recent campaign in Virginia have changed the relative military condition of the belligerents. I am therefore induced to address you in this form of inquiry, whether, in order to stop the further effusion of blood and devastation of property, you are willing to make a temporary suspension of active operations, and to communicate to Lieu-tenant-General Grant, commanding the Armies of the United States, the request that he will take like action in regard to other armies; the object being to permit the civil authorities to enter into the needful arrangements to terminate the exist-ing war.[27]

By calling for the involvement of civil authorities, Davis con-tradicted his own argument that Federal officials would not recognize their Confederate counterparts. He may have inten-tionally done so to sabotage the negotiations and thus keep the struggle for independence alive. His performance during the conference certainly underscored his belief that the peace talks would fail. Before Johnston departed, Davis asked his preference for a line of retreat to the southwest. Undoubtedly to placate the president, Johnston indicated his choice, and Davis promised to have supply depots set up along the se-lected route. After the war, Davis said he made this arrange-ment in case an honorable peace could not be attained. He further explained, "I had never contemplated a surrender, except upon such terms as a belligerent might claim, as long as we were able to keep the field, and never expected a Confederate army to surrender while it was able either to fight or to retreat." Future events would show that Johnston left the 13 April meeting with an entirely different perspective.[28]

This Thursday meeting marked a turning point in Jefferson Davis's status as president. Previously his cabinet had stood by him in his resolve to continue the fight. Since Lee's surrender and after hearing firsthand the condition of Johnston's forces, they had, with the exception of Benjamin, obviously had a change of heart. Davis now stood practically alone in his persistent attachment to the idea of Southern independence. Nevertheless, he walked away from the meeting firm in his belief that all was not lost and determined to exercise the powers of his office regardless of the opinions of others.

The president's attitude complicated an already sensitive political situation in North Carolina. William Graham and David Swain had enlisted the aid of Governor Vance in an attempt to negotiate North Carolina back into the Union. Swain had talked with Vance on 9 April about having the state legislature take appropriate action to facilitate contact with Federal authorities. On 12 April, Vance had invited Swain and Graham to Raleigh for a conference that resulted in a letter from Vance to Sherman suggesting a truce as the first step toward the "final termination of the existing war." The governor appointed his guests as his personal representatives to deliver the letter.[29]

Archer Anderson, assistant adjutant general to Johnston, had learned of the plot when General William Hardee had given the commissioners a permit allowing their special train to pass through the military lines. Anderson telegraphed Johnston and Davis for instructions and ordered General Wade Hampton to detain the train. Davis then ordered the arrest of Vance's commissioners. The order, signed by Johnston, concluded, "No intercourse with the enemy permitted except under proper military flag of truce." Informed of the president's action, Vance wired an explanation to Greensboro, noting that Hardee and Johnston had been informed of his attempt to contact Sherman. "It is not my intention," wrote Vance, "to do anything subversive of your prerogative or without consultation with yourself." His actions disputed his words, and Davis fired off an immediate reply: "I could not attribute to you such purpose as you disclaim, and your military experience and good judgment will render it unnecessary to explain why the commanding general cannot properly allow any intercourse with the enemy except under his authority and with his full knowledge and consent. Such was the purpose of the instructions sent to General Hardee."[30]

As a result of Davis's intervention, the train carrying Swain and Graham was captured by Federal cavalry when it was returning to Raleigh. When Vance heard this news, he abandoned the whole plan and sent Sherman a message authorizing the mayor of Raleigh to surrender the city. Late in the evening of 12 April, the governor left the capital and rode toward Johnston's army.[31]

Meanwhile, Vance's emissaries had met with Sherman. The Union general expressed doubts about calling a truce, but he promised to cooperate with Vance in every way possible. Swain and Graham returned to Raleigh on 13 April and learned that Vance had departed. With the assistance of an escort provided by Sherman, the two searched for the governor, whom they finally located in Graham's home in Hillsboro. Having just received Davis's 11 April message, which apparently, perhaps conveniently, had been misplaced until now, Vance refused to return to Raleigh. He left for Greensboro the next morning to see President Davis.[32]

If he was aware of all these developments, Davis must have felt some degree of satisfaction. The turn of events practically eliminated Graham and Swain from the peace process, and Johnston and Sherman were in contact regarding negotiations. In addition, some North Carolinians viewed the activities of Graham and Swain as traitorous to the Confederacy.[33]

Despite his firmness with Vance and his determination to carry on the war if necessary, President Davis must have been aware of the deteriorating condition of the army in the Greensboro area. For a while morale had merely wavered, but as one soldier said, "With Lee's surrender, all hope fled, and thereafter obedience and discharge of duty were purely mechanical." Yet, until rumors of Johnston's possible surrender surfaced, an observer thought the spirit of the Army of Tennessee "defiant, and more than ready to try conclusions with Sherman in a pitched battle." Once those rumors spread through the camps, however, the number of deserters rapidly multiplied. Government efforts to stem the tide of desertions brought negligible results.[34]

Elsewhere in the Confederacy, the collapse continued. James Wilson's cavalry roamed freely through Georgia. On the night of 11 April, Confederate forces left Mobile; the next day, Federal forces marched in. The Confederate commander at Mobile, General Dabney Maury, took his men to Meridian, Mississippi, where he hoped to regroup and eventually join Johnston. In Virginia, Governor William Smith begged Davis to name him commander of whatever Confederate forces were still in the state. Smith promised to send the men on to Johnston.[35]

Shortly after the 13 April conference, perhaps the same day or the next, Davis received Lee's official message detailing his surrender. Ironically, Lee's son, Robert E. Lee, Jr., was standing near Davis when the wire arrived at headquarters. Young Lee had traveled south with a few companions to join up with Johnston. He noted that before Davis saw the message, he seemed at ease and confident. Indeed, he was reiterating his belief that the war could be carried on successfully west of the Mississippi. After being handed the wire, the president read it and passed it along to Lee and John Taylor Wood. Turning away, Davis "silently wept bitter tears." Lee remembered: "He seemed quite broken . . . by this tangible evidence of the loss of his army and the misfortune of its general. All of us, respecting his great grief, silently withdrew, leaving him with Colonel Wood."[36]

The message from General Lee helped persuade Davis to accept the opinion of his staff and the cabinet: the government must move on southward to Charlotte. No matter what the outcome of Johnston's contact with Sherman, Confederate officials would find themselves in an untenable position. They would not be included in any agreement, and if negotiations failed, they would be practically on the battlefront. Davis assumed that Johnston, as a precaution, would soon begin shifting his army to the discussed line of retreat, using "his superiority in cavalry" to hold back any Federal pursuit. Suggesting that Davis was alone in his view, Mallory noted that the fugitives were leaving Greensboro "with plans unformed."[37]

The only immediate desire of the cabinet and Davis's aides was to get their president to safety. They realized the futility of further military resistance. Furthermore, they knew Davis would have to leave the country if negotiations failed. Colonel Charles E. Thorburn joined the government entourage at Greensboro with the intention of helping Davis escape if it became necessary. Thorburn, an old friend of John Taylor Wood's, had recently been involved in blockade running. He owned a small vessel in Florida, and he and Wood had decided that if Davis could not escape to the west, Thorburn would take him by water from Florida to Texas. Davis may have been aware of the scheme, but he later claimed, "I certainly was not a party to that arrangement."[38]

On Saturday, 15 April, the government once more made arrangements to move on. With Trenholm still out of action, Davis took charge of the Treasury funds. He ordered Confederate States Treasurer John C. Hendren to transfer about $39,000 in silver to Beauregard for deposit in the army wagon train. Micajah Clark assumed responsibility for the $288,000 in bullion and coin to be carried with the government as operational funds. The bulk of the treasury, that part which had been sent from Danville to Charlotte on 9 April, was also on the move again. Under William Parker's command, the specie train had left Charlotte on 13 April. Worried over rumors of Federal cavalry in the area, Parker decided on his own initiative to travel farther south. A break in the track had forced the train to stop at Chester, South Carolina, where the cargo was carried by wagon to Newberry. There, another train carried passengers and funds on to Abbeville. Unknown to the president, his wife and family were traveling with

Parker's command. Varina Davis, fearful of capture by Federals, had decided to leave Charlotte with the treasure train.[39]

Escape from Greensboro proved to be a major problem for the fugitive government. The railroad leading to Charlotte had been cut by Union raiders. With the cooperation of Beauregard's staff, John Taylor Wood worked feverishly to put together a train of wagons and ambulances for transportation of men and baggage. Mallory assisted Wood in obtaining vehicles and played diplomat in talking Samuel Cooper, angry at the cramped traveling accommodations, into taking a seat beside the rotund Benjamin "in a wretched ambulance." George Davis and Benjamin's brother-in-law, Jules St. Martin, also crowded into the shaky vehicle pulled by "old and broken down" horses. Secretary Trenholm rode in an ambulance on a mattress provided by the Morehead family.[40]

Government records filled several wagons. Clark personally packed and loaded presidential files, and other clerks loaded War Department records and files of the Confederate Congress. According to one War Department clerk, several boxes of departmental records had to be left behind. Records of the Engineer Bureau were abandoned in a railroad car.[41]

President Davis, Mallory, Breckinridge, Reagan, and Davis's aides departed Greensboro on horseback. Breckinridge and Beauregard assembled a cavalry escort made up of one brigade each of Tennesseans, commanded by George G. Dibrell, and Kentuckians, led by the secretary of war's cousin, W. C. P. Breckinridge, a total of about thirteen hundred horsemen. Scouting duties fell to Captain Given Campbell's Ninth Kentucky Cavalry Regiment. A small group of Mississippians, probably from Lee's army, also volunteered to ride along as extra protection for the president. Dibrell assumed overall command of the military force.[42]

In two respects, the presidential party relived their flights from Richmond and Danville. On the day of their departure, demoralized and rowdy troops and civilians raided warehouses. Violence erupted when home guards protecting the supplies fired on pilfering cavalrymen. In addition to public disorder, the rains came again. Burton Harrison recalled that "the earth was saturated with water, the soil was a sticky red clay, the mud was awful, and the road, in places, almost impracticable." Another witness concurred, "A bleaker evening's ride . . . , no equestrian party ever took."[43]

Into the late afternoon and evening, the remnant of the Confederate government snaked its way southward toward Charlotte. A Greensboro resident who witnessed the departure wrote: "As these great men passed slowly by me on this gloomy April day with their sad faces turned to the South, and as I gazed for the last time in all . . . probability upon the graceful forms and dignified countenances of the two horsemen [Davis and Breckinridge] riding side by side . . . I wept for them and my country."[44]

Jefferson Davis may have been as depressed as the onlookers who watched him ride out of Greensboro. He had left Richmond with the firm belief that Robert E. Lee would save the day. He had departed Danville knowing that the future was in Joe Johnston's hands. When he had presented his views to Johnston and Beauregard during the 13 April conference, "his heart must have beat with a great anxiety, for he must have known how much depended on these Generals countenancing his plans of continuing the war."[45] Unfortunately for Davis, neither they nor the cabinet supported their president's position. He had been forced to agree to negotiations with General Sherman.

Although he had not prevailed, Davis had assumed the offensive by resorting to the same strategy he had used in February to defuse the peace movement. Confident that he would be vindicated, he agreed to negotiate. He was convinced that Sherman would either refuse to talk or reject the proposed terms. The items in the draft agreement suggested that Davis may have developed a secondary strategy that ironically involved the tactics of the peace movement. If he could not win militarily, then he would try for a *status quo ante bellum* political victory. As an astute politician, Davis did not believe the negotiations would succeed, but he would accept the results if Union authorities agreed to his terms.

Despite the continuation of his forced retreat, Jefferson Davis could feel some degree of satisfaction. Johnston's meeting with Sherman would prove him right or win an acceptable peace. If the terms were accepted, the credit would belong to the Davis administration, not to Swain and Graham. If the conference failed, the struggle would continue, or so Davis thought. He wanted to keep fighting, and he probably truly believed that Johnston would obey orders to carry on the war.

Davis's commitment had not been encouraged by his trek into North Carolina. Rebuff by the local citizenry there had been in sharp contrast to his Virginia experiences. In the long view, however, the stigma that would attach to his cold reception in Greensboro revealed something of the character of the Confederacy's transition from lost war to Lost Cause. In the mind of Jefferson Davis, the transition would have to come later. Others might be quitting the field while embracing the memory; he would ride on.

As Greensboro faded in the distance, President Davis did not know that whatever meager chances still existed for extending the life of the Confederacy had suffered a severe blow with the loss of the port city of Mobile on 12 April. Richard Taylor had wired the government on 14 April, requesting orders on what to do next. He could try to concentrate all available forces in Georgia or attempt to protect supply depots in Mississippi and Alabama. The latter option might preserve communications with the Mississippi River and therefore with Kirby Smith. Since Davis considered retreat to the Trans-Mississippi a last resort, Taylor's request for directives was especially important to the government's future.

While in Danville, the president had at least maintained contact with states in the western theater, but Taylor's message never reached Greensboro. The general tried again on 20 April and still the message did not get through.[46] Davis had not been in touch with Kirby Smith since before the evacuation of Richmond, and now the limits of communications to the west had narrowed further. Virginia had been lost with Lee's army. With every mile of the continuing retreat, the realm of Jefferson Davis and his government ebbed from both east and west. He had now left the eastern border that he had maintained in Greensboro. It would follow him to Charlotte.

1. [Stuart], "Davis' Flight"; OR, ser. 1, vol. 46, pt. 3, p. 1395; Averill, "Richmond, Virginia," 270; Trenholm Diary.

2. Ethel Stephens Arnett, Greensboro, North Carolina: The County Seat of Guilford (Chapel Hill, 1955), 20, 389–91.

3. OR, ser. 1, vol. 51, pt. 2, p. 815; Aaron Thompson to W. P. Nixon, 21 Feb. 1865 in Thomas Nixon Papers, Manuscript Department, William R. Perkins Library, Duke University; Mrs. [?]Walker, "The Federals in Greensboro," Charlotte Daily Observer, 27 Jan. 1901.

4. Greensboro Patriot, 23 March 1866.

5. I. G. Bradwell, "Making Our Way Home from Appomattox," Confederate Veteran 29 (March 1921): 102; Burton N. Harrison, "Capture of Davis," 133–34; Greensboro Patriot, 23 March 1866.

6. Mallory, "Last Days," 107; [Stuart], "Davis' Flight"; Swallow, "Retreat of the Confederate Government," 600; Burton N. Harrison, "Capture of Davis," 132.

7. [Stuart], "Davis' Flight"; Wood Diary, 11 April 1865; Jacob D. Cox, "The Surrender of Johnston's Army and the Closing Scenes of the War in North Carolina," in Sketches of War History, 1861–1865: Papers Read before the Ohio Commandery of the Military Order of the Loyal Legion of the United States, 1886–1888, ed. Robert Hunter, 2 vols. (Cincinnati, 1888), 2:252; Walker, "Federals in Greensboro"; Greensboro Patriot, 23 March 1866.

8. Burton N. Harrison, "Capture of Davis," 132; Durkin, John Dooley, 187.

9. Greensboro Patriot, 23 March 1866.

10. Pollard, Life of Jefferson Davis, 512–13; Clement Eaton, Jefferson Davis (New York, 1977), 260.

11. Mallory, "Last Days," 107; Burton N. Harrison, "Capture of Davis," 132–33; Arnett, Greensboro, North Carolina, 394; Swallow, "Retreat of the Confederate Government," 600; [Stuart], "Davis' Flight"; Wood Diary, 11 April 1865.

12. [Stuart], "Davis' Flight"; Swallow, "Retreat of the Confederate Government," 600; Burton N. Harrison, "Capture of Davis," 132; Mallory, "Last Days," 107.

13. Swallow, "Retreat of the Confederate Government," 600; Mallory, "Last Days," 239.

14. Mallory, "Last Days," 107, 239.

15. Alfred Roman, The Military Operations of General Beauregard in the War between the States, 1861 to 1865, 2 vols. (New York, 1883), 2:390–92.

16. OR, Ser. 1, vol. 46, pt. 3, p. 1393.

17. Rowland, Jefferson Davis, 6:543–44; Roman, Military Operations of Beauregard, 2:393.

18. Johnston, Narrative, 396; Roman, Military Operations of Beauregard, 2:394; Reagan, Memoirs, 199; Wood Diary, 12 April 1865.

19. Johnston, Narrative, 396–97; Roman, Military Operations of Beauregard, 2:394.

20. William C. Davis, Breckinridge, 509; Roman, Military Operations of Beauregard, 2:394; OR, ser. 1, vol. 46, pt. 3, p. 1393.

21. Johnston, Narrative, 397–98; Roman, Military Operations of Beauregard, 2:395; Mallory, "Last Days," 240.

22. Reagan, Memoirs, 199; Mallory, "Last Days," 240; Jefferson Davis, Rise and Fall, 2:679–80.

23. Reagan, Memoirs, 199; Mallory, "Last Days," 240.

24. Jefferson Davis, *Rise and Fall*, 2:680; Johnston, *Narrative*, 398–99; Mallory, "Last Days," 240–42.

25. Mallory, "Last Days," 242; Johnston, *Narrative*, 399; Roman, *Military Operations of Beauregard*, 2:395; Reagan, *Memoirs*, 199.

26. Johnston, *Narrative*, 399–400; Reagan, *Memoirs*, 199; Rowland, *Jefferson Davis*, 8:537; Mallory, "Last Days," 242.

27. *OR*, ser. 1, vol. 47, pt.3, pp. 206–7.

28. Jefferson Davis, *Rise and Fall*, 2:681–82. Supply depots for Johnston's army were set up at several locations in South Carolina. See Rowland, *Jefferson Davis*, 7:360.

29. Barrett, *Civil War in North Carolina*, 372–73; Williams and Hamilton, *Papers of Graham*, 6:298. See also Rowland, *Jefferson Davis*, 9:330–33, 341–44.

30. *OR*, ser. 1, vol. 47, pt. 3, pp. 791–92.

31. Barrett, *Civil War in North Carolina*, 373–74; Williams and Hamilton, *Papers of Graham*, 6:299.

32. Barrett, *Civil War in North Carolina*, 375, 377; Williams and Hamilton, *Papers of Graham*, 6:299; Yates, *Confederacy and Zeb Vance*, 119.

33. Cornelia Phillips Spencer, *The Last Ninety Days of the War in North Carolina* (New York, 1866), 165–66; Barrett, *Civil War in North Carolina*, 373. See also Williams and Hamilton, *Papers of Graham*, 6:321 n. 146.

34. James M. Mullen, "Last Days of Johnston's Army," *Southern Historical Society Papers* 18 (1890): 105; Wise, *End of an Era*, 453; *OR*, ser. 1, vol. 47, pt. 3, p. 799.

35. Long, *Civil War Day by Day*, 673; *OR*, ser. 1, vol. 51, pt. 2, p. 1069.

36. Robert E. Lee [Jr.], *Recollections and Letters of General Robert E. Lee* (New York, 1904), 156–57.

37. Jefferson Davis, *Rise and Fall*, 2:682–83; Mallory, "Last Days," 242.

38. Burton N. Harrison, "Capture of Davis," 141–42; Fairfax Harrison, ed., *The Harrisons of Skimino* (Privately published, 1910), 259n.

39. Rowland, *Jefferson Davis*, 6:545; Clark, "Last Days of Confederate Treasury," 545; John F. Wheless, "The Confederate Treasure—Statement of Paymaster John F. Wheless," *Southern Historical Society Papers* 10 (March 1882): 139; John W. Harris, "Gold of Confederate States Treasury," 160; Strode, *Davis: Private Letters*, 152.

40. Clark, "Last Days of Confederate Treasury," 542–43; [Stuart], "Davis' Flight"; Burton N. Harrison, "Capture of Davis," 134; Trenholm Diary.

41. Clark, "Last Days of Confederate Treasury," 543; Wellford Diary; Irvine, "Fate of Archives," 830.

42. Mallory, "Last Days," 242; Milford Overly, "Escort to President Davis," *Confederate Veteran* 16 (March 1908): 121; Clark, "Last Days of Confederate Treasury," 543; Burton N. Harrison, "Capture of Davis," 133; Juvenis [pseud.] "The Last of the Confederacy," New York *Times*, 7 Jan. 1866. "Juvenis" may have been Confederate war correspondent J. W. Youngblood, who reported under that name during the war. J. Cutler Andrews, *The South Reports the Civil War* (Princeton, 1970), 551; Rowland, *Jefferson Davis*, 8:152.

43. Wood Diary, 15 April 1865; Reagan, *Memoirs*, 199; Burton N. Harrison, "Capture of Davis," 134; [Stuart], "Davis' Flight."

44. Greensboro *Patriot*, 23 March 1866.

45. Pollard, *Life of Jefferson Davis*, 515.

46. *OR*, ser. 1, vol. 49, pt. 2, pp. 1140, 1255.

FIVE

Unseated
but not Unthroned

ON SUNDAY, 16 APRIL, Joe Johnston received word from General Sherman that negotiations based on the Appomattox terms could begin. Johnston hurried to Greensboro to inform President Davis, only to find him gone. No one had bothered to inform Johnston that the Confederate government was evacuating the town. Johnston then telegraphed his news southward hoping to reach Davis somewhere along the way. At General Beauregard's suggestion, he requested that Breckinridge return to assist in the proposed talks. Beauregard felt that the secretary of war's presence would protect Johnston if Davis should later question the results of the conference. Meanwhile, the Johnston and Sherman staffs arranged for the two generals to meet on Monday at a point between Durham and Hillsboro.[1]

As Sherman stepped aboard his train on Monday morning, he received news of the assassination of Abraham Lincoln on 14 April. He ordered the telegrapher to keep this shocking information quiet until he returned from his meeting with Johnston.[2]

Despite their long careers in the United States army, the two military leaders who shook hands at the 17 April conference had not met before, except on the battlefield. After the

93

introductions and amenities, Sherman and Johnston departed for a private meeting at James Bennett's nearby farmhouse. There, Johnston learned of Lincoln's death, and the two discussed possible ramifications. Sherman explained that, because he feared possible vengeful reactions from his men, he had thus far withheld the news. He hastened to add that he did not suspect any Southern military officers of complicity in such an act, although he would not be surprised at Davis's involvement. Johnston did not bother to contest the latter remark, a slight duly noted by Davis in his postwar memoirs.[3]

The talks finally turned to the issue at hand. Fulfilling President Davis's prophecy, Sherman rejected any negotiations involving rebel civil authorities. He offered Appomattox terms, which involved the paroling of Confederate soldiers and allowed their retention of certain personal property, without touching upon civil matters. Johnston responded that circumstances in North Carolina were different from those that had existed in Virginia. Indirectly, the Confederate government was a party to the present convention. Therefore, he proposed that, instead of a "suspension of hostilities," the "terms of a permanent peace" be arranged. Sherman liked the suggestion. As he understood the will of the United States Congress and Lincoln, "the restoration of the Union was the object of the war," and he would agree to any terms achieving that end. Johnston implied that he had Davis's authority to negotiate such an agreement. The only sticking point proved to be Sherman's refusal to include Davis and the Confederate cabinet in any general amnesty for rebel soldiers. Despite the fact that neither the president nor any other government official had requested consideration of their futures, Johnston decided he should consult with Breckinridge before continuing negotiations. At that point, the meeting adjourned until noon the next day.[4]

A similar lack of progress marked the first few miles of the Confederate government's journey toward Charlotte. Horses and wheels continuously sank into the muddy roads. Burton Harrison had to seek help from a nearby artillery camp to get the Benjamin ambulance up a hill. While others struggled in the mire, the secretary of state puffed his cigar and recited Tennyson's poem on the death of the Duke of Wellington. The fugitives camped the night of 15 April near Jamestown, having moved less than fifteen miles that day. Davis and the cabinet lodged at a nearby house, where the owner provided food and sleeping quarters. A servant, mistaking Adjutant General Cooper for the president, provided the weary old soldier with a private bedroom. Davis and "one or two others were presently provided for elsewhere," wrote Harrison, "and the rest of us bestowed ourselves to slumber on the floor, before the roaring fire."[5]

Next morning the trip resumed with better horses now pulling Benjamin's troublesome vehicle and Davis riding a filly presented by his host. The caravan crept along the sloppy roads, leaving Jamestown behind, passing through High Point, and camping about four miles from Lexington. Apparently no housing could be found, because Davis and his party camped in a pine grove by the roadside. Mallory noticed that the president seemed depressed and for the first time appeared to be losing hope for the cause. Sometime later that evening, Breckinridge learned of several messages awaiting him in Lexington. These included a one-line note from Johnston: "Your immediate presence is necessary, in order that I should be able to confer with you." Other wires indicated that Sherman had agreed to a conference. Davis asked Reagan to accompany Breckinridge back to Greensboro.[6]

To save time, Breckinridge decided that he and Reagan should make the return trip by rail. He wired Johnston to have engines ready where destruction by Union raiders had created gaps in the track. Despite this foresight, traveling problems delayed arrival in Greensboro until early Monday morning, when, at 9:30, Breckinridge wired Davis that the party had reached its destination safely. He also sent a message requesting instructions from Johnston in Hillsboro, and shortly before noon, he notified Davis that Johnston was in his meeting with Sherman. At two o'clock the general sent word to Breckinridge to meet him in Hillsboro that evening.[7]

William T. Sherman spent the evening of 17 April discussing the events of the day with his officers. One issue that weighed heavily on his mind was the disposition of Jefferson Davis and his cabinet. One of Sherman's officers suggested that if Johnston insisted on his government's unmolested escape, the rebel president and his colleagues should be provided with a ship for transportation to the Bahamas. Sherman's mind probably drifted back to the conference he had attended with Grant and Lincoln on 28 March, when this very subject had come up. "As usual," Sherman remembered, Lincoln

> illustrated his . . . [view] by a story: "A man had taken the total-abstinence pledge. When visiting a friend, he was invited to take a drink, but declined, on the score of his pledge; when his friend suggested lemonade, [it] . . . was accepted. In preparing the lemonade, the friend pointed to the brandy-bottle, and said the lemonade would be more palatable if he were to pour in a little brandy; when his guest said, if he could do so 'unbeknown' to him, he would not object." From which illustration I inferred that Mr. Lincoln wanted Davis to escape, "unbeknown" to him.[8]

During the early morning hours of Tuesday, 18 April, Breckinridge and Reagan rode up to Johnston's quarters, where the general briefed them on Monday's meeting. Reagan set to work on a draft of the terms discussed at the 13 April Greensboro conference, leaving out any mention of the involvement or fate of Davis and the cabinet. While Reagan wrote, Johnston, Breckinridge, and their escort departed for the day's meeting with Sherman.[9]

Accompanied by Lieutenant General Wade Hampton, Johnston rode up to the Bennett house at two o'clock. Sherman had been waiting since noon. Breckinridge stayed out of sight until Johnston received Sherman's permission for him to join the conference. Convinced by the argument that, although he was a cabinet member, Breckinridge also held the military rank of major general, Sherman reluctantly agreed to his participation.[10]

According to Johnston's account, the meeting became quite congenial after Breckinridge arrived, especially when Sherman uncorked a bottle of liquor. Breckinridge argued the Confederate position so well that, at one point, Sherman protested good-naturedly, "See here, gentlemen, who is doing this surrendering anyhow? If this thing goes on, you'll have me sending a letter of apology to Jeff Davis." When Reagan's written proposal arrived by messenger, Sherman initially rejected it as too "general and verbose." He then sat down and wrote out his own terms, but Johnston noticed that he kept Reagan's paper close by. Sherman's finished document reflected more than the influence of Reagan's proposals. The Union general had an affection for the South gained during the years he had spent in the region before the war. He remembered Lincoln's conciliatory tone during the same March conference when the president had talked of Davis's fate. At that time, Lincoln had said that rebel soldiers who laid down their arms should have their rights as United States citizens restored. Furthermore, he had expressed no objection to allowing the North Carolina state government to govern de facto until other arrangements could be made. Sherman also knew of Lincoln's initial acceptance of Campbell's Virginia plan, but he did not know Lincoln had later changed his mind or why.[11]

Sherman's proposal called for a cease-fire, the collection of arms at state arsenals, recognition of present state governments, reestablishment of federal courts in the South, and the guarantee of United States constitutional rights to and amnesty for Southern citizens who had participated in the Confederate war effort. The document made no mention of Jefferson Davis or his cabinet. The Confederate government had gotten just what it wanted. Only three days earlier, Sherman had wired Grant and the United States secretary of war, Edwin M. Stanton, that he would agree to no terms that might affect civil policy. He had now proceeded to do just that by including such nonmilitary points as recognition of Southern state governments in the surrender document.[12]

After the signing ceremonies, Sherman returned to Raleigh, where he prepared to send a copy of the agreement to Washington. Breckinridge began making preparations to travel on to Charlotte. He had just received a message from President Davis, now at Concord, to join him as soon as possible. Breckinridge sent a return wire informing Davis of

Lincoln's assassination and then, with a copy of the surrender document tucked inside his coat, began what would become a two-day effort to reach Charlotte by rail.[13]

While the negotiations of 17–18 April had been in progress, the Davis caravan had continued its trek southward. By the evening of 17 April, the column had almost reached Salisbury. Frank Vizetelly, an artist-correspondent for the *Illustrated London News*, had joined the fugitives in Greensboro. He had left Virginia just before Lee's surrender to report on the Johnston-Sherman campaign. Vizetelly sketched for his paper the presidential party's anxious crossing of the Yadkin River and felt the tension caused by fear of Union cavalry roaming the area. The weary travelers made camp across the river, except President Davis, who accepted an invitation from a local Episcopal minister to share his home for the night. In a cheerful mood, the president sat up late, chewing on an unlighted cigar and discussing the ill effects of Lee's surrender.[14]

On Tuesday, 18 April, the march continued toward Concord. After a few miles, some of the less hardy travelers transferred to a train carrying excess baggage on to Charlotte. At Concord, Davis pitched his tent by a small pine tree, "for many years thereafter an object of interest to all." A local resident, Victor Barringer, invited the president and the cabinet into his home for the night. Many citizens of the town came by in the evening and the next morning to pay their respects, their warm greetings contrasting with apathetic receptions in Lexington and Salisbury caused by fears of retaliation by George Stoneman's cavalry.[15]

Burton Harrison noted that the president seemed "singularly equable and cheerful" throughout the trip to Charlotte. He appeared "to have had a great load taken from his mind, to feel relieved of responsibilities, and his conversation was bright and agreeable. He talked of men and books, particularly of Walter Scott and Byron; of horses and dogs and sports; of the woods and the fields; of trees and many plants; of roads, and how to make them; of the habits of birds, and of a variety of other topics." The landscape lifted the spirits of the travelers, who saw "men in the fields, white and black, . . . plowing the young corn, beautiful colts . . . following their dams up and down the corn rows, fruit trees and flowers . . . blooming around comfortable homes. The fields were well fenced, and everything bespoke comfort and, to outward appearance, happiness."[16]

The idyllic mood did not last, for new problems awaited the government when it arrived in Charlotte on Wednesday, 19 April. A day earlier, Given Campbell had taken part of the cavalry escort on ahead to check out rumors that Stoneman was threatening the town. Like most of the trip's rumors, these had proved to be false. In fact, the town about to become the new capital of the Confederacy had thus far escaped any wartime destruction. Its location far inland and its lack of major factories were two conditions that had contributed to a government decision in August 1862 to place the Confederate Navy Yard there. Threatened by Union forces operating near the old location in Portsmouth, Virginia, workers produced naval ordnance without incident in Charlotte.[17]

Residents of Charlotte and Mecklenburg County had strongly opposed the election of Abraham Lincoln in 1860 and had enthusiastically supported the secessionist movement. During the war, the county had supplied the Confederacy with over twenty-seven hundred soldiers. In 1863 after the disastrous losses at Vicksburg and Gettysburg, the Davis administration had received a vote of confidence at a public mass meeting in the county courthouse. Past history, then, indicated that the fugitive government could expect a warm reception in Charlotte.[18]

Charlotte impressed the visitors as an agreeable community. A Confederate soldier wrote in his diary, "This town presents quite a pretty appearance; it is ornamented with quite a number of shade trees, a great addition to the natural beauty of the situation. The dwelling houses are examples of taste and beauty, the public buildings are numerous and well situated." Another soldier agreed, "This Charlotte is a sweet little town and Spring in all her loveliness is here, breathing freshness and fragrance through the rose bordered streets."[19]

The people of the town did not similarly strike the visitors. One complained, "Of those citizens that I have seen, only a very small minority possess the air of respectability. Of the ladies the same seems to be the rule. The respectable are in the minority, and as well as I can learn are refugees. In sentiment the regular citizens seem to be quite rotten in regard to the Confederacy and our cause." In fact, finding a house for Jefferson Davis proved to be as big a problem here as in Greensboro. Burton Harrison had sent advance word to Varina Davis, informing her of the approaching column and asking her to assist in procuring quarters. The local quartermaster told Harrison that Mrs. Davis had departed with Parker's train and that her present whereabouts were unknown. The quartermaster also reported that he had found only one person willing to house the president. General Stoneman's men had supposedly issued threats "that whoever entertained [Davis] would have his house burned by the enemy." However, Stephen Mallory thought he and his fellow exiles were received with "kindness and courtesy." Yet, "upon all sides . . . the proofs of the hopelessness of the cause were evident."[20]

Lewis Bates, a Massachusetts native, a bachelor, and superintendent of the Southern Express Company, volunteered to share his home with President Davis. He waited in vain for his guest at the train depot, not having been informed that the presidential party was traveling by horse and wagon. One of his neighbors had to welcome Davis and his staff to his house. A Davis aide noted that some local citizens complained about the president's staying with a Yankee in such a plain-looking house, but, of course, the complainers had not offered their residences to the weary chief executive. In any event, those close to Davis felt that after his Greensboro experience, he no longer cared about irrelevant protocol.[21]

Despite the problem of quarters for the president, the refugees found Charlotte much more cooperative than Greensboro. For example, local officials offered the Charlotte branch of the Bank of North Carolina for use as executive headquarters. The long-suffering Trenholm and his wife lodged with the William Phifer family. Wood, Johnston, and Lubbock stayed with the president in Bates's house. Burton Harrison, Benjamin, and Jules St. Martin moved into the mansion of Abram Weill, the merchant who had befriended

Varina Davis during her stay in Charlotte. George Davis and Mallory also found quarters in private residences.[22]

While Jefferson Davis waited for one of the military officers to enter the rear of Bates's house to unlock the front door, a large crowd gathered in the street and called on their president to speak. He turned, thanked them for the show of affection, especially in light of current circumstances, and promised to continue the struggle as long as the people willed it. He admitted to "having committed errors, and very grave ones," during the course of the war but insisted that he was as dedicated as ever to the one purpose for which he had served, "the preservation of the true principles of constitutional freedom."[23]

As Davis spoke, another event upstaged him. Local telegraph agent J. C. Courtney came running up with Breckinridge's wire announcing Lincoln's death. As William Johnston, a local railroader and former commissary general of North Carolina, remembered the moment, Davis passed the telegram to him, remarking on the "extraordinary" nature of the message. Some of the crowd overheard and called for the wire to be read aloud. With Davis's consent, Johnston read the brief words, and then the president proceeded with his impromptu remarks. By this time, Lewis Bates had arrived from the train depot. Bates, the gracious host, later stirred up a controversy over Davis's reaction to the assassination. He testified that Davis remarked with great satisfaction to the crowd, "If it were done it were well that it was well done," misquoting Shakespeare's *Macbeth*. Bates also claimed that Davis said he hoped the same fate befell Andrew Johnson and Edwin Stanton. William Johnston later charged that Bates, anxious to conciliate the commander of Federal occupation forces in Charlotte, who was seeking to gather evidence connecting Davis with the assassination, gave a false account of the president's response to the news. Having housed the rebel leader, Bates was obviously in an awkward position. Natives of Charlotte who were present that day reacted angrily against Bates, and he eventually returned to Massachusetts to live.[24] News of the incident would soon spread anger across the South.

Witnesses who left accounts of what transpired did not support all the details of Johnston's version. However, all but Bates stated categorically that Davis expressed regret over Lincoln's death. Basil Duke, who had brought his Kentucky cavalry regiment from Virginia to North Carolina in an effort to join Johnston, had been sidetracked into Charlotte. He and his men were among those who stood in the street and called for a speech. Duke did not notice any particular reaction by Davis, other than his doubting the accuracy of the report. Stephen Mallory agreed, writing in his notes that Davis called the news "a canard." When the navy secretary remarked that he feared violence if the story were true, Davis responded, "I certainly have no special regard for Mr. Lincoln; but there are a great many men of whose end I would much rather have heard than his. I fear it will be disastrous for our people, and I regret it deeply." Others heard Davis call the assassination "lamentable" and "awful."[25]

The Confederate president glimpsed what was to come during church services the following Sunday. Davis, his aides, and several members of the cabinet went to Saint Peter's Episcopal Church. The minister spoke of the sad condition of the country, especially condemning the assassination of Lincoln. Calling it a "blot on American civilization," the rector warned that the South would suffer from this unjustifiable event. Davis later said he felt the minister had looked a little too often in his direction during the sermon. He explained to Preston Johnston and Harrison, "I think the preacher directed his remarks at me; and he really seems to fancy I had something to do with the assassination."[26]

After the commotion of the arrival and the news of Lincoln's death, the skeleton government simply marked time while waiting for Breckinridge. Davis received a welcome letter from Varina, who had arrived to a warm reception in Abbeville, South Carolina. Aside from the illness of their young son and depression over the war situation, she wrote that she was safe and well cared for. Relieved at this news, the president busied himself with the routine correspondence that had helped him to pass the time since leaving Greensboro. At Salisbury he had denied the request of a Virginia battalion to be allowed to leave North Carolina for their native state. He explained, "Our necessities exclude the idea of disbanding any portion of the force which remains to us and constitutes our best hope of recovery from the reverses and disasters to which you refer." Davis also worked to get saddles for Duke's cavalry and to procure artillery and cavalry from Beauregard to assist local forces defending Charlotte. He sought information on Federal troop movements in South Carolina and sent a message to Howell Cobb in Macon, Georgia, encouraging his efforts to gather a makeshift force to meet James Wilson's cavalry.[27]

The correspondence with Cobb further defined the ever-narrowing limits of Davis's power. Though cheering the Georgian's efforts, the president was forced to the position of promising to legitimize Cobb's actions with an executive order after the fact. Cobb would make the necessary decisions at his own discretion. A message from Montgomery also demonstrated Davis's helplessness. Authorities in that south Alabama city, the Confederacy's first capital, had been unable to get a message through to Richard Taylor in Meridian, Mississippi. Reinforcements were needed to meet the threat of James Wilson's Federal raiders. Davis could only advise that Cobb might be able to send help from Georgia.[28]

While Davis thus occupied himself, John Breckinridge faced exasperating obstacles in his trek to Charlotte. Gaps in the railroad kept him, Reagan, and their small escort from reaching Salisbury until Thursday, 20 April. From there, Breckinridge sent a message to Davis detailing the difficulties encountered thus far and complaining that the expected train from Charlotte had not yet arrived. He blamed the delay on stragglers, who had probably seized the engine. Davis responded, "Train will start for you at midnight with guard." Next morning, Breckinridge wired back that stragglers and parolees had seized the train at Concord, but the "engine and tender escaped, and will be here presently." He also wired Joe Johnston that something should be done to protect rail traffic.[29]

Early Saturday morning the Breckinridge party finally arrived in Charlotte. One of the first familiar figures they saw, sitting on the front porch of the Weill mansion "hatless, smoking, sleek and smiling," was Judah Benjamin. He called out to Breckinridge and asked if the news about Lincoln was true. Benjamin's ever-present smile faded when Breckinridge confirmed the news. He then went on to the Bates house to present Davis with the long-awaited peace agreement. Called on to speak by a small group that witnessed his arrival, the secretary of war excused himself "with grace and dignity" and retired to Davis's quarters. The president asked about the veracity of the assassination report, and then the two discussed the Johnston-Sherman document. Afterward, Davis scheduled a cabinet meeting for Saturday evening.[30]

At the conference that night in the bank building, President Davis explained the terms of the agreement to the cabinet. After a general discussion, Davis asked that each cabinet officer prepare in writing his views on whether the terms should be accepted and, if so, how best to proceed.[31]

Throughout Saturday night and all day Sunday, cabinet members worked on their documents of opinion. Although Mallory denied any consultation, the similarity of views suggests otherwise. All, including Benjamin, concluded that the convention should be accepted. The only alternative they saw was guerrilla or partisan warfare, which, in Mallory's words, "would be more disastrous to our own people than it could possibly be to the enemy." Perhaps Robert E. Lee's recent wire to Davis was influential. Lee had argued strongly against continuing the war, especially on a partisan scale. On the problem of implementing the agreement, the cabinet generally agreed that Davis did not have the constitutional authority to dissolve the Confederacy. However, their nearly unanimous opinion appeared to be that the circumstances overruled any such consideration. Benjamin suggested that Davis invite the states to consider the matter, but others agreed with George Davis, who argued that the president should act "for the speedy delivery of the people from the horrors of war."[32]

All things considered, the cabinet thought the terms remarkably favorable. Benjamin saw no "dishonor" or "degradation" in the document's language, and Attorney General Davis thought the Southern people would be willing to accept provisions "far less liberal than the convention proposes." Reagan even argued that since no mention was made of slavery, the South would have to make no concession on the issue, leaving the subject in the same legal state "as it was before the war." His analysis was naïve but understandable in light of Sherman's generosity and the fact that the Thirteenth Amendment, abolishing slavery, had not yet been approved.[33]

Jefferson Davis did not share the optimism of his colleagues, in part because he fully expected Federal authorities to reject the agreement. He liked the section recognizing state governments and individual rights, but still his choice of options pained him. "On one hand," he wrote Varina,

> is the long night of oppression which will follow the return of our people to the "Union"; on the other, the suffering of the women and children, and carnage among the few brave patriots who would still oppose the invader, and who, unless the people would rise en-masse to sustain them, would struggle but to die in vain. I think my judgment is undisturbed by any pride of opinion. . . . I have sacrificed so much for the cause of the Confederacy that I can measure my ability to make any further sacrifice required, and am assured there is but one to which I am not equal—My wife and my Children—How are they to be saved from degradation or want is now my care.

He admitted that Lee's surrender "destroyed the hopes I entertained when we parted." The country was now in a state of panic and Beauregard and Johnston talked only of retreat and surrender. He told Varina that it would be a good time for her to try to escape, either to Texas or to a foreign country, whichever "may be more practicable." As for himself, he would try to make it to Texas, and "if nothing can be done there which it will be proper to do," he could go on to Mexico "and have the world from which to choose a location."[34]

The president busied himself trying to reestablish contact with Zeb Vance. The governor had arrived in Greensboro too late to see Davis and, for military reasons, had not been allowed to travel from Greensboro to meet with Johnston,

Breckinridge, and Reagan while the truce was in effect. He spent the interim fighting a war of words with Johnston over the seizure of state supplies by the latter's men.[35]

After receiving a wire from Davis, Vance traveled to Charlotte, arriving sometime late Sunday afternoon. In a meeting with the president and the cabinet, Vance asked what he should do. According to the governor's account of the conference, Davis tried to sound hopeful and talked of going on to the Trans-Mississippi to continue the war. He suggested that Vance come along and bring as many North Carolina troops as possible. A "sad silence" followed Davis's words, and one or two of the cabinet present mumbled halfhearted support. However, Breckinridge insisted that nothing could be accomplished by trying to continue the fighting. Vance, he argued, should stay in North Carolina and do the best he could for his state. Sighing, the president reluctantly agreed. The governor traveled back to Greensboro, but Federal officials prevented his return to Raleigh.[36]

During an informal visit to the camp of fellow Kentuckians in Duke's cavalry, Breckinridge lobbied for peace as he had during the meeting with Vance. When an unconvinced young soldier pressed him, the secretary of war stated firmly, "I think the terms are such as all should accept." A veteran standing nearby thought government officials were only "trying to mollify our bitter discomfiture and crushing humiliation."[37]

Yielding to cabinet arguments, Jefferson Davis sent a wire to Johnston approving the agreement. Perhaps to remind the general that he still had a government to answer to, Davis concluded his 24 April message: "Further instructions will be given as to the details of negotiation and the methods of executing the terms of agreement when notified by you of the readiness on the part of the general commanding U.S. forces to proceed with the arrangement."[38]

These words probably aggravated Johnston's already bad mood. After returning to his headquarters from the meeting with Sherman, he had been handed Davis's order authorizing Treasurer John Hendren to transfer specie to the army baggage train. Johnston ordered the money held for distribution to his army. He later claimed that another message from Davis directed that the money be sent to Charlotte. Johnston also accused the president of ignoring a request for additional funds to pay the troops. After the war, Davis denied both charges, and there is no evidence in the official records to support Johnston. Indeed, Beauregard, in an endorsement on the Davis order to Hendren, informed Johnston that Breckinridge had said that the money could be added to the "military chest of the army" if necessary. The episode, placed in a controversial light when Johnston published his account several years after the war, demonstrates the depth of continuing enmity between the two men.[39]

The several days that had passed without word from Charlotte had also grated on the general's nerves. Johnston wanted a decision from Davis as soon as possible. Perhaps an hour after word from Charlotte had finally arrived, Johnston also received two notes from Sherman. One announced that Federal authorities had rejected the terms, and the other gave notification that the current truce would end in forty-eight hours.[40]

At 6:30 P.M. Johnston wired Breckinridge reporting the latest developments and asking for instructions. He concluded with a warning: "We had better disband this small force to prevent devastation to the country." Possibly upset by the peremptory tone of the message, Breckinridge immediately wired back for a clarification. Did Johnston mean the infantry and artillery should disband, and if so, could not the men retain their small arms and rendezvous elsewhere? Could not the general "bring off the cavalry and all of the men you can mount . . . , with some light field pieces?" Such a force, wrote Breckinridge, should be sufficient against any resistance that might be encountered to the southwest. Clearly, the secretary of war wanted an adequate escort for the continued retreat of the government. Meanwhile, Davis, having abandoned any hope for an acceptable peace, wired Braxton Bragg, apparently in South Carolina, to check the security of Johnston's supply line. He ordered Bragg to secure stores in the Chester area and said, "I expect to join you in a few days." In Louisiana, Kirby Smith called on his men to resist invasion and "protract the struggle."[41]

During the early morning hours of Tuesday, 25 April, Johnston received Breckinridge's message of inquiry. In his reply, the general rejected the Kentuckian's plan, offering only to provide a cavalry escort for the presidential party. Neither he nor his generals believed the army would fight any longer. Furthermore, he contended that the capture of Macon, Georgia, and the surrender of Mobile did not make a large military movement to the southwest feasible. In effect, Johnston was announcing that he would no longer allow Davis or the cabinet to dictate to him. In a follow-up wire, he informed Breckinridge that he had proposed another meeting with Sherman for the purpose of surrender.[42]

Undoubtedly speaking for Davis, Breckinridge requested that Johnston allow Wade Hampton's men to volunteer for further cavalry duty and to provide horses as needed. Hampton, an impetuous South Carolinian, had already contacted Davis to offer his services for the anticipated flight to the Trans-Mississippi. This fiery cavalryman considered that it would be "far better for us to fight to the extreme limits of our country rather than to reconstruct the Union upon any terms." Breckinridge sent orders the same day, detaching him from Johnston's army. When Hampton informed Johnston of these instructions the next day, 26 April, he learned of the third meeting at the Bennett house and the terms surrendering the Confederate army. Confused about how or whether the surrender affected him, Hampton talked with Johnston, who advised him to go to Charlotte for consultations with Davis and Breckinridge.[43]

In Charlotte the Confederate government once more began preparing for retreat. The town and the government itself had become more and more unsettled as word leaked out about the surrender negotiations. Charlotte's refugee population continued to swell with soldiers and civilians. As in other towns along the government's route, hungry people threatened to raid the local military supply depots. A gang of local toughs robbed one man's home, claiming he had been purchasing government stores and hoarding the goods "for private purposes." The refusal of local merchants to accept Confederate paper money infuriated some of the soldiers. The few cavalry officers with silver coins spent their time "jingling their spurs around the hotel . . . [and] living high." The city's economy suffered from the lack of specie; "trade was nearly altogether suspended, and a very promising city bore every symptom of premature decay." The presence of Davis and other government officials afforded no relief. "The government," complained one soldier, "is completely disorganized, and can support neither its soldiers nor paroled officers."[44]

Indeed, the government seemed to be in more disarray than at any time since leaving Richmond. Johnston's signal that he had no intention of continuing the fighting exploded Davis's expectation that the army would retreat along the route discussed at Greensboro. Wade Hampton and Lieutenant General Joseph Wheeler arrived in town, conferred with the anxious president, and received permission to withdraw all the volunteer cavalry they could muster from Johnston's army. Wheeler had six hundred men to answer the call, but Hampton could muster only his staff and a small escort.[45]

While the cavalry chiefs looked for soldiers, the last cabinet meeting in Charlotte took place in the William Phifer house some time on 26 April. Davis chose this site so the bedridden Trenholm could be present. Members of the Phifer family long remembered the "flutter of excitement" in the house at the sight of "these distinguished men, bowed in sorrow, come in a body [to] pass into the sick room to confer together." The cabinet agreed that the only course now open for Davis and those wishing to accompany him was to leave as soon as possible.[46]

Burton Harrison had already left, sent ahead by the president to Abbeville to see to the safety of Varina Davis and her party. North Carolinian George Davis, whose Wilmington home the Federals now occupied, asked and received permission to resign and remain in Charlotte to care for his motherless children, who had been living with friends nearby. With the major Confederate armies now gone, the aged Adjutant General Samuel Cooper also decided to stay in Charlotte. John Taylor Wood wrote sadly in his diary, "So we are falling to pieces."[47]

The effect of Johnston's surrender on the War Department underscored the truth of Wood's melancholy observation, a truth that extended beyond the loss of individuals. The Subsistence Bureau ceased to exist except for the distribution of supplies from commissary depots to returning soldiers and hospitals. The Ordnance Bureau also dissolved. Bureau Chief Josiah Gorgas's last duty was to sit on a board of examiners set up to judge a cadet's qualifications for promotion to lieutenant. "We met a little before sundown in the ample upper story of a warehouse . . . ," recalled Gorgas, "and by the waning light . . . we went through all the stages of an examination of an expectant Lieutenant of the Confederate Armies." The youngster passed the test, and the pathos of the event lingered in Gorgas's mind long afterward. Of all his Confederate experiences, there was no scene he "mused over oftener than that twilight examination of the last Confederate Cadet."[48]

During the bustle of departure preparations, officials decided to store most of the archives in Charlotte. State Department records and the Great Seal of the Confederacy had already been stored in the Mecklenburg County Courthouse, where they would remain until after the war. Breckinridge ordered War Department records brought from Greensboro to be stored in the area and surrendered to Federal authorities if necessary to keep them from being destroyed. C. T. Bruen, secretary of the Confederate Senate, stored his papers with the War Department files. R. G. H. Kean, the War Bureau chief, and a few clerks stayed behind to see to the disposition of the records and then returned to their native Virginia.[49]

As the government loaded wagons and mounted horses for the trip southward into South Carolina, its treasury train was moving north on a course that would eventually bring about a junction with the presidential column. After leaving Varina Davis in Abbeville, William Parker and his men moved on via Washington, Georgia, to Augusta. There, on 20 April, Parker had deposited the specie in a local bank vault. He had resisted pressures to divide the money among his men and ignored a wire from Stephen Mallory ordering him to disband. When word of the surrender talks had reached Augusta, Parker had consulted with his officers and decided that Johnston's surrender might encourage paroled soldiers and desperate citizens to try to steal the specie. On Sunday, 23 April, Colonel Parker and his troops had begun retracing their route back to Abbeville, where he hoped to find additional soldiers to protect his cargo.[50]

In Charlotte, at noon on a clear, hot Wednesday, 26 April, even as Johnston completed his surrender, the government caravan, "ready for another flitting," began moving slowly southward. Five wagons; ambulances; the cavalry escort, consisting now of five brigades totaling about three thousand men; and Davis, his staff, and cabinet members who preferred the saddle made up the skeletal remains of the Confederate government that passed along the streets of its third temporary capital since the loss of Richmond twenty-four days earlier.[51]

Events had dramatically altered the status of the man who rode at the head of the procession. His government had not operated as a functional bureaucracy since leaving Danville. In Greensboro and Charlotte only the Executive and War Departments had conducted routine business on a small scale. Despite the decline in government activity at that time, Jefferson Davis had managed to remain president in fact as well as in title. Now, however, the cabinet's support of the initial surrender agreement and Johnston's unilateral decision to surrender on 26 April virtually eliminated Davis's influence as chief executive. Johnston's actions not only defied Davis but left him with no army east of the Mississippi to carry out his determination to continue the war. In addition, Davis had refused even to consider the option offered by Sherman at the Bennett House and delivered by Breckinridge at Charlotte that would have allowed him to leave the country in a boat. Lincoln's death had meanwhile destroyed any chance the Confederate leader had to flee on a ship unhindered by Federal forces. In Washington, United States officials, no doubt influenced by public reaction to the assassination, had already begun compiling evidence that supposedly linked Davis to the John Wilkes Booth conspiracy. Ironically, the anti-Davis triumvirate of Campbell, Swain, and Graham found that the hard-line Federal reaction to Lincoln's death also severely crippled their continuing efforts to influence the political reconstruction of the South.[52]

In spite of the destruction of his dream of Southern independence, Jefferson Davis did not ride out of Charlotte a dispirited man. One observer thought he looked "sad and, indeed, hopeless," but a few days earlier, Davis had said to Harrison, "I *cannot* feel like a beaten man." This statement would appear at first glance to cast doubt on the president's previous sincerity, but Davis never allowed his personal feelings to interfere with his convictions. He had made up his mind to defend the Southern cause to the last man, no matter what. In his own words, he would make any sacrifice, except to compromise the safety of his family. He had been under no illusion that his respite in Charlotte would be lengthy. In the letter to Varina, he had confided, "My stay will not be prolonged a day beyond the prospect of useful labor here." Although expecting to retreat, he had not anticipated being without Johnston's army. Nevertheless, the enthusiasm of the cavalry escort lifted his spirits. Mallory worried when he saw the president respond to the cavalry's cheers and their boasts of carrying on the fight across the Mississippi. Davis, wrote Mallory, seemed to lose all concern for his personal well-being.[53]

Others also expressed concern over what they saw as Davis's flight from reality. A Confederate soldier sadly noted: "Poor President, he is unwilling to see what all around him see. He cannot bring himself to believe that after four years of glorious struggle we are to be crushed into the dust of submission." Another witness thought Davis's stubborn attitude went deeper than mere denial of military defeat: "The principle he had contended for was still as dear to him as ever, only the opportunity to give it honor or stability, or to reflect its feautures [*sic*] himself was irrevocably gone. He felt himself unseated but not unthroned."[54]

Since leaving Greensboro, the president had had experiences that had reinforced such a feeling. The many well-wishers en route to and within Charlotte had no doubt convinced Davis that if hope for victory had vanished, affection for the cause had not. He probably did not perceive the transfer of the cause from the battlefield to the minds and hearts of Southerners. Certainly there is no evidence that he had begun to see himself as a symbol or a martyr. With Johnston's surrender, however, Davis did understand that if he gave up, all vestiges of resistence and hope would disappear. Characteristically, this latest setback made him more determined to continue, and his determination in light of the facts gave the impression that he had lost touch with reality. His behavior may have been naïve, but it was consistent. He remained confident because he simply refused to abandon his goal of saving the Confederacy. His friends did not share his confidence, and they were relieved to get him out of Charlotte to the hoped-for safety of the Deep South.

1. *OR*, ser. 1, vol. 47, pt. 3, p. 307; Johnston, *Narrative*, 401.

2. William T. Sherman, *Memoirs of William T. Sherman, Written by Himself*, 2 vols. in 1 (New York, 1891), 2:347–48; *OR*, ser. 1, vol. 47, pt. 3, pp. 220–21.

3. Sherman, *Memoirs*, 2:348–49; Johnston, *Narrative*, 402; Jefferson Davis, *Rise and Fall*, 2:686.

4. Johnston, *Narrative*, 402–4; Sherman, *Memoirs*, 2:349–50.

5. Burton N. Harrison, "Capture of Davis," 134–35; Given Campbell, "Memorandum of a Journal, Kept Daily during the Last March of Jefferson Davis," 15, 16 April 1865, Library of Congress; [Stuart], "Davis' Flight"; Wood Diary, 16 April 1865; Mallory, "Last Days," 242.

6. *OR*, ser. 1, vol. 47, pt. 3, pp. 801, 803; Jefferson Davis, *Rise and Fall*, 2:683; Reagan, *Memoirs*, 201.

7. Reagan, *Memoirs*, 201; *OR*, ser. 1, vol. 47, pt. 3, pp. 806.

8. Sherman, *Memoirs*, 2:326–27, 350–52.

9. Reagan, *Memoirs*, 201; Johnston, *Narrative*, 403–4; *OR*, ser. 1, vol. 47, pt. 3, pp. 806–7.

10. Sherman, *Memoirs*, 2:352; Johnston, *Narrative*, 405.

11. Wise, *End of an Era*, 450–52; Johnston, *Narrative*, 405; Sherman, *Memoirs*, 2:327–31; *OR*, ser. 1, vol. 47, pt. 3, p. 257.

12. H. V. Boynton, *Sherman's Historical Raid: The Memoirs in Light of the Record* (Cincinnati, 1875), 229–30; *OR*, ser. 1, vol. 47, pt. 3, p. 221.

13. Sherman, *Memoirs*, 2:354, 357; *OR*, ser. 1, vol. 47, pt. 3, pp. 809, 812,

814; Rowland, *Jefferson Davis*, 6:551; Roman, *Military Operations of Beauregard*, 2:399.
14. Campbell Journal, 17 April 1865; Wood Diary, 17 April 1865; W. Stanley Hoole, *Vizetelly Covers the Confederacy* (Tuscaloosa, 1957), 133–34; "The Last Days of the Confederate Government," *Illustrated London News*, 22 July 1865, 70; Burton N. Harrison, "Capture of Davis," 136; Varina Davis, *Jefferson Davis*, 2:627.
15. Campbell Journal, 18 April 1865; Wood Diary, 18 April 1865; "President Davis in Concord," Charlotte *Daily Observer*, 3 Feb. 1901; Burton N. Harrison, "Capture of Davis," 136.
16. Burton N. Harrison, "Capture of Davis," 136; Haw, "Last of the Ordnance Department," 452.
17. Campbell Journal, 18, 19 April 1865; Dannye Romine, *Mecklenburg: A Bicentennial Story* (Charlotte, 1975), 48; Violet G. Alexander, comp., "The Confederate States Navy Yard at Charlotte, N.C., 1862–1865," *Southern Historical Society Papers* 40 (Sept. 1915): 186–87.
18. D. A. Tompkins, *A History of Mecklenburg County and the City of Charlotte from 1740 to 1903*, 2 vols. (Charlotte, 1903), 1:136–37, 140–41.
19. Harry C. Townsend, "Townsend's Diary—January–May 1865," *Southern Historical Society Papers* 34 (1906): 124; Durkin, *John Dooley*, 200.
20. Townsend, "Townsend's Diary," 124; Burton N. Harrison, "Capture of Davis," 136; Mallory, "Last Days," 243–44.
21. Joseph G. Fiveash, "When Mr. Davis Heard of Lincoln's Death," *Confederate Veteran* 15 (Aug. 1907): 366; Romine, *Mecklenburg*, 49; LeGette Blythe and Charles Raven Brockmann, *Hornets' Nest: The Story of Charlotte and Mecklenburg County* (Charlotte, 1961), 404; Harrison, "Capture of Davis," 136; [Stuart], "Davis' Flight."
22. Blythe and Brockmann, *Hornets' Nest*, 404; Wood Diary, 19 April 1865; Burton N. Harrison, "Capture of Davis," 136–37; Meade, *Benjamin*, 316; Mrs. James A. Fore, "Cabinet Meeting in Charlotte," *Southern Historical Society Papers* 41 (Sept. 1916): 62–64; Varina Davis, *Jefferson Davis*, 2:578; Mallory, "Last Days," 243.
23. Rowland, *Jefferson Davis*, 9:158; R. V. Booth, "Last Address of President Davis, C.S.A.," *Confederate Veteran* 22 (July 1914): 304.
24. Swallow, "Retreat of Confederate Government," 603; Rowland, *Jefferson Davis*, 9:157–58, 439; Francis Richard Lubbock, *Six Decades in Texas; or, Memoirs of Francis Richard Lubbock*, ed. C. W. Raines (Austin, 1900), 564; Burton N. Harrison, "Capture of Davis," 136; Fiveash, "When Mr. Davis Heard of Lincoln's Death," 336; New York *Times*, 31 May 1865.
25. Swallow, "Retreat of Confederate Government," 603; Basil W. Duke, *Reminiscences of General Basil W. Duke, C.S.A.* (Garden City, N.Y., 1911), 380–83; Lubbock, *Memoirs*, 564; Burton N. Harrison, "Capture of Davis," 136–37; Mallory, "Last Days," 244, [Stuart], "Davis' Flight"; Juvenis, "Last of the Confederacy."
26. A. J. Hanna, *Flight into Oblivion* (Richmond, 1938), 47–48; Wood Diary, 23 April 1865; Burton N. Harrison, "Capture of Davis," 137.
27. *OR*, ser. 1, vol. 47, pt. 3, pp. 810, 816; Rowland, *Jefferson Davis*, 6:556–57; Strode, *Davis: Private Letters*, 153.
28. *OR*, ser. 1, vol. 49, pt. 2, pp. 1257, 1267.
29. *OR*, ser. 1, vol. 47, pt. 3, pp. 812, 874, 819–20.
30. [Stuart], "Davis' Flight"; Durkin, *John Dooley*, 197; William C. Davis, *Breckinridge*, 515; Mallory, "Last Days," 245.

31. Mallory, "Last Days," 245, Rowland, *Jefferson Davis*, 6:577.

32. Mallory, "Last Days," 245; Rowland, *Jefferson Davis*, 6:569–85; Dowdy and Manarin, *Papers of Lee*, 938–39.

33. Rowland, *Jefferson Davis*, 6:571, 579, 581–82.

34. Ibid., 559–61.

35. *OR*, ser. 1, vol. 53, p. 418, ser. 1, vol. 47, pt. 3, pp. 810–11, 815–16; Johnston to Vance, 19 April 1865, Vance to Johnston, 20 April 1865, Zebulon Vance Papers, North Carolina Division of Archives and History, Raleigh.

36. Clement Dowd, *Life of Zebulon Vance* (Charlotte, 1897), 485–86.

37. Duke, *Reminiscences*, 383–84; Durkin, *John Dooley*, 198.

38. *OR*, ser. 1, vol. 47, pt. 3, p. 834.

39. Johnston, *Narrative*, 408–9; Jefferson Davis, *Rise and Fall*, 2:690–92; *OR*, ser. 1, vol. 47, pt. 3, p. 801.

40. *OR*, ser. 1, vol. 47, pt. 3, pp. 293–94, 831, 834–35; Johnston, *Narrative*, 410–11.

41. *OR*, ser. 1, vol. 47, pt. 3, pp. 835–36.

42. Johnston, *Narrative*, 411–12; *OR*, ser. 1, vol. 47, pt. 3, p. 836.

43. *OR*, ser. 1, vol. 47, pt. 3, pp. 813–14, 837, 845–46.

44. Rowland, *Jefferson Davis*, 9:158; Vandiver, *Diary of Josiah Gorgas*, 181; [Stuart], "Davis' Flight"; Townsend, "Townsend Diary," 124; Tench Tilghman Diary, 20 April 1865, Southern Historical Collection, University of North Carolina at Chapel Hill; Wood Diary, 21 April 1865; Durkin, *John Dooley*, 194.

45. Jefferson Davis, *Rise and Fall*, 2:689; *OR*, ser. 1, vol. 47, pt. 3, pp. 845–46; Joseph Wheeler, "An Effort to Rescue Jefferson Davis," *Century Magazine* 56 (May 1898): 86.

46. Fore, "Cabinet Meeting in Charlotte," 66–67; Mallory, "Last Days," 245.

47. Burton N. Harrison, "Capture of Davis," 137; Reagan, *Memoirs*, 208; Wood Diary, 24 April 1865.

48. Rowland, *Jefferson Davis*, 7:355–56, 8:332.

49. Irvine, "Fate of Archives," 826–27; Blythe and Brockmann, *Hornets' Nest*, 403; Younger, *Inside the Confederate Government*, 206–7; Wellford Diary, 24 April 1865. The United States Treasury Department purchased the Confederate State Department records after the war. The Great Seal eventually came into the possession of the Museum of the Confederacy, Richmond, Virginia. Irvine, ibid.

50. John W. Harris, "Gold of Confederate States Treasury," 160; Wheless, "Confederate Treasure," 140; Parker, "Gold and Silver," 307–9.

51. Tilghman Diary, 26 April 1865; Trenholm Diary; Duke, *Reminiscences*, 385; Younger, *Inside the Confederate Government*, 207; Rowland, *Jefferson Davis*, 8:152.

52. Jefferson Davis to John Reagan, 9 Aug. 1877, Davis-Reagan Papers, Dallas Historical Society, Dallas, Tex.; John Campbell to R. M. T. Hunter, 21 April 1865, R. M. T. Hunter Papers, Microfilm Edition, 13 reels (reel 7), Troy Middleton Library, Louisiana State University (originals at University of Virginia); Williams and Hamilton, *Papers of Graham*, 6:310–11. Some in the peace movement adopted a new strategy to appease the conquering North. The same day the Confederate government left Charlotte, a North Carolina unionist bitterly wrote that the old secessionists were eulogizing Lincoln and "now think that he was one of the greatest men . . . we ever had." John A. Hedrick to [Benjamin S. Hedrick], 26 April 1865, Benjamin Sherwood

Hedrick Papers, Manuscript Department, William R. Perkins Library, Duke University.

53. [Stuart], "Davis' Flight"; Burton N. Harrison, "Capture of Davis," 137; Rowland, *Jefferson Davis*, 6:561; Mallory, "Last Days," 245–46.

54. Durkin, *John Dooley*, 198; [Stuart], "Davis' Flight".

Jefferson Davis and family in Canada, 1867, shortly after his release from prison

Jefferson and Varina Davis   *Museum of the Confederacy*

The Davis Children, l-r, Jefferson, Jr., Margaret (Maggie), Billy, and Winnie   *Miller's Photographic History of the Civil War*

The Confederate Cabinet during the final days

George Davis, Attorney General
Museum of the Confederacy

John C. Breckinridge, Secretary of War *Library of Congress*

Judah P. Benjamin,
Secretary of State
Museum of the Confederacy

Stephen R. Mallory, Secretary of
the Navy *Museum of the Confederacy*

George A. Trenholm, Secretary
of the Treasury *Library of Congress*

John H. Reagan,
Postmaster General
Library of Congress

Jefferson Davis's personal staff during the final days

William Preston Johnston
Howard-Tilton Memorial Library, Tulane University

Micajah H. Clark
Museum of the Confederacy

Francis R. Lubbock
Texas State Library

Burton N. Harrison
Museum of the Confederacy

John Taylor Wood, pictured on the left during his U.S. Naval Academy days with his brother Robert, a West Pointer. *Southern Historical Collection, University of North Carolina at Chapel Hill*

William T. Sutherlin Home, Danville, Virginia, Jefferson Davis's headquarters 3–10 April 1865 *Danville Museum of Fine Arts and History*

A. B. Springs Home, Fort Mill, South Carolina, where Davis spent the night of 26 April 1865   *Marshall Doswell and Anne Springs Close, Fort Mill, South Carolina*

Armistead Burt Home (also known as the Stark Home), Abbeville, South Carolina, where Varina Davis spent the night of 28 April 1865 and where Jefferson Davis rested several hours and met with his cavalry commanders on 2 May 1865.   *South Caroliniana Library, University of South Carolina*

Georgia Bank Building, Washington, Georgia, which contained the Robertson family quarters where Jefferson Davis dissolved the Confederate government on 3 May 1865.   *Mary Willis Library, Washington, Georgia*

Monument marking the spot at Irwinville, Georgia where Jefferson Davis and his party were taken prisoner by Federal cavalry on 10 May 1865.   *Mrs. Oscar Powell, Ocilla, Georgia*

The captured Davis family is conveyed through the streets of Macon, Georgia, in an ambulance on 13 May 1865. *Library of Congress*

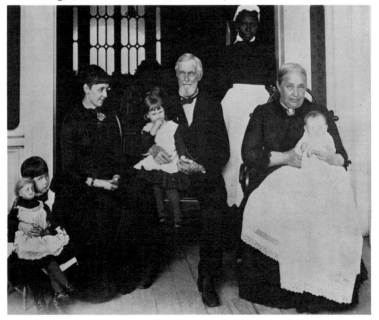

Jefferson and Varina Davis with daughter Maggie and grandchildren at Beauvoir, their Mississippi Gulf Coast home, 1885 *Library of Congress*

SIX

Walking in a Dream

BASIL DUKE GREW FRUSTRATED at the slow pace of the government column that snaked into South Carolina. One of his officers reminded him that at least the leisurely gait gave the impression that Jefferson Davis was "travelling like a president and not like a fugitive." Francis Lubbock had promised the president that when the government arrived in Lubbock's native South Carolina, there would be no more cool receptions, and indeed, in this region largely untouched by war, the fugitives did notice a much friendlier atmosphere. The first night out of Charlotte was spent in the town of Fort Mill, a few miles from the Catawba River. Davis, his staff, and most of the cabinet, stayed in the A. B. Springs home a few miles north of town. Teamsters parked the wagon train in a "nice clover lot" and enjoyed a dry night under the stars.[1]

George Trenholm and his wife went on to Fort Mill and roomed in the home of William E. White. Trenholm's condition worsened during the night, and the next morning he wrote out his resignation. In the brief note, Trenholm thanked Jefferson Davis for his "kindness and courtesy." In accepting the resignation, the president wrote candidly, "You may have forgotten that I warned you when you were about to take office that our wants so far exceeded our means that you could not expect entire success and should anticipate censure and perhaps the loss of financial reputation." From Fort Mill, Trenholm and his wife traveled first to Chester and eventually

117

to Columbia, the state capital, recently razed during Sherman's march. Within a few weeks, he would be arrested there by Federal officials.[2]

A hurriedly assembled cabinet conference under a big tree on the lawn of the White home led to the selection of John Reagan as interim secretary of the treasury. Reagan must have arrived at the meeting late, because he complained that the appointment had been made in his absence. He argued that his mail and telegraphic duties left him little time for seeing to the Treasury. Davis countered "that there would not be much for the Secretary of the Treasury to do" anyway. Reagan reluctantly relented and assumed responsibility for about $800,000 in worthless paper and some $80,000 in bullion.[3]

Minus another cabinet member, the fugitive government continued southwestward, crossing streams and traveling dusty roads to a point near the Broad River. There the weary column camped on the evening of 28 April. With the exception of a warm reception in the town of Yorkville, the retreat from Charlotte had been demoralizing thus far. News of Johnston's official surrender on 26 April had reached the exiles. One of the wagon drivers wrote sadly in his diary, "The cause has gone up. God only knows what will be the end of all this."[4]

President Davis and Secretary of War Breckinridge were also concerned about the future. While Reagan and Stephen Mallory were passing time pitching "silver half dollars for five cents 'Eleven Up,' " Davis and Breckinridge huddled on the front porch of a local residence and discussed the cavalry escort situation. After their conference, the Kentuckian wrote to Wade Hampton, who was worried over the effect Johnston's surrender might have on his status: "If my letter to [Johnston] of [April] 25th, which you carried, was not rec'd before completion of terms, the Gov't, with its imperfect knowledge of the facts, cannot interfere as to the body of the troops; but, in regard to yourself, if not present nor consenting, it is the opinion of the Government that you, and others in like condition, are free to come out." Regardless of the government's desperate condition, this last war between gentlemen must remain chivalric to the end.[5]

The fear of losing part of the escort prompted Breckinridge to encourage, with stipulations, Hampton's desire to join the retreat. Some of the cavalry were indeed talking of going home. One Virginian decided to discuss the situation with General George Dibrell. Dibrell listened while the young soldier told him of some Tennesseans who were thinking about leaving. Dibrell replied firmly and sharply, "We are not going home." The intimidated youngster "beat a retreat to the tattoo of a very rapid pulse." Perhaps to reduce notions of desertion, Davis and members of the cabinet began to mix freely with soldiers and teamsters, and morale noticeably improved.[6]

While the president worked to hold his column together, Varina Davis answered from Abbeville the letter her husband had sent with Burton Harrison a few days earlier from Charlotte. Her spouse's words must have been a tonic after her very trying trip southward. She, too, had seen signs of the collapse. At Chester, the presence of Lieutenant General John Bell Hood, Brigadier General John Preston, former head of the Conscription Bureau in Richmond, and Brigadier General James Chesnut, Jr., an aide to Beauregard during the Fort Sumter crisis of 1861 and husband of famous diarist Mary Boykin Chesnut, lifted the First Lady's spirits. All the officers, "as they stood calm in the expectation of our great woe," offered to help her in any way possible. Nevertheless, she had trouble finding transportation for her family. The railroad was inoperable southward out of Chester, so she needed a good wagon or, preferably, an ambulance. Finally she obtained one of each, putting the baggage in the wagon and loading her maids, children, sister, and herself in the ambulance. Together they proved to be too much weight for the vehicle to carry on the muddy trail. She never forgot that "as my maid was too weak to walk and my nurse was unwilling, I walked five miles in the darkness in mud over my shoe tops, with my cheerful little baby in my arms." Rumors of Yankee cavalry apparently kept Captain William Parker and his men too occupied with the safety of the treasury to be of much assistance to Varina, although she did remember Parker being kind and helpful. En route, she encountered exorbitant food prices charged by merchants and private citizens. Finally, catching a train for the last leg of the journey the party arrived "more dead than alive" in Abbeville, where they were welcomed into the home of the Armistead Burt family.[7]

Varina wrote her husband that she planned to leave early the next morning, 29 April, for Georgia. She anticipated sailing to England to put the two eldest children in school and then returning with the two youngest for a reunion with her husband in Texas. She cautioned him to be careful if his path took him close to Augusta. "I get rumors that [Governor Joseph E.] Brown is going to seize all Government property, and the people are averse—and mean to resist with pistols—They are a set of wretches together, and I wish you were safe out of their land." In Abbeville, however, "they *are all your friends.*" She held doubts about success in the Trans-Mississippi, "but the spirit is there, and the daily accretions will be great when the deluded of this side are crushed out between the upper and nether millstone."[8]

While his family prepared to continue their flight, President Davis and his convoy crossed the Broad River on 29 April and pressed on toward Abbeville. He and the cabinet talked resignedly of the personal monetary and property losses they had suffered as a result of the war. In the village of Unionville, they lunched in the home of Brigadier General William H. Wallace, one of Lee's surrendered officers who had not yet returned home. Here, accompanied by his wife, Braxton Bragg joined the retreat. He told Davis and the cabinet that he believed continuing the struggle was useless. Scouting reports from Georgia and Alabama appeared to confirm Bragg's opinion. Strong Federal cavalry forces operating in those states forced a reassessment of the government's projected line of retreat to the Mississippi.[9]

During a rest stop the next day at the Lafayette Young home south of Martin's Depot, President Davis received more news from Varina and Burton Harrison. In messages brought from Abbeville by family friend Henry Leovy, Harrison reported that he would take his charges to Atlanta by way of Washington, Georgia. There they would wait for presidential instructions. On this same day, Sunday, 30 April, Richard Taylor agreed to a truce to discuss the surrender of Confederate forces in Alabama, Mississippi, and east Louisiana. If consummated, the surrender would further reduce the possibilities of a Davis escape overland to the Trans-Mississippi.[10]

While future prospects dimmed, crowds along the retreat route cheered the caravan. Mallory ruefully noted that word of mouth brought people from all around. Women and children lined the road, scattering flowers and cheering. At one home, two of the wagon drivers received fresh strawberries. Touched by the outpouring of goodwill, Davis stopped to speak. A witness remembered, "Great tears rolled down his haggard cheeks as he bade us be cheerful—trusting always in the wisdom and goodness of God who doeth all things well." In Cokesbury, the president received "generous gifts of fruit and flowers, and the warmest expressions of sympathy and affection." The image of Jefferson Davis and the cause he represented shone brightly in the eyes of these South Carolinians.[11]

In the early morning hours of 2 May, the weary column drifted into Abbeville, a town Burton Harrison described as "a beautiful place, on high ground; . . . [where] the people lived in great comfort, their houses embowered in vines and roses, with many flowers everywhere." Enthusiasm for secession in 1860 had permeated western South Carolina as it had other parts of the state. In Abbeville, in November of that year, a large prosecession rally of several thousand people had gathered at what came to be called Secession Hill. As the exhausted president and his men came into view, "the whole town was thrown open to the party," and the Burt family invited Davis to establish his quarters in the home that his wife had left just two days before. The cabinet stayed in the home of T. C. Perrin, and Preston Johnston, and probably others of the staff, lodged with the Leovys. Expecting to stay a while, the drivers unpacked their wagons, bathed, and changed clothes.[12]

Shortly after arriving, John Breckinridge discussed the situation with his cavalry commanders and decided to have President Davis call a council of war. Despite attempts to maintain morale, rumblings of discontent among officers and men had increased. Convinced that the war was over, the cavalrymen considered it foolish to continue the retreat. Stephen Mallory learned that some of the officers had told Davis that many of their soldiers could not be counted on to fight. In later years, Basil Duke denied that any men would have shirked their duty but admitted that they had grown increasingly impatient over the slow pace of the retreat. They thought the only chance for a successful escape was to strip the column to the bare necessities and ride hard for the west.[13]

Such talk disturbed Breckinridge, so he decided to clear the air. Between 4:00 and 4:30 P.M., he had President Davis call a meeting in the Burt house. The five cavalry commanders, S. W. Ferguson, J. C. Vaughn, W. C. P. Breckinridge, Dibrell, and Duke attended, and Davis, Secretary Breckinridge, and Braxton Bragg were also present. Some versions of the meeting contend that other cabinet members were also there, but the most reliable cite only Breckinridge. The nature of the retreat had changed since leaving Charlotte. Now military considerations predominated, and none of the other cabinet members had any expertise in this area. In Basil Duke's opinion, "none of them knew what was going on, what was going to be done, or what ought to be done." Thus, there was no reason for them to be present.[14]

The president's opening statement clearly demonstrated the haphazard nature of the flight: "It is time that we adopt some definite plan upon which the further prosecution of our struggle shall be conducted. I have summoned you for consultation. I feel that I ought to do nothing without the advice of my military chiefs." Each officer responded with a report on the condition of his command. Davis listened and remarked that the cause was not yet lost. The times were no worse than during the dark days of the American Revolution. Even if he could find no more soldiers than he now had, he continued, "three thousand men are enough for a nucleus around which the whole people will rally when the panic which now afflicts them has passed away."[15]

As in other presidential conferences of the past few weeks, an embarrassing silence followed Davis's words. "We looked at each other in amazement and with feelings a little akin to trepidation," remembered Basil Duke, "for we hardly knew how we should give expression to views diametrically opposed to those he had uttered." The officers finally spoke up, each stating that it was not possible to continue the war. News of Wilson's success in Alabama made further retreat westward risky at best. And according to W. C. P. Breckinridge, the officers concluded from what was known that "the munitions of war were in the hands of the enemy, and there remained no resources, and . . . no people." An offended Davis responded by asking why they were still in the field. "We answered," wrote Duke, "that we were desirous of affording him an opportunity of escaping the depredation of capture. . . . We said that we would ask our men to follow us until his safety was assured, and would risk them in battle for that purpose, but would not fire another shot in an effort to continue hostilities." Davis's efforts to sway his commanders failed, and he finally arose and exclaimed "that all was indeed lost." He became "very pallid, and he walked so feebly as he proceeded to leave the room that General Breckinridge . . . offered his arm." The president's cabinet had been melting away, and now most of his escort would soon be gone.[16]

Secretary Breckinridge and Bragg had remained silent, apparently adopting the strategy that it would be more effective for the president to hear the hard facts from the cavalry chiefs. After Davis left, the two concurred with the opinions of the officers. They agreed that each cavalry regiment should be allowed to vote on whether to continue the march or to disband. Breckinridge proposed to take those men who remained and create diversions to confuse pursuing Union cavalry.[17]

Having addressed the problem of disgruntled cavalry, government officials now examined the sensitive issue of the Treasury funds. At the afternoon conference, the officers had agreed to divide the specie brought from Charlotte by the president's escort equally among the men. A few days earlier, however, William Parker had arrived in Abbeville with the main Treasury funds, and he now turned the money over to Acting Secretary of the Treasury John Reagan. Basil Duke posted a guard around the railroad car where the specie had been stored. Sensing the volatile mood of the men, Duke chose representatives from each brigade to avoid feelings of jealousy.[18]

While all this activity was transpiring in Abbeville, Varina Davis and Burton Harrison packed up their wagon train in Washington, Georgia, to continue their hectic journey. After departing from Abbeville they had received a scare unrelated to rumors of Union cavalry threats. There were reports of smallpox in the area, and the youngest Davis daughter, Winnie, had never been vaccinated. So they had halted at a house near the road, where "Mrs. Davis had the operation performed by the planter, who got a fresh scab from the arm of a little negro called up for the purpose."[19]

When the party had entered Washington, they had "found the whole town in a state of most depressing disorder." Quartermaster and commissary depots had been sacked at the news of Johnston's surrender. Varina Davis's brother, Jefferson Howell, and other paroled soldiers and available teamsters offered to join the outbound wagon train. Harrison initially had a difficult time securing additional vehicles, but he finally obtained some sturdy wagons. His success probably further annoyed some Kentucky drivers who had joined them in Abbeville, for they had already complained about being slowed by too many wagons too heavily loaded. To pay the cost of enlarging the train, Harrison withdrew some government specie that Secretary Trenholm earlier had deposited in Washington.[20]

During the stopover, Varina wrote a brief letter to her husband. She expressed her "intense grief at the treacherous surrender [by Johnston] of this Department" and wished Davis safe conduct through "this maze of enemies." Harrison had decided, she wrote, "to go on a line between Macon and Augusta and to make towards Pensacola, and take a ship or what else I can." In an accompanying message, Harrison explained to Davis that Johnston's surrender had changed his mind about going to Atlanta. The area around the city was now officially in Union hands.[21]

While in Washington, Harrison took time from his duties to converse with Robert Toombs, the first Confederate secretary of state, who lived there. After leaving the cabinet, Toombs had become a brigadier general in the army and a persistent foe of the Davis administration. Harrison also talked with Brigadier General Humphrey Marshall, a Kentucky congressman, who, he recalled, had come up and sat beside him in a narrow doorway on the town square, almost squeezing "the breath out of my body in doing so," for Marshall was very fat. They discussed the current state of affairs, and Marshall concluded, "Well, Harrison, in all my days I never knew a government to go to pieces in *this* way." He seemed to speak, Harrison amusedly noted, with the authority of one whose "life had been strewed with the wrecks of empires, comminuted indeed, but nothing like this!" Marshall eventually escaped across the Mississippi by lying flat in a dug-out log, accompanied by swarms of mosquitoes.[22]

Finally, on 2 May, Varina Davis's train, more encumbered than ever with additional wagons and baggage, rolled in a southwesterly direction out of town. As Harrison rode along, he waved to Robert Toombs, who stood dressed in a black, worn "Websterian" coat and a "broad-brimmed shabby hat." Toombs said he planned to travel in his "old buggy, drawn by two ancient gray horses" down to Crawfordsville to see Alexander Stephens. As he rode away, Harrison heard Toombs fill the morning air "with blasphemies and with denunciations of the Yankees!"[23]

To the east in Abbeville, Jefferson Davis recovered the composure he had lost at the afternoon meeting. For the most part, he had remained faithful to his pledge not to feel like a beaten man. Micajah Clark noticed Davis trying to cheer up those he met along the trail. Francis Lubbock thought the president to be "entirely calm and unaffected by the desperate state of our fortunes." In Abbeville, William Parker recalled, "I had several interviews with President Davis and found him calm and composed, and resolute to a degree."

Basil Duke gave an illuminating analysis: "Mr. Davis seemed overwhelmed with a sense of the national calamity; he at times exhibited some impatience and irascibility, but I never witnessed in a man a more entire abnegation of self, or selfish considerations. He seemed to cling obstinately to the hope of continuing the struggle in order to accomplish the great end of Southern independence—his whole soul was given to that thought, and an appearance of slackness upon the part of others seemed to arouse his indignation." Yet, Duke concluded, "I think the very ardor of his resolution prevented him from properly estimating the resources at his command."[24]

After the disappointing meeting with his officers, Davis's thoughts probably turned to the help he might still receive from Wade Hampton and Joe Wheeler. Several days before, Wheeler and his six hundred volunteers had started southward from Greensboro to join the government column. The original rendezvous point had been changed from Cokesbury to Washington. On Sunday night, 30 April, Wheeler led his men into Hampton's hometown of Yorkville, where he learned that Hampton had not yet returned from North Carolina. Wheeler decided to set up camp and wait. Hampton meanwhile had ridden to Charlotte only to find President Davis gone. He ordered his small force to rest overnight and ride for Yorkville the next day. He rode on ahead, arriving at his home early Monday morning. Wheeler came in from camp and was shocked by Hampton's "broken appearance." After discussing their situations, they agreed that Wheeler should ride on ahead and try to catch up with Davis. Hampton wrote out a brief message. He said he was still uncertain of his own status and advised Davis to rely on a small, carefully selected escort to accompany him to the Mississippi. He personally had but few men, but he would wait for word from the president before doing anything further. Having already lost much valuable time, Wheeler and his men rode hard out of town.[25]

On the evening of 2 May, John Breckinridge decided that the government column should hurry on to Washington, Georgia. Rumors of Union cavalry in the area continued to abound, and Breckinridge continued to fear for Davis's safety.

The president's lack of concern worried his friends. Davis rejected all plans based on securing his personal escape. He told William Parker that he would never desert the Southern people or take any action that might be construed as "an inglorious flight." His fixation on the Trans-Mississippi had always been based on the idea of carrying on the war there. He did not see the area as a personal haven. His companions believed he could still escape, noted Basil Duke, "but we feared that his pride would prevent his making the attempt."[26]

An offer to help Davis evade capture came from two Confederate agents, John W. Headley and Robert M. Martin, who had been operating in the North and in Canada and had just arrived in Abbeville. The course of the war had pushed them southward, and they now volunteered to conduct President Davis to Talladega, Alabama, from where they believed he could safely escape westward to Mexico. They talked to Breckinridge, who promised to urge Davis to agree to the plan. In the ensuing haste to evacuate Abbeville, however, the secretary did not have an immediate chance to pursue the matter.[27]

Breckinridge set the departure for 11 P.M., and the teamsters and cavalry worked to get ready for the road. Officials had already been busy destroying archival records packed in some of the wagons to quicken the pace of the retreat. One of Colonel Perrin's daughters watched Judah Benjamin burn papers in the fireplace of her family's home. Davis's staff burned the least valuable of the executive documents and left the rest in the care of Henry Leovy's wife.[28]

Shortly before eleven, Breckinridge went to get Davis, who was speaking to a group of local ladies, and the two men rode with the rest of the cabinet at the head of the column. As the government left town, the usual raids on supply depots followed, and John Reagan observed, "I was forced to the thought that the line between barbarism and civilization is at times very narrow." During the night ride, Breckinridge discussed with Davis the Headley-Martin and other plans for the president's personal escape. Davis's situation had become more desperate than either man knew. On this very day, the

United States government had offered a reward of $100,000 for the capture of Jefferson Davis, charged with complicity in the assassination of Abraham Lincoln. Federal cavalrymen would certainly redouble their efforts to find the rebel president. Unable to sway Davis, Breckinridge rode to the rear of the column to check on the Treasury wagons. He would not see the president again.[29]

At dawn, the column reached and crossed the Savannah River. Since there appeared to be no Federal cavalry in the area, the sleepy riders stopped to rest and have breakfast. Before eating, Davis sent a note to General Vaughn requesting a detachment to investigate reports of Union cavalry in Washington. Vaughn was uncertain whether Johnston's surrender prevented him from sending his men on such a mission and took the note to Dibrell. The men had already been promised they could vote on surrendering, so Dibrell and Vaughn "concluded it would be wrong to force . . . [them] into service again and notified Mr. Davis."[30]

Back with the Treasury train, Breckinridge was having similar problems. The escort had halted near the river, and some of the men wanted to be paid off immediately. They feared that the specie might fall into Federal hands, and facing an uncertain future, they wanted their money now. "In an old Kentucky hunting jacket," wrote one witness, Breckinridge "appeared before the men, now almost a mob. He told them they were Southern gentlemen and Confederate soldiers. They must not become highway robbers. They knew how to die bravely; they must live honorably." His words cooled tempers, but, sensing the still-hostile mood, Breckinridge ordered the wagons parked, and the men received twenty-six dollars each in silver specie.[31]

Unaware of the problems across the Savannah, Davis and the rest of the cabinet finished breakfast at a farmhouse. During this stopover, Judah Benjamin left the column. Some of the cavalry felt relieved to see him escaping. They had grown fond of the ebullient secretary, "who could not comfortably ride horseback," and they had feared that he might be captured when the Federals closed in. Benjamin shared their fear, and he also knew that his lack of horsemanship would eventually hinder the retreat west. As he climbed aboard a carriage to depart, he responded in typical Benjamin fashion to inquiries about where he would go: "To the farthest place from the United States, if it takes me to the middle of China." Disguised as a sightseeing Frenchman and taking along Henry Leovy to act as his interpreter, Benjamin set out with orders from Davis "to perform certain public duties in Nassau and Havana, and then to rejoin [the president] in Texas."[32]

While the rest of the government was mounting up to ride on to Washington, one advance scout entered the Georgia town. He found no Union cavalry and, under intense questioning, admitted to local citizens that President Davis would soon be arriving. Bank cashier J. J. Robertson's wife volunteered their home in the bank building for use as Davis's headquarters. The scout and a family representative rode out to present a written invitation to the president.[33]

A "beautiful little village," the town of Washington stood at the center of an area populated by several wealthy planters. One contemporary visitor wrote, "It is the quaintest and smuggest . . . town you can think of. All is in prime, promising condition around it." A local resident estimated the town's population in 1865 to be around twenty-two hundred. Most activity centered around an open square dominated by the Wilkes County Courthouse. The bank building containing the Robertson home stood on the north side of the square.[34]

Until April 1865, the town had escaped the physical effects of the war. Located some fifty miles northwest of Augusta, Washington sat well north of the wide swath William T. Sherman's army had cut through eastern Georgia during the march to the sea. Thus far, Mrs. Robertson remembered, "the foot of a Federal soldier had never trodden our streets." However, Lee's surrender had sent streams of Confederate soldiers through Washington on their way to homes farther west. As a result, the town had become infested with lice that crawled thickly on grass, sidewalks, and houses. On a more positive note, William Parker and his treasure wagons and the Varina

Davis party had stirred the emotions of Washingtonians. Now the president, resting only a short distance away, would soon be riding into town.[35]

Around noon, Jefferson Davis and his party rode into the town square, throwing the residents into "the wildest excitement." Many citizens removed their hats as a show of respect for their beleaguered chief executive. Attired in a "full suit of Confederate grey," the tired president went immediately to the room awaiting him in the Robertson home and collapsed into a deep sleep. A mixture of curiosity and anxiety brought townspeople to the bank to see their famous visitor, but they were asked to leave while Davis rested.[36]

His fellow travelers probably ate while Davis slept, since, according to one account, they all appeared to be "half-starved." Neighbors sent extra food to the Robertsons, and Mrs. Robertson produced her own supplies of ham, turkey, lobster, salmon, chicken, eggs, fresh vegetables, tea, and something rare in the Confederacy, real coffee. It had been saved from a purchase her husband had made in Macon in 1863. The Robertsons had already been sharing their food with paroled soldiers passing through. In explaining the family's bounty, Mrs. Robertson wrote, "It must be remembered we were in a little out-of-the-way village, in a farming country, where the hardships and deprivations of the war, for food, had never penetrated."[37] The Confederate experiment in nationhood had clearly not affected the localism of Southern towns like Washington and Abbeville and other smaller communities the government had passed through since leaving Richmond.

The column soon spread out and settled in around the little Georgia town. The wagon train set up camp about a mile away along a stream called Silver Springs. Local quartermasters issued much-needed supplies to the cavalry. Francis Lubbock busied himself gathering new clothing for a wounded friend from Texas he had met in town. John Reagan talked with his host Robert Toombs, who had returned from Crawfordsville. Toombs recalled his past differences with Davis but vowed to do whatever he could, financially or otherwise, to help the president escape. Informed of Toombs's remarks, Davis said he was not surprised at his old adversary's generosity. "This was the interchange of feeling of two noble patriots in the hour of misfortune," wrote Reagan. Certainly, the exchange offered a marked contrast to the Johnston-Davis feud.[38]

John C. Breckinridge spent 3 May supervising the disposition of funds to the cavalry back at the Savannah River. He sent two reports to Davis during the day. The first, written at 9:45 A.M., said that no enemy forces had been sighted and the condition of the troops was still not satisfactory. He again urged Davis to consider the escape plans discussed the previous night. Receiving no response, Breckinridge sent his second message at 8 P.M. His inability to continue as far as Washington was "due to the condition of things here, together with great fatigue." He had paid the troops in silver and would turn over the gold to Reagan in the morning. Many of the men had thrown away their arms, he reported, having decided to stay and surrender. Only a few hundred might be counted on to continue.[39]

On Thursday morning, 4 May, Preston Johnston asked Micajah Clark to report to Davis's quarters. When Clark arrived, the president informed him of his appointment as acting treasurer of the Confederate States. This proved to be Davis's last official act as president, though he did not realize it at the time. The new treasurer rode out to Basil Duke's camp about a mile from town to take charge of the disbursement of funds. From his office beneath a large elm tree, Clark distributed specie to the cavalry and sent money to Augusta to assist paroled soldiers returning home. He also transmitted funds for future use in the Trans-Mississippi to Braxton Bragg and Breckinridge. John Reagan, who had suggested Clark for the treasurer's job, helped supervise the burning of thousands of dollars in worthless paper money. Richmond bank funds were deposited in the local Washington bank. Clark's last official act involved turning over $86,000 in specie to navy officer James Semple, who loaded the money into a false carriage bottom for transportation to either Charleston or Savannah. From there, the funds were to be shipped to Confederate agents in foreign ports and credited to the account of the Confederate government.[40]

After his appointment of Clark, Jefferson Davis pondered other matters weighing heavily on his mind, particularly his wife's safety. Just before leaving Abbeville, Davis had sent a message by courier to Burton Harrison. He had approved his secretary's decision to change the route of Varina Davis's flight but admitted that lacking reliable information, he could only speculate. He had become convinced that all the Federal activity in the area was aimed toward his capture, so he wanted to stay away from his family. "I have the bitterest disappointment in regard to the feeling of our troops," he wrote, "and would not have any one I love dependent upon their resistance against an equal force." The news that Federal General Emory Upton had traveled to Augusta after Johnston's surrender to issue paroles further depleted the cavalry's morale. As the tidings spread, Davis worried over the effect, for as one of General Ferguson's staff remembered, "The men did not know what to do. Their officers, no doubt, talked to them. . . . and demoralized them." Breckinridge finally advised the commanders to discharge their men honorably after making sure they had all received their pay.[41]

The president now called a conference with his staff, Mallory, Reagan and several of the officers. He had finally decided to dissolve the government and continue his retreat with a small escort. He planned to move into south Georgia, turn west, and link up with Confederate troops still operating in Alabama. He could then move on to the Mississippi if necessary. He did not know that even as he spoke, in Citronelle, Alabama, Richard Taylor was surrendering his Department of Alabama, Mississippi, and East Louisiana.[42]

The president's plans indicated only a temporary dissolution of the government with the intent to reassemble it when circumstances permitted. The morning meeting, however, had an air of finality about it. After he left the conference, Quartermaster General A. R. Lawton told his assistant, "It is all over; the Confederate Government is dissolved." The irony of dissolving the government in a town called Washington did not escape those who met with Davis. One of them recalled, "Providence has the most inscrutable ways of exhibiting His purposes."[43]

A few miles away to the northeast, Ordnance Bureau chief Josiah Gorgas also mused over his future. He had traveled to Winnsboro, South Carolina, after the government had left Charlotte, perhaps to check on supplies there but probably because he had not made up his mind whether to follow the rest of the government or go home. On 4 May, not knowing that the government had broken up in Washington, Gorgas entered his thoughts in his diary. What he wrote could have been Jefferson Davis's words: "The calamity which has fallen upon us in the total destruction of our government is of a character so overwhelming that I am as yet unable to comprehend it. I am as one walking in a dream, and expecting to awake. I cannot see its consequences nor shape my course, but am just moving along until I can see my way at some future day."[44]

In Washington, the president talked with Given Campbell, who had already collected sixty volunteers for further escort service. Davis now informed him that he wanted only ten men. He gave Campbell specie to purchase additional guns and fresh horses for the special detachment and a pair of revolvers for his personal use. Campbell chose the horsemen from his own company.[45]

Before leaving, Davis disposed of some of his personal baggage, giving several items to the Robertson family. Mrs. Robertson recorded presents of books, tea, coffee, and brandy, but she wrote, "the gift most valued and treasured is the inkstand used by him as President, and his dressing case, containing many mementos of him. There was also a framed certificate of his honorary membership with the Mobile Cadets." Micajah Clark then supervised the disposition of the executive papers, most of which were sewn between layers of blankets. Burton Harrison's trunk, still packed with executive documents, was left with Mrs. Robertson.[46]

By midmorning of this clear, warm Thursday, 4 May, the presidential column, reduced to fewer than twenty men, gathered to continue what had clearly become an undisguised flight to avoid Davis's capture. The remnants of the government prepared to descend into an area under tight Federal control. Just the day before, Governor Brown had tried to call the state legislature together to "prevent anarchy," but Union military authorities had blocked his effort. Davis's staff, including Colonel Charles Thorburn, mounted to ride with the president, Campbell's escort, and the wagon train, consisting of one wagon and two ambulances. Reagan, Breckinridge, and Clark were to follow later after attending to last-minute administrative details.[47]

Stephen Mallory and Confederate senator and former brigadier general Louis T. Wigfall had already departed, bound for Mallory's home in La Grange, Georgia. Convinced that he could no longer be of service to Davis, Mallory had written out his resignation in Abbeville and had turned it over to the president in Washington. Mallory had offered to stay on to help Davis get to Florida, but he decided to leave when it became apparent that the president had no definite plans about his destination. The departure of this trusted adviser capped a trying day for Davis. Preparing to mount up, he turned with tears in his eyes to many members of the old cavalry escort who had gathered to wish him well and to offer to stay with him. He "begged them to seek their own safety and leave him to meet his fate."[48]

John Headley later wrote a powerful account of the farewell scene:

> It was a moment when many a veteran sighed and gazed prayerfully upon the little cavalcade until it passed from view. But the tender-hearted sons and daughters of Georgia, the young and the old stood about in groups and spoke in whispers and some wiped away tears. There was for the moment the stillness of a benediction and there was a look of despair on every face as if suddenly had been severed the cord that bound them to the distant past of happiness and hope. But never a murmur of lost respect or of blame for the vanquished President fell from the lips of citizen or soldier. Even the mothers of buried boys and the widows whose husbands were among the slain . . . did not chide or weep alone for their own. This disconsolate hour was bitter in sorrow, in desolation and in terror, and the spirits of all were transfixed

upon the cause of the common woe. There was no contemplation now save over the past, present, and future wreck and ruin of homes and people.[49]

Like others along the way, the crowd in Washington was coming to terms with military defeat. They could have turned their backs on the past and looked to the future. But they did not. They mourned the cause, thought about the cause, and ultimately resurrected the cause in their mind's eye. The emotions Headley witnessed would reconnect the severed cord and make a hero of the vanquished president.

As they rode out of Washington, Davis asked Given Campbell what he thought about their chances. Campbell replied that with the baggage train slowing progress, he could make no guarantees. Writing after the war, Basil Duke commented, "I have never believed . . . that Mr. Davis really meant or desired to escape after he became convinced that all was lost." The president "knew well that his only chance of escape was in rapid and continuous movement." Duke believed that Davis was deliberately procrastinating, that "he had resolved not to escape." Davis had rejected a Reagan-Breckinridge plan to go by horseback with a single escort to Florida and then take a boat to Texas, where the two cabinet members, traveling overland, would meet him. He had also shown no interest in the Headley-Martin proposal. The president had insisted that he would not desert Confederate soldiers still in the field east of the Mississippi. His plan of going into Alabama to join up with Confederate forces there was consistent with this position. At a rest stop during the afternoon of 4 May, Davis felt a renewed optimism about the future. He had convinced himself that even if Alabama fell, he could still join Kirby Smith and "carry on the war forever."[50]

Basil Duke had misjudged Davis's intentions. What he saw as procrastination had probably been a pause to rethink options. The president's decision to abandon the large unreliable escort for a smaller, faster detachment clearly indicated he now intended to make a run for safety. He had broken up the government not because he considered the cause lost but because it presently served no useful purpose. When Jefferson Davis left Washington he still walked in his dream of continuing the struggle. He hoped to assemble around Forrest and Taylor large numbers of Lee's and Johnston's men who had declined paroles and then "strike blows" from the Trans-Mississippi "which would secure to the South what had been refused, a peace with rights recognized by Treaty." The harsh realities of his plight had not lessened his stubborn resolve.[51]

Back in Washington, John Reagan and Micajah Clark had finished their business around midnight and were preparing to follow Davis with what was left of the Treasury. Having dissolved the last vestige of the War Department, John C. Breckinridge proposed to Reagan that they take the remaining cavalry west to Texas as originally planned. Reagan rejected the idea, arguing that the demoralized cavalry would not follow anyone. Reagan and Clark then rode off, accompanied, at Breckinridge's insistence, by a cavalry escort. A few hours down the trail, they sent the soldiers back to Washington and went on until daybreak, locating the Davis party at its campsite in a "miserable out of the way place" south of Powelton, Warren County.[52]

Following a few hours sleep at the Robertsons', Breckinridge consulted with Basil Duke and W. C. P. Breckinridge about his plan to draw Federal attention away from Davis's march. He suggested diversionary moves eastward, with each commander following a different route and merging later on. However, in implementing the plan, Colonel Breckinridge soon ran into a strong Union cavalry force, and his cousin John advised him to surrender. The war secretary had decided by this time to leave the area, and he mounted up and headed south to look for the president's party. Shortly afterward, Basil Duke surrendered his Kentuckians.[53]

Sometime late in the evening of 4 May, Joseph Wheeler and his cavalry cautiously approached Washington only to learn they had missed the president by about twelve hours. Finding the area crawling with Federal cavalry, Wheeler broke up his command into small groups and attempted to ride to safety. Within a few days, he was forced to surrender.[54]

The clear, hot weather continued to hold as the Davis party, Reagan, Clark, and the Treasury wagon moved out on the morning of 5 May. The fugitives traveled some thirty-five miles, stopping to camp a few miles north of Sandersville. John Taylor Wood wrote in his diary that the entourage had decided to assume the collective identity of members of congress from Texas on their way home. Since Given Campbell's scouts had reported Union cavalry activity in the Macon area, settlements containing suspected Federal informants were bypassed.[55]

On the morning of 6 May, President Davis left the wagon train and rode ahead with his staff, Reagan, and a few pack mules in an attempt to increase the pace of the retreat. The scouting reports disturbed him, and he hoped to catch up with and see to the safety of his family. Micajah Clark, fearing that his cumbersome Treasury wagons would be easy prey for enemy horsemen, gave Davis's three staff members and Colonel Thorburn expense money and fifteen hundred dollars in gold specie each for safekeeping. Given Campbell accepted three hundred dollars in gold for himself and his men, and Reagan packed thirty-five hundred dollars in gold in his saddlebags. According to Clark's records, the president, probably at his own insistence, received no funds. With over twenty-five thousand dollars left, Clark now separated his train from the government column and headed for the Florida panhandle where he hoped to rejoin it.[56]

With Campbell's men scouting ahead, Davis and his men put in a hard day's ride. Around noon, the scouts reported to Campbell that Varina Davis's wagons were only a few miles ahead near the Oconee River just above Dublin. They also relayed rumors that a band of stragglers and deserters were stalking Mrs. Davis's party. When the president heard the news, he determined to find his wife.[57]

After leaving Washington, Varina Davis and Burton Harrison had been threatened more than once by outlaws. Harrison had become ill with dysentery and fever during part of the trip, leaving him at times "utterly demoralized," according to one of the wagon drivers. Others in the party blamed Harrison for not insisting that the wagon loads be lightened to increase the speed. Harrison's health, the slow pace of the wagons, and the welfare of her husband deeply worried Varina Davis. After leaving Washington, she had received his note stating that all was well and regretting that he had not been able to see her. She had written a reply urging him not to try to join her and advising him to take two or three men and make his escape.[58]

On the evening of 6 May, Burton Harrison led the train into camp in a wooded area off the road near the village of Dublin. Around midnight, while the rest of the party slept, Harrison and two teamsters sat on picket duty north of the camp. "After awhile," Harrison wrote later,

> we heard the soft tread of horses in the darkness approaching over the light, sandy soil of the road. The teamsters immediately ran off to arouse the camp, having no doubt the attack was about to begin. I placed myself on the road to detain the enemy as long as possible and, when the advancing horsemen came near enough to hear me, called "Halt." They drew rein instantly. I demanded "Who comes there?" The foremost of the horsemen replied "Friends," in a voice I was astonished to recognize as that of President Davis, not suspecting he was anywhere near us.[59]

After a separation of more than a month, the Davis family had at last been reunited.

The president and his staff remained in camp for the night. Meanwhile, Campbell and his men scouted the area around the Oconee River ferry. As Davis enjoyed the reunion with his family, he did not know that on this day General Taylor had published his General Orders Number 54 announcing the surrender of his forces.[60]

The next morning, Sunday, 7 May, the combined trains moved on to the southwest. Campbell wanted to detach four of his men to accompany Varina Davis's slow wagons, while the president moved on with his reduced escort. Davis rejected the idea. He did not want to leave his family so quickly, and he rode most of the day with Varina in an ambulance. The fugitives continued slowly through the sparsely settled piney woods and camped in the evening between Dublin and Abbeville, Georgia. They had covered barely thirty miles, and Campbell's scouts reported the disturbing news that Federal cavalry in the area had learned of the Davis train. Two scouts were sent out to investigate further, and Davis decided it was again time to leave Varina.[61]

At dawn on 8 May, the president and his escort mounted up, leaving Varina Davis and Harrison "to pursue," wrote Harrison, "our journey as best we might with our wagons and encumbrances." Heavy rains and high water created problems for Davis and his men at the Ocmulgee, and the delay allowed Varina Davis's train to catch up with the president's at Abbeville that evening. Davis and his men occupied a half-finished dwelling in the village, which contained only three or four houses. Campbell and the escort camped in the river bottom half a mile away. Harrison and Varina crossed the river and set up camp on its bank.[62]

Around midnight Davis sent a courier who awoke Harrison with the news that scouting reports about Federal cavalry in the area had been confirmed. A few hundred bluecoats had been sighted in Hawkinsville twenty-five miles to the northwest. Harrison immediately put wagons and ambulances on the road "in the midst of a terrible storm of thunder, lightning, and rain." As the train passed through Abbeville, Harrison dismounted at the president's quarters and was surprised to find him wrapped in a blanket on the floor. Davis told Harrison to keep the wagons moving. As soon as their horses were rested, he and his men would follow. Throughout the rainy night, the train plodded southward, fighting mud and fallen trees and depending on lightning to show the way. Before dawn, the hard-riding presidential party caught up with the wagons.[63]

After eating breakfast, the weary travelers moved on, not stopping until five o'clock in the afternoon about a mile north of the hamlet of Irwinville. Davis wanted to keep moving, but the animals needed a rest after the hard trip through the storm. In conversations with Harrison, Lubbock, Thorburn, and John Wood, Davis gave assurances that he and his escort would ride on after dark to make up time lost during the previous night. He later wrote, "I did not tell anybody what road I would follow or what would be my objective point, . . . a caution which the circumstances sternly imposed as much for their safety as my own." He delayed his departure when Preston Johnston reported rumors that "marauders" in the area planned to attack the camp.[64]

The scouts rode on ahead to forage and to find a crossing

on the Alapaha River west of Irwinville. Back at camp, Preston Johnston foraged in the immediate area, while Lubbock stalked around, complaining about the danger of being with Varina Davis's train. Finally, the fugitives settled in for the night, pitching their tents on either side of a road running north and south. Harrison lay on the ground "and fell into a profound sleep," confident that when he awoke, the president would be safely on the trail miles away. In another part of camp, Jefferson Davis lay down in his traveling clothes. If no trouble occurred, he would leave before dawn. He did not know that earlier in the day, in Gainesville, Alabama, Nathan Bedford Forrest had written a farewell message to his cavalry corps. There were now no Confederate forces to unite with in Alabama. Determined to stay awake and keep watch, the Confederate president soon fell fast asleep.[65]

The sleeping Davis and his fellow refugees were safe from outlaw raids the night of 9 May, but not from the long arm of the United States government. Lincoln's assassination, Davis's suspected involvement in the plot, and the Confederate government's continuing retreat after Johnston's surrender had spurred efforts to capture the fleeing rebels. The Union navy received orders to patrol the west and east coasts of Florida. Detachments from George Stoneman's cavalry had trailed the Davis column since its departure from Charlotte. One Union trooper described the problems of the pursuit: "The country swarmed with Confederate cavalry moving across farms and by parallel roads and paths, in companies, battalions, and regiments, and all in the same general direction. Every road was worn by recent hoofprints, and it was impossible to ascertain by which of those many paths the [Confederate] President's party had passed."[66]

In Georgia, James Wilson's cavalry joined the hunt. From his headquarters in Macon, Wilson ordered his men to scout a wide area reaching from north Georgia to the Florida panhandle. Nevertheless, he had not learned of Davis's presence in Washington until 6 May, two days after the rebels had left town. Correctly surmising that Davis would travel southward through the area east of Macon, Wilson sent detachments out toward Dublin and along the Ocmulgee.[67]

One hundred and fifty men of the First Wisconsin Cavalry, Lieutenant Colonel Henry Harnden commanding, had arrived in Dublin on the evening of 7 May. Most of the local residents had refused to provide any information about the rebel fugitives, but an elderly black man finally told Harnden where the Davis party had crossed the Oconee. After forcing another local man to guide them through a swampy area, the Federals rode rapidly southward. On 9 May the column had crossed the Ocmulgee and rested in Abbeville. There, Harnden learned that just a few hours earlier a wagon train and riders had passed through on the way to Irwinville. Waiting until evening to move out, Harnden's men had met the advance of Lieutenant Colonel B. D. Pritchard's Fourth Michigan Cavalry riding up from Hawkinsville. Still not sure that they were actually on the trail of the Davises, the two colonels decided to scout in different directions. Pritchard took his four hundred troopers down the Ocmulgee, and Harnden kept on the main road to Irwinville. After a short ride, Pritchard received intelligence reports that convinced him that the travelers at Irwinville were the Davis party. He and his men rode in the direction Harnden had taken.[68]

Darkness concealed the approach of the two Federal columns, each unaware of the other's location. Pritchard had left the bulk of his force to picket the ferries along the Ocmulgee and with 150 of his best mounted men reached Irwinville about one o'clock on the morning of 10 May. Pretending to be Confederates, the Federals learned the location of the Davis camp from local residents. They approached and deployed for an early morning attack. About a mile away to the north, Henry Harnden and the First Wisconsin camped and waited for sunrise, when they too would move in on the unsuspecting Confederates.[69]

The final drama in the Confederate government's long, disintegrating retreat from Richmond began in the dim light and drizzle of dawn, Wednesday, 10 May 1865. The crack of musketry suddenly erupted to the north along a small creek that bordered the camp. Davis's coachman, James Jones, sounded the alarm. The absence of Campbell's men, still scouting to the south, had left the camp unguarded, despite the threat of outlaws and pursuing Federals. Colonel Pritchard came riding into the midst of the camp. Harrison raised his pistol to fire, but changed his mind when he saw large numbers of Union cavalry burst out of the woods. Federal soldiers quickly surrounded the Davis party, and Pritchard rode forward to investigate the rifle fire.[70]

During the confusion, John Taylor Wood told Varina Davis that since the president had not yet been recognized, he should try to escape into the woods about a hundred yards away to the east. Giving in to his wife's pleadings, Davis agreed to try, and throwing on a rain cloak, he walked away, moving eastward at a right angle to the road. From behind, Varina ran up and threw a shawl over his bare head. She then instructed her mulatto maid, Helen, to pick up a bucket and walk with the president to make it look as if the two were going to the creek for water. Varina tried to create a diversion by engaging nearby bluecoats in conversation. However, one horseman saw the two figures walking away and ordered them to halt. They changed directions but kept moving towards the woods. Another of the Federals rode toward the two and threatened to shoot. Davis stopped and faced his pursuer, while Varina came running up to embrace him, pleading for the soldier not to fire. Davis later claimed that he had hoped to knock the cavalryman from his horse, mount up, and thus make his escape.[71] Varina Davis made sure he took no such risk. By now he had been recognized, and the chance to get away would not come again. The last flicker of life left the Confederate government. Its president had fallen into the hands of the enemy, while trying to escape under the cloaked illusion of helping a black servant fetch water.

The shooting finally stopped when the Federals discovered that they were firing at each other. The mistaken identity caused by the dim light of morning cost the Union cavalry two dead and several wounded. Once order had been restored, the survivors rounded up the prisoners and looted the camp. Davis berated Pritchard for attacking and pillaging a party containing women and children, but according to the accounts of the captives, the colonel made little effort to stop the sacking. Most of the party had their money taken, but

Francis Lubbock resisted so strongly that he was allowed to keep some of his funds. Preston Johnston had his father's saddle, trappings, and pistols stolen. Harrison took advantage of quarreling between Federal officers over booty and emptied personal and official papers into a nearby campfire. The soldiers also took all of the captives' horses. Lubbock later summed up their behavior as "anything but soldierly." Pritchard promised that all the stolen possessions would be returned, recalled Lubbock, but he did not keep his word.[72]

Some of the fugitives managed to escape. Wood bribed a cavalryman with specie and made it safely to the woods and freedom. One young South Carolina officer Barnwell walked away with Wood. Charles Thorburn had left camp before the attack and was now riding for Florida and the boat he had hidden away. He had been fired upon as he rode through the Federal lines but had safely escaped. By the time Campbell and his scouts returned, the camp had been taken. Federals captured some of the Kentuckians, but Campbell and most of his men escaped.[73]

The Union officers restored order and managed to allay the fears of the captives somewhat, allowing them to eat breakfast before beginning the trip back to Wilson's headquarters at Macon. To facilitate the journey, Confederates rode their personal mounts. The women and children were assigned to two ambulances. Colonal Pritchard allowed President Davis to accompany his family in one of the vehicles.[74]

Since leaving Charlotte, Jefferson Davis had seen the remnants of his government and his once-large cavalry escort gradually evaporate. He had been unable to garner any support for his desire to continue the fight. His only hope had been to join Kirby Smith in the Trans-Mississippi district, but the surrender of Confederate forces in Alabama and Mississippi had blocked his anticipated escape route. Had Davis not been captured at Irwinville, his decision to go west would likely have resulted in his apprehension before he could have reached the Mississippi.

The comic-opera nature of the Confederate president's capture contrasted sharply with the dignity of Lee's and Johnston's surrenders. Yet, the strength of Davis's popularity as the living symbol of the dead Confederacy had been evident among the people who had greeted him in South Carolina and Georgia. Beyond the tragedy they seemed to see something heroic in his stubborn refusal to admit defeat. Even the circumstances of his arrest would soon cause fellow Southerners to support and defend him. From Charlotte to Irwinville, then, positive factors affecting his image had persisted and had even been strengthened.

The conventional view of historians that Davis was ostracized throughout the South at the end of the war is not totally erroneous. A hue and cry came from among his old political and personal enemies and from others who were simply frustrated and had to blame someone. The criticism would dissipate, however, and for the most part dissipate quickly. From the dawn of 1865 until his capture, Davis had tried desperately to save the cause at all costs, and he had kept on trying long after most of his detractors had given up. During the government's retreat, many Southerners had shown that they appreciated their president's zeal. In the coming months and years, Davis would rise in stature, while criticism of his presidency would be reduced to a whisper. But for now, a prison cell awaited him, and there he would reach the pinnacle of his long journey to martyrdom.

1. Basil W. Duke, "Last Days of the Confederacy," in *Battles and Leaders of the Civil War*, ed. Robert U. Johnson and Clarence B. Buel, *Battles and Leaders of the Civil War*, 4 vols. (New York, 1956), 4:764; Rowland, *Jefferson Davis*, 8:168; Lubbock, *Memoirs*, 566; Tilghman Diary, 26 April 1865; James P. Sloan, "Jefferson Davis Slept Here—and Here—and Here: An Account of South Carolina's Hospitality to the President of the Confederacy," Columbia, S.C., *State Magazine*, 31 Jan. 1954, 4–5, copy in Monroe Fulkerson Cockrell Papers, Manuscript Department, William R. Perkins Library, Duke University. Except where otherwise cited, all information hereinafter relating to the route of Davis through South Carolina is taken from Sloan's article, a synthesis of the work of several historians on the retreat.

2. Trenholm Diary; Rowland, *Jefferson Davis*, 6:564–65.

3. Reagan, *Memoirs*, 208–9; Lubbock, *Memoirs*, 564.

4. Tilghman Diary, 27, 28 April 1865; Johnston, *Narrative*, 415–16; Wood Diary, 26 [27] April 1865.

5. Campbell Journal, 28 April 1865; Duke, "Last Days," 764; "Last Letters and Telegrams of the Confederacy—Correspondence of General John C. Breckinridge," *Southern Historical Society Papers* 12 (March 1884): 105.

6. Haw, "Last of the Ordnance Department," 452; Duke, "Last Days," 764.

7. Varina Davis, *Jefferson Davis*, 2:611–12: John K. Aull, "Journey of Mrs. Jefferson Davis across South Carolina Retraced," Columbia, S.C., *The State*, 13 Sept. 1931.

8. Rowland, *Jefferson Davis*, 6:566–67.

9. Tilghman Diary, 29 April 1865; Reagan, *Memoirs*, 210; Campbell Journal, 29 April 1865; Swallow, "Retreat of Confederate Government," 604; Rowland, *Jefferson Davis*, 8:251; Wood Diary, 28 [29] April 1865.

10. Varina Davis, *Jefferson Davis*, 2:615; *OR*, ser. 1, vol. 47, pt. 3, p. 1269, vol. 49, pt. 2, pp. 531, 558.

11. Mallory, "Last Days," 246; Tilghman Diary, 1 May 1865; Emma Davis Diary quoted in Sloan, "Davis Slept Here," 4; Wood Diary, 1 May 1865; Campbell Journal, 2 [1] May 1865.

12. Burton N. Harrison, "Capture of Davis," 137–38; Cauthen, *South Carolina Goes to War*, 61–62; Clark, "Retreat of Cabinet from Richmond," 294; Wood Diary, 2 May 1865; Clark, "Last Days of the Confederate Treasury," 544; Campbell Journal, 3 [2] May 1865; Walmsley, "Last Meeting of the Confederate Cabinet," 344; Tilghman Diary, 2 May 1865.

13. Mallory, "Last Days," 246; Rowland, *Jefferson Davis*, 8:158–59.

14. Duke, "Last Days," 764; Parker, *Recollections*, 366; Rowland, *Jefferson Davis*, 8:159; S. W. Ferguson, "Escort to President Davis," *Confederate Veteran* 16 (June 1908): 263; John H. Reagan to William P. Calhoun, 7 July 1903, in William Patrick Calhoun Papers, Manuscript Department, William R. Perkins Library, Duke University.

15. Duke, "Last Days," 764; Ferguson, "Escort to Davis," 263. Davis reportedly chastised Bragg for earlier dismissing some South Carolina soldiers who had traveled for a time with the column. Rowland, *Jefferson Davis*, 8:172.

16. Duke, "Last Days," 764–65; Rowland, *Jefferson Davis*, 8:149, 154, 158, 188. See also Walmsley, "Last Meeting of the Confederate Cabinet," 344.

17. Duke, "Last Days," 765; Rowland, *Jefferson Davis*, 8:148, 158, 189.

18. Parker, *Recollections*, 363–66; John W. Harris, "Gold of the Confederate States Treasury," 161; Rowland, *Jefferson Davis*, 8:148; Duke, "Last Days," 765.

19. Burton N. Harrison, "Capture of Davis," 138; Strode, *Davis: Private Letters*, 61.

20. Varina Davis, *Jefferson Davis*, 2:616–17; Burton N. Harrison, "Capture of Davis," 138–39; Hathaway Recollections, vol. 7.

21. Strode, *Davis: Private Letters*, 161; Rowland, *Jefferson Davis*, 6:587–88.

22. Burton N. Harrison, "Capture of Davis," 139; Warner, *Generals in Gray*, 212–13, 306–7.

23. Burton N. Harrison, "Capture of Davis," 139.

24. Clark, "Retreat of Cabinet from Richmond," 294; Lubbock, *Memoirs*, 567; Parker, "Gold and Silver," 209; Rowland, *Jefferson Davis*, 8:171.

25. Wheeler, "Effort to Rescue Davis," 86–87; Wade Hampton, "An Effort to Rescue Jefferson Davis," *Southern Historical Society Papers* 27 (1899): 134–35; Strode, *Davis: Private Letters*, 160.

26. Duke, "Last Days," 765; Rowland, *Jefferson Davis*, 8:162; Lubbock, *Memoirs*, 567; Mallory, "Last Days," 246; Parker, *Recollections*, 367; Swallow, "Retreat of the Confederate Government," 604; Duke, *Reminiscences*, 385.

27. John W. Headley, *Confederate Operations in Canada and New York* (New York, 1906), 432–35.

28. Rowland, *Jefferson Davis*, 8:162; Walmsley, "Last Meeting of the Confederate Cabinet," 345; Wood Diary, 2 May 1865; M. H. Clark to William P. Calhoun, 19 June 1903, Calhoun Papers; Irvine, "Fate of Archives," 823. No doubt some valuable documents perished during the hurried sorting. See Rowland, *Jefferson Davis*, 7:548.

29. William C. Davis, *Breckinridge*, 520; Rowland, *Jefferson Davis*, 8:150; Reagan, *Memoirs*, 211; Clark, "Last Days of the Confederate Treasury," 546; Juvenis, "Last of the Confederacy"; Campbell Journal, 3 May 1865; Wood Diary, 3 May 1865; *OR*, ser. 1, vol. 49, pt. 2, pp. 566–67.

30. Jefferson Davis, *Rise and Fall*, 2:694; Rowland, *Jefferson Davis*, 8:148–49. According to one source, Dibrell and Vaughn were the main dissenters among the five commanders to Davis's pleas to keep the cavalry together. Rowland, *Jefferson Davis*, 8:191.

31. Clark, "Last Days of the Confederate Treasury," 546; "Confederate Gold," *Southern Historical Society Papers* 39 (April 1914): 24; Duke, "Last Days," 766.

32. Reagan, *Memoirs*, 211; Duke, *Reminiscences*, 385; Reagan, *Memoirs*, 211; Jefferson Davis, *Rise and Fall*, 2:694; Judah P. Benjamin to Varina Davis, 1 Sept. 1865, Jefferson Hayes-Davis Papers, Transylvania University Library; Davis to Reagan, 21 Aug. 1877, Reagan-Davis Papers.

33. Mrs. M. E. Robertson, "President Davis's Last Official Meeting," *Southern History Association Publications* 5 (July 1901): 293–94.

34. Tilghman Diary, 3 May 1865; [Stuart], "Davis' Flight"; Eliza Frances Andrews, *The War-time Journal of a Georgia Girl, 1864–1865*, ed., Spencer Bidwell King, Jr. (Macon, 1960), 175.

35. Robertson, "Davis's Last Meeting," 292–93; Andrews, *War-time Journal*, 183–84.

36. Andrews, *War-time Journal*, 201–2; Campbell Journal, 3 May 1865; Robertson, "Davis's Last Meeting," 294–95.

37. Andrews, *War-time Journal*, 201; Robertson, "Davis' Last Meeting," 295–96.

38. Tilghman Diary, 3 May 1865; Swallow, "Retreat of the Confederate Government," 605; Lubbock, *Memoirs*, 568; Reagan, *Memoirs*, 215.

39. *OR*, ser. 1, vol. 49, pt. 2, pp. 1277–78.

40. Clark, "Last Days of the Confederate Treasury," 544–53; Otis Ashmore, "The Story of the Confederate Treasury," *Georgia Historical Quarterly* 2 (Sept. 1918): 125; Otis Ashmore, "The Story of the Virginia Banks Funds," *Georgia Historical Quarterly* 2 (Dec. 1918): 173–74; I. W. Avery, *The History of the State of Georgia from 1850 to 1881* (New York, 1881, rptd., 1972), 326–28; Jefferson Davis, *Rise and Fall*, 2:695; Lubbock, *Memoirs*, 568; Reagan, *Memoirs*, 216; Hanna, *Flight into Oblivion*, 91.

41. *OR*, ser. 1, vol. 49, pt. 2, p. 1277; Jefferson Davis, *Rise and Fall*, 2:695; Rowland, *Jefferson Davis*, 8:264–65; Tilghman Diary, 3 May 1865. Despite a later claim that he followed Varina Davis's party only because of rumors that robbers were stalking her wagons, Davis knew that Harrison was right. The only safe route was southward through Georgia.

42. Robertson, "Davis's Last Meeting," 296; Andrews, *War-time Journal*, 205; Jefferson Davis, *Rise and Fall*, 2:697; *OR*, ser. 1, vol. 49, pt. 2, p. 609.
43. W. F. Alexander, interview in Augusta *Chronicle*, ca. 1903, handwritten summary, Calhoun Papers; [Stuart], "Davis' Flight."
44. Vandiver, *Diary of Josiah Gorgas*, 182–86. On 14 May Gorgas rode into Washington and received his parole.
45. Campbell Journal, 4 May 1865; Jefferson Davis, *Rise and Fall*, 2:695; W. R. Bringhurst, "Survivor of President Davis's Escort," *Confederate Veteran* 34 (Oct. 1926): 368.
46. Robertson, "Davis's Last Meeting," 298; Hanna, *Flight into Oblivion*, 88; Rowland, *Jefferson Davis*, 7:549. The trunk had become a repository for messages received since leaving Richmond. After the war, Harrison reclaimed the trunk, but many of the stored papers had by then disappeared. Rowland, *Jefferson Davis*, 7:550–51.
47. Campbell Journal, 4 May 1865; Tilghman Diary, 4 May 1865; *OR*, ser. 4, vol. 3, pp. 1182–83; Swallow, "Retreat of the Confederate Government," 606; Reagan, *Memoirs*, 212.
48. Mallory, "Last Days," 247–48; "Last Days of the Confederate Government," 70.
49. Headley, *Confederate Operations*, 437.
50. Campbell Journal, 4 May 1865; Duke, "Last Days," 766; Reagan, *Memoirs*, 212; Tilghman Diary, 4 May 1865; Juvenis, "Last of Confederacy."
51. Davis to Reagan, 21 Aug. 1877, Reagan-Davis Papers.
52. Robertson, "Davis's Last Meeting," 296; William C. Davis, *Breckinridge*, 522–23; Reagan, *Memoirs*, 213; Clark, "Last Days of the Confederate Treasury," 553; Tilghman Diary, 4 May 1865; Campbell Journal, 4 May 1865. Breckinridge's biographer, William C. Davis, suggests that the secretary wanted to assist in the surrender of western Confederate troops.
53. William C. Davis, *Breckinridge*, 523–24; Duke, "Last Days," 766.
54. Wheeler, "Effort to Rescue Davis," 87–88.
55. Tilghman Diary, 5 May 1865; Wood Diary, 4, 5 May 1865; Campbell Journal, 5 May 1865.
56. Campbell Journal, 6 May 1865; Wood Diary, 5 May 1865; Clark, "Last Days of the Confederate Treasury," 553–54; Hanna, *Flight into Oblivion*, 94; Tilghman Diary, 6 May 1865.
57. Campbell Journal, 6 May 1865; Wood Diary, 6 May 1865; Lubbock, *Memoirs*, 569–70.
58. Burton N. Harrison, "Capture of Davis," 140; Hathaway Recollections, vol. 7; Varina Davis, *Jefferson Davis*, 2:617–19; Strode, *Davis: Private Letters*, 162.
59. Burton N. Harrison, "Capture of Davis," 140–41.
60. Burton N. Harrison, "Capture of Davis," 141; Campbell Journal, 6 May 1865; *OR*, ser. 1, vol. 49, pt. 2, pp. 1283–84.
61. Campbell Journal, 7 May 1865; Wood Diary, 7 May 1865.
62. Campbell Journal, 7 May 1865; Burton N. Harrison, "Capture of Davis," 141; Wood Diary, 8 May 1865.
63. Burton N. Harrison, "Capture of Davis," 141; Campbell Journal, 7 May 1865; Wood Diary, 8 May 1865.
64. Burton N. Harrison, "Capture of Davis," 141–42; Wood Diary, 8 May 1865; An Eyewitness, "The Capture of President Jefferson Davis," *Register of the Kentucky Historical Society* 64 (Oct. 1966): 271; Fairfax Harrison, *The*

Harrisons of Skimino, 259n; Rowland, *Jefferson Davis*, 8:54.

65. Campbell Journal, 6 May 1865; Wood Diary, 9 May 1865; Burton N. Harrison, "Capture of Davis," 142, 144; Jefferson Davis, "Autobiography of Jefferson Davis," *Confederate Veteran* 15 (May 1907): 221; Fairfax Harrison, *Harrisons of Skimino*, 260n; *OR*, ser. 1, vol. 49, pt. 2, pp. 1289–90. (Note: The entries in Given Campbell's Journal for the period 7–10 May all appear under the date 7 May.)

66. *OR*, ser. 1, vol. 49, pt. 1, p. 546, pt. 2, p. 407; Frank H. Mason, "Stoneman's Last Campaign and the Pursuit of Jefferson Davis," in *Sketches of War History, 1861–1865: Papers Prepared for the Ohio Commandery of the Military Order of the Loyal Legion of the United States, 1888–1890*, ed. Robert Hunter (Cinncinati, 1890), 3:34–35; *Official Records of the Union and Confederate Navies in the War of the Rebellion*, 30 vols. (Washington, D.C., 1894–1922), ser. 1, vol. 17, p. 838.

67. *OR*, Ser. 1, vol. 49, pt. 1, pp. 515–16; James Harrison Wilson, *Under the Old Flag: Recollections of Military Operations in the War for the Union, the Spanish War, the Boxer Rebellion, etc.*, 2 vols. (New York, 1912), 2:305–11.

68. Wilson, *Under the Old Flag*, 2:318–24; *OR*, ser. 1, vol. 49, pt. 1, pp. 526, 535.

69. *OR*, ser. 1, vol. 49, pt. 1, pp. 518, 535–36; Wilson, *Under the Old Flag*, 2:326–27.

70. Burton N. Harrison, "Capture of Davis," 141–43; Fairfax Harrison, *Harrisons of Skimino*, 259–60n; *OR*, ser. 1, vol. 49, pt. 1, p. 536; Lubbock, *Memoirs*, 571.

71. Wood Diary, 10 May 1865; Chester D. Bradley, "Was Jefferson Davis Disguised as a Woman When Captured?," *Journal of Mississippi History* 36 (Aug. 1974): 255; Burton N. Harrison, "Capture of Davis," 142; Fairfax Harrison, *Harrisons of Skimino*, 260n; Rowland, *Jefferson Davis*, 8:176; Walthall, "True Story of Capture," 111.

72. Burton N. Harrison, "Capture of Davis," 144; Lubbock, *Memoirs*, 572–73; *OR*, ser. 1, vol. 49, pt. 1, p. 537.

73. Wood Diary, 10 May 1865; Jefferson Davis, *Rise and Fall*, 2:702; Lubbock, *Memoirs*, 573; Burton N. Harrison, "Capture of Davis," 144; Campbell Journal, 7 May 1865; Rowland, *Jefferson Davis*, 9:598.

74. Burton N. Harrison, "Capture of Davis," 144; *OR*, ser. 1, vol. 49, pt. 1, p. 537.

SEVEN

Old Enmities
Were Forgotten

THE JOURNEY BACK TO MACON TOOK FOUR DAYS. Traveling only during daylight hours, the caravan moved slowly in a column of two's via Abbeville and Hawkinsville. During a stop at a Union cavalry camp, a regimental band struck up "Yankee Doodle." A Confederate officer riding beside Burton Harrison remembered the last time he had heard that tune. "It was at Fredericksburg," he said, "when a brass band came across the pontoon bridge with the [Union] column and occupied a house within range of my guns." A shot from rebel cannon had stopped the music that day in December 1862. There would be no such interruption in May 1865.[1]

During the afternoon of 11 May, a few miles from Hawkinsville, the rest of Pritchard's brigade joined the march. They brought word of the $100,000 reward for the Confederate president's capture. Davis remembered that the news caused "vociferous demonstrations of exultation." His wife later wrote, "There was a perceptible change in the manner of the soldiers from this time, and the jibes and insults heaped upon us as they passed by, notwithstanding Colonel Pritchard's efforts to suppress the expression of their detestation, were hard to bear." The captive president thought Pritchard behaved as badly as his men did. "So far as I know,"

149

he recalled, "never in the annals of civilized war did a commanding officer treat a prisoner of high rank among his own people in a manner so little in accordance with the usages of a soldier and the instincts of a gentleman." John Reagan even accused Pritchard of stealing his saddlebags, but the confrontation ended quickly when the Union officer threatened to put the rebel prisoner in irons.[2]

The bitterness of the accounts written by the captives years afterward indicates that ill-treatment of the prisoners by Union soldiers was either bad enough to have a lasting effect or enhanced to sell memoirs. Varina Davis's recollection of Pritchard's behavior implies that criticism of the Federal colonel by the rebel president and others in his party may have been slanted, and Jefferson Davis's critical comments were typical of the defensive tone of his postwar writings.

The column halted briefly outside Macon on Saturday afternoon, 13 May, while Pritchard prepared an escort for the trip to General James Wilson's headquarters. Varina Davis remembered how her children huddled closely around their father. Outside the ambulance, Union soldiers stood at ease, expressing "in words unfit for a woman's ears all that malice could suggest."[3]

The march into town resumed. The local newspaper reported, "At every step the crowd increased." Soldiers used drawn swords and rifles to clear the way. "From all parts of the city, men, women, and children, soldiers, and negroes, flocked to the sidewalks and blocked up the way." An armed detachment of guards lined the sidewalk to the entrance of the hotel building where Wilson had set up his quarters. As Davis started up the walk, the Union guard presented arms. Perhaps on Wilson's orders, the soldiers of the North had ceased taunting the rebel leader. A local reporter wrote, "Not a shout or token of exultation was manifested during the whole time by the Federal soldiery, while the citizens looked on with countenance generally expressing regret."[4]

A "commodious room" awaited the Davis family, and there, after resting, they were served dinner. A black employee brought in a tray of flowers with the food. The moment stuck in Varina's memory: "With tears in his eyes . . . [the

waiter] said, 'I could not bear for you to eat without something pretty from the Confederates.' " After eating, Davis went
to see Wilson in the general's suite.[5]

Before the war, Jefferson Davis had been part of a United
States congressional inquiry into affairs at the United States
Military Academy at West Point. While there, he had met
Wilson, then a cadet. Now in Macon, Georgia, the two men
met under dramatically different circumstances. They talked
of old times, as well as the present. Wilson mentioned the
reward, and Davis remarked bitterly that Andrew Johnson
knew that the charges of his complicity in the assassination
were not true. Johnson knew, argued Davis, that he preferred
Lincoln to his successor. Wilson thought his prisoner seemed
more concerned about possible treason charges. In a letter
written later that same evening, Wilson described Davis's
appearance as "quite cheerful and talkative, but in his whole
demeanor [he] showed no dignity or great fortitude. . . . The
thought struck me once or twice that Jefferson Davis was a
mad man. The indifference with which he seemed to regard
the affairs of our day savored of insanity." Wilson had observed Davis's ability to shut out everything he chose to ignore.[6]

In his later memoirs Wilson portrayed Davis differently,
perhaps because time had mellowed his memory. "He looked
bronzed and careworn," wrote the general as he recalled the
Macon meeting, "but hardy and vigorous, and during the
conversation behaved with perfect self-possession and dignity." Wilson remembered having the impression that, "although he was the fallen chief of the Confederacy who had
lost and become a prisoner of war, he still felt that he would in
some way remain an important factor in the political reconstruction of the Union." He also recalled that Davis spoke
highly of Pritchard's conduct![7]

While their fallen leader met with Wilson, members of the
former official family waited for decisions on their fate. Francis Lubbock spent part of the afternoon writing his wife in
Texas, advising her to sell some cattle for specie. He did not
know yet what course he would take, concluding, "I can not
say much at present." Burton Harrison felt relieved to learn

that one of Wilson's brigadiers was an old classmate from Yale. Friendly conversations about the past helped relieve tension.[8]

Later in the afternoon word leaked out that only Jefferson Davis would be sent on to Washington. John Reagan immediately went to Wilson and protested. As the only remaining cabinet member, Reagan said he felt obligated to go with Davis. Harrison also insisted on accompanying the former president. Eventually, word came through official channels that all the prisoners would be transferred together.[9]

Asked how he wanted to travel, Davis told Wilson that he preferred going by water, because it would be easier on the children. Wilson assented, and at seven o'clock that evening the prisoners were taken to the train station to begin their journey to the Georgia coast via Atlanta. Along the route to the depot, soldiers in blue lined the streets and "yelled and hooted in derision." One of them called to a former Confederate standing nearby, "Hey, Johnny Reb, we've got your President!" Came the quick response, "And the devil's got yours!"[10]

Colonel Pritchard detailed himself, three other officers, and twenty men as a special guard for the prisoners, and 150 more soldiers rode along as extra security as far as Atlanta. There waited another heavily guarded train, to which the prisoners were transferred at daylight on 14 May. Arriving in Augusta that evening, Pritchard and the escort put the captives onto the steamer *Standish*, which chugged into Savannah at 1 A.M., 16 May. Another boat then took them to the *William P. Clyde*. Three days later, the *Clyde* anchored near Fortress Monroe, Virgina. On the afternoon of 22 May, Jefferson Davis left the boat and was led to his prison cell in Fortress Monroe.[11]

Along the way, others had joined the party. Clement C. Clay and his wife, Virginia, had boarded the same train as the Davises at Macon. En route to Savannah, Alexander H. Stephens, Joseph Wheeler, and three of Wheeler's staff had swelled the ranks. Davis and Stephens did not attempt to smooth over their past differences. Stephens later recalled that when they first met on the *Clyde,* Davis's "salutation was not unfriendly, but it was far from cordial. We passed but few words; these were commonplace." The two did manage a cordial and somewhat emotional farewell when they later parted company. Wheeler thought the trip proved more enjoyable than might have been expected under the circumstances. The prisoners spent much time planning possible escapes, but Davis's apparent disinterest quelled their enthusiasm. Wheeler observed, "It was evident that [Davis] felt his relief from responsiblity, and, amid all his trials and troubles, he evidently enjoyed the pleasure of having a few days which he could so entirely devote to his family." Virginia Clay, however, thought her old friend at times seemed depressed and quite restless.[12]

Upon arrival, Federal authorities had dispersed the prisoners to several locations. Clay joined Davis in Monroe, although he was placed in a different section of the fort; Stephens and John Reagan were taken to Fort Warren in Boston Harbor; Harrison was jailed in the Old Capitol Prison in Washington; Lubbock, Wheeler, Preston Johnston, and the rest served their time in Fort Delaware on the west side of Delaware Bay. Denied permission to live near where their husbands were incarcerated, Virginia Clay, Varina Davis, and her children sailed back to Savannah on the *Clyde,* accompanied by paroled rebel soldiers.[13]

Other participants in the Confederate government's retreat from Richmond met a variety of fates. Because of his ill health, George Trenholm initially received a parole from his cell in Fort Pulaski near the Georgia coast. The terms confined him to the city limits of Columbia, South Carolina. However, he returned to prison after Secretary of War Edwin M. Stanton overruled his parole. At his Georgia home, Stephen Mallory surrendered to Union officials and was taken to Fort LaFayette in New York. In October 1865 George Davis, who had left Charlotte after seeing to the safety of his children, turned himself in rather than remain on the run. He served several weeks in Fort LaFayette and was released on 1 January 1866. By then, all the imprisoned cabinet members had been freed except Mallory, whose role in Confederate privateering had angered Secretary of War Stanton. Mallory was not liberated until 10 March 1866.[14]

Judah P. Benjamin and John C. Breckinridge escaped. Benjamin found temporary refuge at a plantation on Florida's western coastline near the Manatee River. Following a harrowing ocean trip to Saint Thomas in the Virgin Islands, he sailed for England on the *Britannia*. There he embarked on a very successful legal career. He never returned to the United States.[15]

As he had ridden southward, Breckinridge had picked up an escort of Confederate soldiers on their way home. To avoid being recognized, the former war secretary had clipped his bushy moustache, reduced his rank to colonel, and abandoned his last name, calling himself John Cabell. On 10 May, the day of Jefferson Davis's capture, Breckinridge and his men were camped some forty miles east of Irwinville. Upon hearing the news, Breckinridge had gone on to Florida, meeting John Taylor Wood along the way. With other refugees, they eventually reached Cuba and then traveled to Canada. Wood lived out his days with his family in Halifax, Nova Scotia. Breckinridge's family also joined him in Canada. He spent several months traveling in Europe and in the Middle East. Returning to Canada, he received amnesty from the United States in 1868. A year later he returned to his native Kentucky.[16]

Almost two weeks after the fact, Micajah Clark and the men of the baggage and treasury trains learned of the Irwinville capture. At their camp on the David Yulee plantation near Gainesville, Florida, Clark and the teamsters engaged in a heated discussion over the disposition of the Treasury funds. The men wanted to divide the money equally, less one-quarter of the total for Davis's wife and children. Clark wanted to pay the rest of the party a fair sum "for the risk and trouble incurred by them" and take the balance to England where he would wait for instructions from Davis and Reagan. Outnumbered and outvoted, Clark relented.

Returning to Abbeville, the former treasurer gave Mrs. Leovy some documents for safekeeping in her New Orleans home. Federal officials captured baggage and papers left at the Yulee home. Clark later reported to Varina Davis in Augusta after her return there from Fortress Monroe. She probably felt relieved to hear about the money, but apparently the teamsters never sent it to her. Clark eventually returned home to Clarksville, Tennessee.[17]

Northern newspapers reported the capture of all the prominent Confederates and speculated on the whereabouts of those still at large. Most headlines, however, concerned the arrest of Jefferson Davis. When the news flashed across the North, papers enthusiastically played up reports that the rebel leader had tried to escape dressed as a woman. The story had apparently originated in the ranks of the First Wisconsin, which had arrived in Macon ahead of the Fourth Michigan and the prisoners. General Wilson had heard the tale and had immediately fired off a telegram to Secretary of War Edwin M. Stanton. He had learned, wrote Wilson, that Davis had "hastily put on one of Mrs. Davis' dresses and started for the woods" before being apprehended.[18]

After Pritchard's arrival on the afternoon on 13 May, Wilson had sent another message to Stanton informing the secretary of plans to send Davis on to Fortress Monroe. This wire had made no mention of the dress story. After arriving at Monroe, Pritchard had received orders to bring the now famous dress to the War Department in Washington. Department officials then had to change the First Wisconsin version of the story when word leaked out that the "dress" was in fact a cloak and shawl. The altered account, reported by the *Army and Navy Journal*, perhaps inspired by the War Department and quickly supported by the Northern press, now held that Davis had been captured wearing female clothing. In his official report to Stanton dated 25 May, Pritchard made no other reference to the incident, except to report that he had obtained the cloak and shawl from Mrs. Davis.[19]

The Davises and their supporters hotly denied the story. Davis later argued that he had picked up Varina's waterproof cloak, mistaking it for his own. Rain had been falling the morning of 10 May; so it would have been logical for him to wear protective clothing. However, in another recounting of the story, he wrote that Varina Davis had thrown the cloak over his shoulders and the shawl over his head. She had also sent along her servant girl carrying the water bucket. Since both articles of clothing were not worn exclusively by women during this period, the apparel alone does not prove that Davis had tried to escape disguised as a woman. Several years later, he wrote, although "there was no impropriety in using a disguise to escape capture, . . . there was no time to have assumed one."[20]

The key question is Varina Davis's intent. In his diary John Taylor Wood, an eyewitness, indicated that he thought the president was disguising himself as a woman and observed that Davis would only have tried the ploy to placate his wife. Yet, in a letter written nearly a month after the capture, Varina claimed she had thrown the clothes on him so "that in the grey of the morning he would not be recognized."[21] Was she trying to pass her husband off as a woman, or was she merely attempting to conceal his identity by covering him with a cloak and a shawl? In the excitement of the moment, perhaps she only wanted to keep him from being recognized. Since their versions of the story came after the news had been spread across the country by newspapers, the Davises naturally reacted defensively. Thus the true nature of her actions that morning may never be known.

The effect of the incident is more significant than the story itself. Former Confederates saw the story as a vicious attempt by Northerners to discredit their president. Francis Lubbock wrote that he wished "to emphatically brand as false the statement that Mr. Davis was disguised in female apparel." John Reagan called the story "wicked and foolish" and just another Yankee attempt to make the "Confederate cause odious." When he heard the news, Preston Johnston recalled that he "was astounded and denounced it as a falsehood."[22] Of course, none of these three men witnessed the incident. They knew only that Davis had not been wearing a dress when they saw him moments after his capture. They could not have known the Davises' motives.

Secretary of War Stanton's decision to lock the cloak and shawl in his safe, away from public view, demonstrated his desire to make the most of the dress story. Items of potential embarrassment to the Federal administration had a way of disappearing in Stanton's office. Documents related to the Kilpatrick-Dahlgren raid on Richmond in 1864, for instance, had vanished after being sent to the secretary. The papers allegedly revealed a Union scheme to kill Jefferson Davis and the Confederate cabinet. The articles of clothing, obviously not as sensitive as the missing papers, did survive, however, although government red tape kept them from public inspection until 1961. They are now housed in Beauvoir, the Davis's postwar home on the Mississippi Gulf Coast.[23]

Another example of the Federal government's attempts to discredit Davis involved former Confederate congressman W. S. Oldham of Texas. On 11 February 1865, Oldham had written President Davis regarding a scheme "of annoying and harassing the enemy by means of burning their Shipping, Towns, etc." Oldham especially emphasized attacks on shipping. Davis had expressed unspecified objections to the plan in an earlier discussion, and in his letter, Oldham attempted to allay the president's doubts. Davis told Judah P. Benjamin to investigate the matter further, and there the idea apparently died. After the evacuation of Richmond, Oldham's correspondence fell into Union hands and eventually wound up on Secretary Stanton's desk. On 20 May 1865, ten days after Davis's capture, the New York *Times* published an editorial condemning the rebel leader for endorsing a plan that included "a phosphoric preparation for smothering Northern women and children in their beds." The remarks typified anti-Davis writing in some of the Northern press. To Southerners who had lived through Union raids in the Shenandoah Valley or found themselves in the path of Sherman's Georgia and Carolina marches, the *Times*'s charges must have seemed hypocritical indeed. Others probably dismissed the incident as yet another Yankee attempt to disparage their former president. As proof, they could point to the fact that the letters were presented as evidence in the trial of the Lincoln conspirators.[24]

The most significant incident involving the United States government's treatment of Jefferson Davis occurred on 23

May, the second day of his imprisonment at Fortress Monroe. The day before, Assistant Secretary of War Charles A. Dana and Major General Henry W. Halleck, commander of the military district that included the fort, had discussed security problems. The possibility of putting shackles on Davis had been discussed, but Halleck had expressed his opposition to the idea, calling it unnecessary. However, in his written instructions to the prison commandant, General Nelson A. Miles, Dana authorized the placing of "manacles and fetters upon the hands and feet" of Davis and Clay if Miles deemed such action necessary "to render their imprisonment more secure." The next day, guard Jerome E. Titlow, a member of the Third Pennsylvania Artillery, came into Davis's cell accompanied by a blacksmith. Titlow told Davis that General Miles had ordered shackles for Davis's ankles. According to later accounts by Titlow and prison doctor John J. Craven, Davis at first expressed disbelief, then heated indignation, and finally offered violent resistance. Titlow called in four unarmed guards to subdue the prisoner, and the shackles, made of heavy iron, were hammered on. Davis then broke down and shook with heavy sobs. In later years, Davis contended that Craven, whose 1866 account appeared several years before Titlow's, had based the story on unreliable prison gossip. Admitting that he had resisted, Davis denied losing control of himself and becoming argumentative. Although Craven had not been present, he did base his version on what the Union soldiers in the cell had told him, but Craven's book was actually written by New York *Citizen* editor Charles G. Halpine, who in several instances augmented Craven's notes and diary with fictional details. In any case, Titlow's later account of the incident generally supported the story in Craven and Halpine's book.[25]

Philadelphia newspapers first broke the story. The New York *Herald* hoped the news was not true, commenting that "no good and strong government does an unnecessary act." Secretary Stanton received a letter and clipping from the Union League in Philadelphia. The letter told Stanton of the "most prejudicial feelings" the story had aroused among

League members. If the article were not true, the secretary should immediately publish a denial.[26]

On 28 May Stanton reacted to the public outcry with a sharply worded message to Miles. "Please report whether irons have or have not been placed on Jefferson Davis," he wrote. "If they have been, when was it done, and for what reason, and remove them." Miles immediately replied that he had given the order because he had been concerned over security problems caused by wooden doors and the lack of locks in Davis's cell area. These problems had now been solved, he continued, "and the anklets have been removed." Three days earlier, Dr. Craven had recommended to Miles that the irons be taken off for the sake of Davis's health. When the shackles came off on 28 May, Craven was pleased, but he did not know that Miles had acted only after receiving the terse orders from Stanton.[27]

The influential New York Republican politican, Thurlow Weed, put the episode into perspective in a 29 May letter to Stanton:

> I could not believe the accounts of Ironing Davis, but they *seem* authentic. If true, it is a great error and a great calamity. All else is well, and I hope that this dreadful cloud may not obscure the glory of other Achievements.
>
> The Fact—if fact it be—is even less revolting than the details. Until now, our country is honored every where. The World is with us. But this wholly unnecessary severity with a *State* Prisoner will loose [*sic*] us a great advantage.[28]

Weed clearly understood the possible ramifications of the incident. Doubt had been cast on the North's ability to heal the nation's wounds and restore a united country to its former place of power in the world. Weed worried that victory, in effect, had been tainted.

Overshadowing all the incidents related to Davis's capture and imprisonment was the issue of his ultimate fate. The Northern press did not have a unanimous opinion on this question. Initially, the New York *Times* called for hanging the chief rebel. He deserved no sympathy, said the *Times*, for he would be known "hereafter as the representative man of the rebellion." Other papers echoed the call for the death penalty. However, Henry J. Raymond, Republican editor of the *Times*, soon began to have second thoughts. In a 25 May editorial, Raymond discussed arguments that were being made against the imprisonment and execution of Davis. Some people seemed to believe that Davis had committed no crime since he had acted in the belief that secession was a constitutional right. Raymond dismissed this reasoning on the grounds that the act of treason took precedence over all other considerations. Others argued that executing Davis would make him a martyr and delay the reunification of the country. Raymond admitted that this notion had merit. In summary, he believed that the passage of time would soothe the virulent anti-Davis feelings of the Northern public, and therefore, no rash action should be taken.[29]

Horace Greeley, the eccentric editor of the New York *Tribune*, also called for moderation. Immediately after learning of Davis's capture, Greeley had written, "We trust that he will be treated as a prisoner, under the protection of the dignity and honor of a self-respecting people." Greeley reminded those who called for Davis's immediate hanging of the usual course of due process—that is, arrest, trial, verdict, carrying out of sentence. "Many persons," said Greeley, "seem intent on beginning at the wrong end."[30]

Southern newspapers reacted cautiously to the plight of their former president. Many editors had been forced to cease publication; others were publishing in temporary locations away from their hometowns; and some had been purchased by anti-Confederate owners. The Charleston *Daily Courier*, pro-Davis during most of the war, now railed against the former Confederate president. The Richmond *Whig*, anti-Davis for most of the war, continued to criticize his administration after his capture. However, these papers were an exception to the position of most other Southern journals.[31]

The Lynchburg *Daily Virginian* sounded the major theme of the Southern press, noting that the Southern people sympathized with Davis, and "they earnestly desire that no harm may be visited upon him, *for their offense.*" Calling the charge of involvement in Lincoln's assassination "absurd," the *Vir-*

ginian warned Northern officials that the execution of the former president would make him as strong a martyr for the South as Lincoln had become for the North. Moreover, pardoning Davis would speed the healing of the nation's wounds.[32]

Other papers expressed similar sentiments. The Macon, Georgia, *Daily Telegraph* did not comment editorially but did print a quote from the fiercely pro-Union, anti-Davis editor of the Louisville *Journal*, George D. Prentice: "We are afraid now that his capture and [the] treatment he is destined to receive will render the restoration of national harmony much more difficult than it would be if he were upon a foreign shore." The *Telegraph* also printed an excerpt from the London *Morning Herald*, which argued that the creation of the Confederacy was an "act of the people at large." Furthermore, "the execution of Jeff. Davis would be simply a political murder; and a murder more wicked, cruel and cowardly than that of Abraham Lincoln, inasmuch as it would be the act not of one desperate fanatic, but of a national government. It would fix upon every citizen of the northern States, and especially on the president and his advisers, a guilt in every respect corresponding to that of John Wilkes Booth."[33]

The reaction of Southern women to the imprisonment of Davis foretold the significant role they would play in the postwar deification of the fallen rebel president. In diaries across the South, women wrote their thoughts on the misfortune of the leader of the Southern cause. "I trust that God will take Mr. Davis to Himself," wrote Georgianna Walker, "before our enemies can bring him to an ignominious death. But what they would consider ignominy, we would think a halo of glory." South Carolinian Emma Holmes decried Southerners who blamed Davis for losing the war. It was terrible, she said, "that not only must he bear in his living tomb the consequences of his own misuse of power, but the execrations of thousands of his countrymen, who lay all the blame of our fearful failure on his shoulders. If there is anyone I pity & feel for from the depths of my heart, it is Jefferson Davis." Cornelia McDonald of Virginia wrote that Southerners expected Yankees to implicate them in Lincoln's murder "but were not prepared for the extent of diabolical rage which they manifested in the treatment of President Davis when he fell into their hands."[34]

In October 1865 women of Petersburg, Virginia, sent President Johnson a petition, signed by more than six hundred women of the town, pleading for clemency and a pardon for the Confederate president. Davis, said the petition, "is bound to each one of our section by the indissoluble ties of friendship, love and veneration. . . . He has our love for every virtue which adorned the Christian, the gentleman, and the patriot, shown forth in every act with the brilliancy of the morning sun, reflecting honor upon his country, dignity upon his government, and purity upon the social circle." An East Tennessee unionist wrote in June 1865 that he thought Davis to be in disfavor in the South, "except with the women, who speak much of his great piety."[35]

No creditable evidence of Davis's involvement in the assassination of Abraham Lincoln could be found; so Federal officials decided to try the rebel leader for treason. They hoped to use his case to obtain a specific Supreme Court ruling establishing secession as treason. Legal questions and jurisdictional problems caused many delays, but finally, on 13 May 1867 Jefferson Davis walked out of prison, free on a bail bond signed by, among others, Horace Greeley and prewar abolitionist Gerrit Smith. There were further futile attempts at continuing the case, but in February 1869 it was dismissed for good.[36]

Edward Pollard, Davis's old enemy, perhaps summed it up best in his biography of the president:

> The imprisonment of Mr. Davis was the best thing that could have happened for his fame. What he suffered lying as a prisoner in a casemate of Fortress Monroe for two years, and for the first few weeks degraded by fetters, and especially the manner of his suffering, not only disarmed much of the old resentment of his countrymen, but displayed him in an attitude so touching, and in conduct so becoming and noble, that, when released on bail . . . , he found himself welcomed by nearly every heart in the South, and hailed with a pride

and tenderness that his countrymen had not before shown him, even in the best of his former estate.

Old enmities were forgotten, old offenses were forgiven, and not an injurious memory of the past war was allowed to disturb the tribute which the whole south seemed now anxious to pay to the martyr of the "lost cause."[37]

Certainly the imprisonment of Davis had been an important event in assuring his martyrdom. The necessary groundwork, however, had already been laid before the event occurred. Before being forced from Richmond, Davis had successfully met the challenges of the peace movement, the states' rights philosophy, the slave-soldier issue, Robert E. Lee's promotion, and Joe Johnston's reinstatement. After the evacuation, the Confederate president had rejected surrender and issued a defiant call to arms from Danville. In Greensboro inhospitable treatment by local citizens had backfired in his favor. In Charlotte his reaction to the news of Lincoln's assassination, based on Lewis Bates's false testimony, had helped lead to the placing of a price on his head and assured his capture. Lincoln's death had thus produced Davis's imprisonment, the crowning touch to his martyr image.

All along the way from Charlotte to Irwinville, the president's determined devotion to the cause had impressed citizens who saw him. Moreover, the sight of the bedraggled remnants of the Confederate government had evoked deep sympathy and pity for Davis and his followers. Finally captured, he had been the victim of stories intended to humiliate him and had suffered the unspeakable cruelty of having iron shackles placed on his ankles. This series of events kept Davis's image afloat while the Confederacy sank around him.

Through the weary months of 1865 until his capture, Davis had shown that as a politician and a leader, he could deal more effectively with situations than with people. Throughout the war, he had erred in the handling of his generals, and he had often been too strident in his relationships with congressmen. The issues he had faced in Richmond prior to the evacuation and the events of the retreat were compatible with the strong will that dominated his personality. His firmness did not necessarily make him a distant, foreboding individual. He had charmed his way through Richmond parties, had evoked strong loyalties in his staff and cabinet, and had had a close, affectionate relationship with his family. But Davis could be distant and unyielding when he thought such behavior essential to winning, whether the battle was political or military. During the last days of the Confederacy, he had found himself in several situations that called for a hard line, and he had responded accordingly. When political issues during the early months of 1865 had called for flexibility, he had been flexible, because saving the cause required him to do whatever was necessary to prevail. Later, when his only options were surrender and fighting on, he fought on, showing fellow Southerners the side of him they needed to see—a leader solely and irrevocably dedicated to the cause. As one study has characterized him, "In portraiture Davis fared best in stone. Granite and marble befitted him well, for though stone might crack or even crumble, it would never bend."[38]

Devotion to duty played a key role in the enhancement of the deposed president's image. "Mr. Davis is a man of principle, not of policy. He would not swerve an inch from what he believed to be right to oblige the world," wrote an acquaintance shortly after the war.[39] Davis had accepted the goal of Southern independence and, convincing himself that it was right, had clung tenaciously to that object until it was beyond his reach. He had no patience with those who would not stand with him. Although devoted to states' rights, he had been willing to accept necessary changes, to centralize the war effort, to use the military draft, and to free the slaves if necessary to attain victory. This unshakable devotion to the cause of independence kept him going during the trying days of the retreat from Richmond. When despair and reality occasionally intervened, Davis always turned his thoughts again to his dream, and he always rebounded.

In addition, the mood of the South at the end of the war helped mythologize Davis. From its attempt at nationhood, the region had collapsed into several distinct worlds. In Danville, a woman had taken to the streets to complain of hunger.

In Washington, Georgia, another woman had set a bountiful table for the refugee government. In towns along the way, soldiers, civilians, and criminals had sacked or attempted to sack supply stores. Between towns, the fugitives from Richmond had noticed the serenity of the countryside, fields being tended, and people going about their business as if unaware of the war. The routine of everyday life, interrupted occasionally by paroled soldiers casually making their way home, contrasted with the anxious, sometimes aimless flight of the Confederacy's elite. A sense of anarchy had enveloped the South, exhibited in a curious mixture of desperation and continuity.

Thus, the course of the war had reinforced feelings of dependence on local and state authority, key ingredients for a reaffirmation of states' rights. There was but one unifying factor—the Lost Cause. All Southerners had not suffered equally. Some could recall the past four years with affection, and those who had lost much needed to feel that they had lost it in a good and noble cause. In either case, an idealized past offered a pleasant escape from current realities. In the end, the people of the South rejected Jefferson Davis's appeal to fight on, but they embraced the cause he was trying to save.

As Davis languished in his cell, the Lost Cause state of mind that eventually became an orchestrated movement gathered momentum in the defeated South. Even before the guns fell silent, Southerners began to search for meaning among the ruins. Why had the innate superiority of the Southern people failed to triumph over the inferior Yankee? Why had their trusted God turned his back on the noble and righteous Confederate crusade?

Edward Pollard, whose constant railing against the Davis administration had contributed to destructive dissension within the Confederacy, gave direction and title to the answers his fellow citizens sought in his 1866 book, *The Lost Cause*. Now that a military war had settled the slavery issue, wrote Pollard, the South would fight a "war of ideas," and this conflict would be fought with the written word, not guns. True to Pollard's prophetic call to action, Confederates began writing their stories in an outpouring of defenses and analyses that justified the Southern cause while rationalizing defeat.[40]

Their words showed that the spirit of the Confederacy had survived its death. The triumph of the North was compatible with the prevalent fatalism of religious thought in Dixie. God's chosen people had been tested by disappointment and oppression in the past, but severe trials had never been just cause for abandoning faith. Southern ministers recalled Isaiah's "man of sorrows," his "arm of the Lord," who was "despised and rejected of men," who bore man's grief and carried his sorrows, who "was wounded for our transgressions, he was bruised for our iniquities: the chastisement of our peace was upon him; and with his stripes we are healed." They held up "the Confederate Man of Sorrows as a moral lesson on suffering, humiliation, defeat, and death." But would the South be healed? Perhaps God was teaching that the sacred Southern way of life must not be taken for granted. In any event, the crusades must be continued against outside evil, namely, the Yankee and his immoral society, and for the preservation of Southern good, including agrarianism, close family ties, fundamental religion, chivalry, the honoring of womanhood, paternalism toward the less fortunate, and white supremacy.[41]

The "dream of a cohesive Southern people with a separate cultural identity" replaced the vision of an independent nation. The cause became a kind of "civil religion," drawing from the past a "basis for a Southern religious-moral identity as a chosen people." This civil religion, a spiritual reflection of the war experience, containing "ritualistic, mythological, theological, institutional, educational, and intellectual elements," permeated Southern society. By romanticizing and glorifying what had been, Southerners made the "postbellum adjustment" to their war experience less painful; they found a way to avoid being reconstructed in the image of the conquering Yankee. The "experience of defeat . . . had created a spiritual and psychological need for Southerners to reaffirm their identity."[42]

The centerpiece of the Lost Cause movement was the Confederate veteran and the memory of his war exploits, real and imagined. Organizations of veterans began springing up shortly after the war ended, culminating in the establishment of the United Confederate Veterans in 1889. Members made speeches extolling Lee, Jackson, and other heroes; raised money for monuments; assaulted Reconstruction policies; pronounced the sacredness of their cause; and waved rebel flags in celebration of their participation in the war epic. Southern women supported the veterans, eventually forming their own organization, the United Daughters of the Confederacy. Soldiers were transformed into holy warriors. Concludes one historian, the "day of the Confederacy . . . offered the materials from which the Myth of the Lost Cause would take its greatest strength."[43]

Confederate dead received special attention, and when Robert E. Lee joined their ranks in 1870, the South practically came to a standstill to pay homage. Many Northerners, too, praised the rebel general who had worked for conciliation between the sections since Appomattox. These reactions to Lee's death indicated that the Lost Cause might in some respects take on a national hue. Indeed, the mythological Old South of moonlight, magnolias, and mint juleps would eventually be embraced by non-Southerners. Blue and gray veterans would meet and reminisce together about their war. Such developments have been analyzed as Northern attempts to place the South in a reunited nation.[44]

Nationalization of the Lost Cause was for the future, however. In the immediate postwar period, the cause was the sole property of the South. It was a cause molded from defeat and dominated by the Southern mind. From his prison cell, Jefferson Davis stepped into its milieu and ultimately became its principal figure.

After leaving Fort Monroe, Davis kept the low profile that, except during the shackling incident, he had maintained while incarcerated, partly because of ill health and no doubt because he feared reprisals by his captors that might go beyond a jail cell and chains. His troubles during the retreat from Richmond, at Monroe and afterward, won praise from

Southerners who viewed him as the personification of their suffering homeland. To the people he had led, Davis's trials made God's testing of the South more apparent.

After his release, Davis received a letter from a friend who wrote: "True greatness never manifests itself more nobly than in conforming with resignation to its attendant requirements." During the ensuing years, many other letters echoed this sentiment. A lady correspondent proclaimed her "admiration for the noble gentleman who has always been chief among us, and who has had even the sad pre-eminence in the common pain and suffering." Others acknowledged Davis as the "chief victim and sufferer" of the lost war and praised "the noble manner in which he has borne himself since the South fell." Perhaps the crowning benediction to this theme appeared in 1885 in the Montgomery, Alabama, *Advertiser:* "Jefferson Davis is one of history's few great men, great in the noon, grand in the solemn hush of night that has fallen on his hopes. Heroically and uncomplainingly he treads his thorny way to the grave, bearing on his single head, the weight of a thousand wrongs and wearing in his single heart a million shafts and wards them from his people."[45]

While applauding Davis's humble bearing, fellow Southerners did not hesitate to fight his battles for him. As early as 1866 Albert Taylor Bledsoe, a Virginia lawyer, published a treatise entitled *Is Davis a Traitor, or Was Secession a Constitutional Right previous to the War of 1861?* Bledsoe's work actually defended several prominent Confederates, including Lee, Jackson, and Sidney Johnston, for their roles in the war, but it is significant that Davis's name appears in the title. When a Massachusetts senator argued in the United States Senate against including Jefferson Davis among beneficiaries of a Mexican War pension bill, Mississippi Senator L. Q. C. Lamar, a champion of sectional reconciliation, launched a spirited defense of the former president.[46]

In 1881, however, Davis in self-defense published his own account of the war, *The Rise and Fall of the Confederate Government.* The two-volume work defended Davis's actions during the war while opening old wounds with criticism of Joe Johnston and Beauregard, among others. Davis also condemned a few of the war enemy, singling out William T. Sherman for several offenses, including his "barbarous cruelty" in ordering the evacuation of the civilian population of Atlanta in 1864 and his disregard for "the common dictates of humanity" in burning Columbia, South Carolina, in 1865. Davis's words precipitated heated exchanges with Sherman then and later.[47]

In 1886, for example, Sherman said in an interview that Davis "never was a secessionist. He was a conspirator. . . . His object was to get a fulcrum from which to operate against the Northern States; and if he had succeeded, he would to-day be the master spirit of the continent, and you [the North] would be slaves." As proof, Sherman claimed that he had seen a wartime letter from Davis to a man who was now a United States senator (later identified as Zebulon Vance), in which Davis wrote that Lee's army would be used to keep any Confederate state from leaving the Confederacy.

Davis blasted the charge as a "reckless, shameless falsehood," the motive for which was "personal malignity." Let Sherman bring forth the alleged letter "or wear the brand of a base slanderer." Davis proceeded to write a lengthy exposé attempting to show that the letter had never existed. Vance denied receiving any such letter during his days as war governor. Sherman could not produce the evidence, and Davis's stinging and convincing counterattack was cheered in the South.[48]

Friends nevertheless cautioned Davis against becoming too involved in such an exchange. When Joe Johnston accused Davis in 1881 of stealing over two million dollars in Confederate gold during the retreat from Richmond, a Davis defender warned that recriminations against Johnston and his kind must be avoided. "You are our Representative man of the 'Lost Cause,' and any self-inflicted wounds upon yourself, will be keenly felt by your many friends whose feelings in your behalf are grossly outraged by Johnston's cruel and unmanly attack."[49]

Jefferson Davis never recanted; he never saw any reason to. If he tried to avoid controversy, he also made known at every opportunity his firm belief that the Confederate movement was right and proper. In speeches and countless letters, he expounded on this theme and, in the process, confirmed perhaps the most vital of Lost Cause principles: the South had no desire to fight again, but it had no reason to apologize for the events of 1861–1865.

Characterizing himself as "a Confederate whose heart-love lies buried in the grave of our cause," Davis constantly sought to justify the dream of Southern independence. In an 1878 speech he frankly asserted, "The course pursued by the Federal Government, after the war had ceased, vindicates the judgment of those who held separation to be necessary for the safety and freedom of the Southern States." In his Preface to *The Rise and Fall*, Davis wrote that his purpose was to show that the South had had a right to secede and that the North's refusal to acknowledge that right violated the Constitution and the principles of the Declaration of Independence.[50]

On the subject of personal repentance, Davis thundered to the Mississippi state legislature in 1884: " 'Tis been said that I should apply to the United States for a pardon, but repentance must precede the right of pardon, and I have not repented. Remembering as I must all which has been suffered, all which has been lost, disappointed hopes and crushed asperations, yet I deliberately say, if it were to do over again, I would again do just as I did in 1861." To an inquiry by the Reverend Edward Bailey of Philadelphia about whether Davis regretted the war, the former president responded that he had worked to avoid the conflict but had had no qualms over the South's right to leave the Union. As for his personal role, "If suffering for the cause I espoused could produce repentance, I have surely borne enough for that end, but martyrs have gloried in their faith when yielding up their lives for its assertion and if I mistake not your character, you would scorn the man who recanted and called it repentance."[51]

During an 1886 speaking tour through Alabama and Georgia, Davis asserted that the war had not destroyed state sovereignty. He argued further that when reason prevailed, "it must be decided that the General Government had no constitutional power to coerce a State and that a State had the right to repel invasion." Words like these took attention away from the more moderate remarks Davis made during the same speeches, and though they met uproarious approbation in the South, they provoked an uproar of protest in the North. Biting editorials and Union veterans who remembered the horrors of war condemned the "unrepentant old villain and Union-hater."[52] The Springfield, Massachusetts, *Republican*, however, tried to present a balanced view of the tour:

> We have reached that distance when we can recognize the genuine convictions that filled the men of the south, when twenty-five years ago they essayed to found a nation of their own. . . . Doubtless they underestimated the courage and the persistence of the north, but they addressed themselves to oppose the power of the nation with as serious purpose as ever any people had in revolution, and bore themselves bravely and resolutely to the end. . . . Now that time has removed that dire destruction to a historic distance, they gather to commemorate the lost cause with no desire to recall it, only to recognize it for what it was to them, to assert it to the world, and to go about their affairs again, content and proud in the greater and nobler patriotism of their and our common country.
>
> This is the way we read the honors to Jefferson Davis. . . . How could we respect the southern people if they did not believe in the thing they undertook to do, if they were not attached to its memory, if they did not honor their leaders and their soldiers, nor exalt their services and sacrifices? They do well to cherish the sentiment that hallows their story.[53]

The editorial was accurate as far as it went and clearly indicated that the Lost Cause was becoming nationalized. Nevertheless, it is doubtful that the editor really understood the depth and breadth of the Lost Cause mythology or the extent of the South's affection for its former president. Sentiments in the South went beyond mere attachment to memory. Three years later the significance of the Davis tour became more apparent.

Virginia minister J. William Jones, the "Evangelist of the Lost Cause," compiled a memorial volume in Davis's honor after the president had "laid down his cross to receive a crown." He published the thick volume in 1890, a year after Davis's death. The many eulogistic remarks assembled by Jones demonstrated the nature of the South's remembrance of Jefferson Davis. During disasters, "President Davis was calm, brave, and determined." On the retreat from Richmond, he "bore himself grandly." While in North Carolina, "he could not believe that the star of the Confederacy had fallen . . . , and with an intensity and eloquence born of genius he stood out for another base of operations." He was praised for the "martyrdom which he suffered for principles dear to us all," for "his fearless and constant advocacy of principles which he deemed great," and for "his devotion to the ideas he represented." Davis's "burden—grievous as it was—was bravely and uncomplainingly borne," and he "stood by his convictions and by his devotion to the South until his dying hour."[54]

With a romantic flair, the New Orleans *Times Democrat* epitomized the laudatory outpouring: "Tenacious of principle, the slave of conscience, resolute, yet filled with the inspiration that comes from unyielding belief, the giant figure of the ex-President of the Confederacy stalked across the nineteenth century as some majestic spirit, that strong in the consciousness of its own right-doing, scorned the plaudits of a world; and lived only that in himself duty might be deified. Such was Jefferson Davis, and such will history declare him to be."[55]

More accurately, such was the *image* of Jefferson Davis at his death. The Monroe irons had become "anklets of gold"; his clanking chains had a "martyr ring." These relics of Davis's sufferings had become to Southerners as the wood of the cross to Christians. So went the hyperbolic incantations of one eulogizer. But such sentiments should not be dismissed lightly. At the unveiling of Davis's monument in Richmond in 1907, a crowd estimated at 200,000 gathered, the largest assemblage ever to honor a Confederate hero. The shrine's inscription restated the thrust of his perceived memory. In part it reads, "With dignity he met defeat, with fortitude he met imprisonment and suffering, with entire devotion he kept the faith." As one historian has concluded, "While Lee was becoming a national hero between 1900 and 1920, Davis was advancing in reputation as a symbol of the South's holiness.[56]

The influence of Davis's performance during the sunset of his presidency on the development of his image in the Lost Cause movement is apparent. Not so obvious is the effect of the government's retreat on the tenets of the Lost Cause. The Lost Cause developed into a complex movement, but it sprang from the basic reactions of Southerners to what they viewed as subjugation. Their responses included grief, hero worship for the military men and civilians who had led the crusade, attempts to understand the meaning of defeat, and a resolve to honor the effort.

Where was the evidence of these responses during the flight of Davis and the government? It was written on the shocked faces of Richmond residents watching bonfires of archival records. Fleeing government officials saw it in the eyes of those who stood reverently as the government train passed by. Danville residents expressed it by opening their homes to the Richmond refugees. In Greensboro, a man felt it as he watched President Davis and Secretary of War Breckinridge ride out of town. Soldiers and civilians alike displayed it when they called on their president to speak in Charlotte. Throughout South Carolina, it was evidenced by rural and small-town residents who gathered along the retreat route and gave affectionate and emotional receptions to the regnant fugitives. John Headley noted it in the desperate faces of the crowd that gathered to watch the remnants of its government ride out of Washington, Georgia. Even a black servant manifested it in his special attention to the captured Confederate president and his wife in a Macon, Georgia, hotel room. Finally, the uproar over prison chains on a martyr's ankles was a sign that seeds of a cause were germinating.

For the Confederacy that lived on in the minds of Southerners was the Confederacy of Jefferson Davis, not the dissension-ridden nation of Joe Brown and Alexander Stephens. It was the good South victimized by the evil Yankee, a holy South stripped of all the faults that had doomed its disastrous experiment in nationhood. Jefferson Davis remembered and defended it that way. So did the Southern people, and they began to remember it that way even as it was collapsing around them.

Thus, the long trek from Richmond to Fort Monroe had proved more than a formative period for the Jefferson Davis of later years. Reactions to the retreat reflected attitudes that would shape the character of the Lost Cause movement. Enhanced by these sentiments, Jefferson Davis arose from the ashes of Confederate defeat to cast a long shadow across the post–Civil War South.

1. Burton N. Harrison, "Capture of Davis," 144–45.

2. *OR*, ser. 1, vol. 49, pt. 1, p. 537; Jefferson Davis, *Rise and Fall*, 2:703; Varina Davis, *Jefferson Davis*, 2:642; Rowland, *Jefferson Davis*, 8: 178; Reagan, *Memoirs*, 220–21. According to Harrison, Pritchard had obtained a generous share of booty from the Davis camp. Burton N. Harrison, "Capture of Davis," 144.

3. Varina Davis, *Jefferson Davis*, 2:642.

4. Macon *Daily Telegraph*, 14 May 1865; Jefferson Davis, *Rise and Fall*, 2:703.

5. Jefferson Davis, *Rise and Fall*, 2:703; Varina Davis, *Jefferson Davis*, 2:643n.

6. Jefferson Davis, *Rise and Fall*, 2:703; James P. Jones, ed., " 'Your Left Arm': James H. Wilson's Letters to Adam Badeau," *Civil War History* 12 (Sept. 1966):243–44.

7. Wilson, *Under the Old Flag*, 2:336, 338. The difference in the two accounts can be attributed to several factors. Time had helped remove whatever vengeful feelings Wilson may have had in 1865. Also, in the 7 July 1877 issue of the Philadelphia *Weekly Times*, Wilson had written an error-filled, anti-Davis account of the retreat and capture of the Confederate government. Some of Davis's friends, including several who had participated in the retreat, convincingly attacked Wilson's article in the *Southern Historical Society Papers*. Thus, Wilson's milder 1912 view of Davis may have been an attempt to back away from the *Times* story. Finally, Jefferson Davis had been dead some twenty-three years when General Wilson's memoirs were published. The former Confederate president had become more and more revered in the South since the end of the war. He had indeed become "an important factor" in the politics of the South. Moreover, the North and the South had romanticized prominent war figures on both sides. The different accounts probably reflect the different times in which they were written. See Walthall, "True Story of Capture," 97–126; C. Vann Woodward, *Origins of the New South, 1817–1913* (Baton Rouge, 1971), 142–74; Paul H. Buck, *The Road to Reunion* (Boston, 1937), 236–62.

8. Lubbock, *Memoirs*, 474–75; Burton N. Harrison, "Capture of Davis," 145.

9. Reagan, *Memoirs*, 221–22; Jefferson Davis, *Rise and Fall*, 2:704.

10. Jefferson Davis, *Rise and Fall*, 2:703–4; *OR*, ser. 1, vol. 49, pt. 1, p. 537; [Clay], *Belle of the Fifties*, 256.

11. *OR*, ser. 1, vol. 49, pt. 1, pp. 537–38; Jefferson Davis, *Rise and Fall*, 2:704. Four days later, Kirby Smith surrendered the Trans-Mississippi. *OR*, ser. 1, vol. 48, pt. 2, pp. 600–601.

12. [Clay], *Belle of the Fifties*, 256, 261; Wheeler, "Effort to Rescue Davis," 88–90; Myrta Lockett Avary, ed., *Recollections of Alexander H. Stephens: His Diary Kept When a Prisoner at Fort Warren, Boston Harbour, 1865* (New York, 1910), 113–14; Wheeler quoted in Lubbock, *Memoirs*, 576.

13. Wheeler, "Effort to Rescue Davis," 90; Lubbock, *Memoirs*, 577; Reagan, *Memoirs*, 222; Jefferson Davis, *Rise and Fall*, 2:704–5; [Clay], *Belle of the Fifties*, 269. Before boarding the *Clyde* for the trip to Monroe, the Davises had decided to leave Jim Limber with old family friend Union General Rufus Saxton, fearing that unfriendly Federal officers might try to take him by force. Apparently, they never saw him again. Varina Davis, *Jefferson Davis*, 2:645n.

14. *OR*, ser. 2, vol. 8, pp. 664, 692, 763, 799; Patrick, *Davis and His Cabinet*, 361–62; Hanna, *Flight into Oblivion*, 209–23, 249; Joseph T. Durkin, *Stephen R. Mallory: Confederate Navy Chief* (Chapel Hill, 1954), 375, 379.

15. Benjamin's escape is detailed in Hanna, *Flight into Oblivion*, 194–208.

16. Royce Gordon Shingleton, *John Taylor Wood: Sea Ghost of the Confederacy* (Athens, 1979), 197–205; William C. Davis, *Breckinridge*, 525–92.

17. M. H. Clark to Burton N. Harrison, 20 Feb. 1866, Clark to Harrison, 26 Aug. 1867, Burton Norval Harrison Family Papers, Library of Congress. Watson Van Benthuysen, who with his brother Alfred had been a part of Clark's party, kept some of the funds intended for the Davises. The Benthuysen's aunt had married Joe Davis, the president's brother. See Hanna, *Flight into Oblivion*, 109, 164n.

18. Bradley, "Was Davis Disguised?" 246; *OR*, Ser. 1, vol. 49, pt. 2, pp. 721–22, 743. Bradley's is the most thorough account available of the dress controversy.

19. *OR*, ser. 1, vol. 49, pt. 1, pp. 536–38, pt. 2, pp. 743, 888; Bradley, "Was Davis Disguised?" 250–51. See also Rowland, *Jefferson Davis*, 7:447–49.

20. Jefferson Davis, *Rise and Fall*, 2:701; Rowland, *Jefferson Davis*, 8:35, 176; Bradley, "Was Davis Disguised?" 264–65.

21. Wood Diary, 10 May 1865 (Shingleton, *John Taylor Wood*, 162, agrees that Wood so interpreted Davis's action); Varina Davis to Francis P. Blair, 6 June 1865, quoted in part in Bradley, "Was Davis Disguised?" 255. See also Rowland, *Jefferson Davis*, 7:441–45.

22. Lubbock, *Memoirs*, 572; Reagan, *Memoirs*, 220; Walthall, "True Story of Capture," 121.

23. Bradley, "Was Davis Disguised?" 258–61; James O. Hall, "The Dahlgren Papers: A Yankee Plot to Kill President Davis," *Civil War Times Illustrated* 22 (Nov. 1983), 33, 39.

24. W. S. Oldham to Jefferson Davis, 11 Feb. 1865 (including note by Davis on back of letter dated 20 Feb. 1865), B. J. Sweet to W. H. Ryder, 9 May 1865 both in Ryder Collection of Confederate Archives, Tufts University Archives; New York *Times*, 19, 20 May 1865.

25. *OR*, ser. 2, vol. 8, pp. 564–65; Chester D. Bradley, "Dr. Craven and the Prison Life of Jefferson Davis," *Virginia Magazine of History and Biography* 62 (Jan. 1954):72–74; Varina Davis, *Jefferson Davis*, 2:656–58; John J. Craven, *Prison Life of Jefferson Davis* (New York, 1866), 33–39. In 1868 Robert Barnwell Rhett, Jr., editor of the Charleston *Mercury* during and after the war, accused Craven of fraud because of Halpine's authorship of the book. The controversy is discussed in Bradley, "Dr. Craven," 50–94; David Rankin Barbee, "Dr. Craven's 'Prison Life of Jefferson Davis'—an Exposé," *Tyler's Quarterly Magazine* 32 (April 1951):282–95; William Hanchett, "Reconstruction and Rehabilitation of Jefferson Davis: Charles G. Halpine's *Prison Life*," *Journal of American History* 56 (Sept. 1969):280–89.

26. Bradley, "Dr. Craven," 53; New York *Herald*, 27 May 1865; Rowland, *Jefferson Davis*, 7:22.

27. *OR*, ser. 2, vol. 8, p. 577; Craven, *Prison Life*, 51–65.

28. Rowland, *Jefferson Davis*, 7:26.

29. New York *Times*, 16, 25 May 1865; *Harper's Weekly Illustrated Magazine*, 27 May 1865; Chicago *Tribune*, 19, 26, May 1865.

30. New York *Tribune*, 15, 17 May, 4 July 1865.

31. Charleston *Daily Courier*, June–July 1865, *passim*; Richmond *Whig*, May–June 1865, *passim*.

32. Lynchburg *Daily Virginian*, 17, 24 May, 16 June 1865.

33. Macon *Daily Telegraph*, 17, 18 June 1865. See also Jackson (Miss.) *Daily Clarion*, 9 Aug. 1865, and New Orleans *Daily Picayune*, 24 May 1865. See also Sparks, "John P. Osterhout," 22.

34. Dwight Franklin Henderson, ed., *The Private Journal of Georgiana Gholson Walker, 1862–1865, with Selections from the Post-war Years* (Tuscaloosa, Ala., 1963), 123–24; Marszalek, *Diary of Emma Holmes*, 260–61; McDonald, *Diary*, 260–261. See also Anderson, *Brokenburn*, 355; Andrews, *War-time Journal*, 253.

35. "Petition for Mr. Davis' Release," *Southern Historical Society Papers* 24 (1896):240–42; Martin Abbott, ed., "A Southerner Views the South, 1865: Letters of Harvey M. Watterson," *Virginia Magazine of History and Biography* 68 (Oct. 1960):482.

36. Roy Franklin Nichols, "United States vs. Jefferson Davis, 1865–1869," *American Historical Review* 31 (Jan. 1926):266–84.

37. Pollard, *Life of Jefferson Davis*, 526–27.

38. Nash K. Burger and John K. Bettersworth, *South of Appomattox* (New York, 1959), 304.

39. Juvenis, "Last of the Confederacy." The most balanced analysis of Davis as a war leader is Escott, *After Secession*, 256-74, esp. 273–74.

40. Rollin G. Osterweis, *The Myth of the Lost Cause, 1865–1900* (Hamden, Conn., 1973), 11; Edward A. Pollard, *The Lost Cause: A New Southern History of the War of the Confederates* (New York, 1866), 750; Thomas L. Connelly and Barbara L. Bellows, *God and General Longstreet: The Lost Cause and the Southern Mind* (Baton Rouge, 1982), 1–2. See also Lawrence Goodwyn, "Hierarchy and Democracy: The Paradox of the Southern Experience," in *From the Old South to the New: Essays on the Transitional South*, ed. Walter J. Fraser, Jr., and Winfred B. Moore, Jr. (Westport, Conn., 1981), 235.

41. Charles Reagan Wilson, *Baptized in Blood: the Religion of the Lost Cause, 1865–1920* (Athens, 1980), 57, 77, 98–99; Osterweis, *Myth of Lost Cause*, ix, 143, 152.

42. Wilson, *Baptized in Blood*, 1, 13, 26; Connelly and Bellows, *God and General Longstreet*, 5; Osterweis, *Myth of the Lost Cause*, x.

43. William W. White, *The Confederate Veteran* (Tuscaloosa, 1962), *passim;* Osterweis, *Myth of the Lost Cause*, 43.

44. Connelly and Bellows, *God and General Longstreet*, 5.

45. Rowland, *Jefferson Davis*, 7:261, 529, 8:51–52, 211, 9:336, and see 8:240, 9:404, 430.

46. Albert Taylor Bledsoe, *Is Davis a Traitor, or Was Secession a Constitutional Right Previous to the War of 1861?* (Baltimore, 1866), v; "Lamar's Defense of Jefferson Davis," *Confederate Veteran* 29 (April 1921):125–26; Rowland, *Jefferson Davis*, 8:366.

47. Jefferson Davis, *Rise and Fall*, 2:564, 627.

48. Rowland, *Jefferson Davis*, 9:474–90, 492–95.

49. Ibid., 9:29.

50. Ibid., 8:229; Jefferson Davis, *Rise and Fall*, 1:v.

51. Rowland, *Jefferson Davis*, 9:280, 403.

52. Ibid., 436; New York *Tribune*, quoted in Raymond B. Nixon, *Henry W. Grady: Spokesman of the New South* (New York, 1943), 230. The Davis tour is discussed in Michael B. Ballard, "Cheers for Jefferson Davis," *American History Illustrated* 16 (May 1981):8–15.

53. Rowland, *Jefferson Davis*, 9:443–44.

54. J. William Jones, *Davis Memorial Volume*, 480, 378, 394, 523–25, 606, 639. On Jones and the Lost Cause see Wilson, *Baptized in Blood*, 119–38.

55. J. William Jones, *Davis Memorial Volume*, 478.

56. Ibid., 514; Wilson, *Baptized in Blood*, 19, 51; "The Jefferson Davis Monument," *Confederate Veteran* 15 (May 1907):198.

Bibliography

PRIMARY SOURCES

Manuscript Collections

University of Alabama, W. S. Hoole Special Collections Library
    Davis, Jefferson. Papers.
Dallas Historical Society
    Reagan-Davis. Papers.
Duke University, Manuscript Department, William R. Perkins Library
    Beauregard, Pierre Gustave Toutant. Papers.
    Calhoun, William Patrick. Papers.
    Clay, Clement Claiborne. Papers.
    Davis, Jefferson. Papers.
    Hedrick, Benjamin Sherwood. Papers.
    Holmes, Theophilus Hunter. Papers.
    Munford-Ellis Family. Papers.
    Nixon, Thomas. Papers.
Emory University, Special Collections Department, Robert W. Woodruff Library
    Davis, Jefferson. Papers.
Library of Congress, Manuscript Division
    Campbell, Given. Journal.
    Harrison, Burton Norval, Family. Papers.
Louisiana State University, Troy Middleton Library
    Hunter, R. M. T. Papers. Microfilm edition. 13 reels. Originals at the University of Virginia.
Miami University, Walter Havighurst Special Collections, Miami University Library, Oxford, Ohio
    Richey, Samuel. Collection.
Museum of the Confederacy, Manuscript Collections, Richmond, Virginia
    Davis, Jefferson. Papers.
    Potts, Frank. Letter.
    Sublett, Emmie. Letter.
University of North Carolina at Chapel Hill, Southern Historical

Collection
Campbell and Colston Family. Papers.
Hathaway, Leeland. Recollections.
Mallory, Stephen Russell. Papers and Diaries.
Mayo, Peter Helms. Recollections.
Miles, William Porcher. Papers.
Stamps, Mary. Papers.
Tilghman, Tench. Diary.
Wellford, B. R. Diary. In White, Wellford, Taliaferro, and Marshall Family Papers.
Wood, John Taylor. Papers and Diary.
North Carolina Division of Archives and History, Raleigh
Vance, Zebulon. Papers.
University of South Carolina, South Caroliniana Library
Trenholm, Anna. Diary. In George A. Trenholm Papers.
Transylvania University Library
Hayes-Davis, Jefferson. Papers.
Tufts University Archives
Ryder Collection of Confederate Archives.
Tulane University, Special Collections Department, Howard-Tilton Memorial Library
Davis, Jefferson. Papers.

Newspapers and Periodicals

Charleston *Daily Courier,* 1865.
Chicago *Tribune,* 1865.
Danville *Register,* 1865, 1965.
Greensboro (N.C.) *Patriot,* 1865.
Harper's Weekly Illustrated Magazine, 1865.
Jackson (Miss.) *Daily Clarion,* 1865.
Louisville (Ky.) *Journal,* 1865.
Lynchburg *Daily Virginian,* 1865.
Macon (Ga.) *Daily Telegraph,* 1865.
Macon *Southern Confederacy,* 1865.
Mobile *Register and Advertiser,* 1865.
New Orleans *Daily Picayune,* 1865.
New York *Herald,* 1865.
New York *Times,* 1865.
New York *Tribune,* 1865.
Richmond *Whig,* 1865.

Books

Anderson, John Q., ed. *Brokenburn: The Journal of Kate Stone, 1861–1868*. Baton Rouge, 1955.

Andrews, Eliza Frances. *The War-time Journal of a Georgia Girl, 1864–1865*. Edited by Spencer Bidwell King, Jr. Macon, 1960.

Avary, Myrta Lockett, ed. *Recollections of Alexander H. Stephens: His Diary Kept When a Prisoner at Fort Warren, Boston Harbour, 1865*. New York, 1910.

Basler, Roy P., ed. *The Collected Works of Abraham Lincoln*. 8 vols. New Brunswick, N.J., 1959.

Bergh, Albert Ellery, ed. *The Writings of Thomas Jefferson*. 20 vols. in 10. Washington, D.C., 1907.

Campbell, John A. *Recollections of the Evacuation of Richmond, April 2d, 1865*. Baltimore, 1880.

———.*Reminiscences and Documents Relating to the Civil War during the Year 1865*. Baltimore, 1887.

[Clay, Virginia.]*A Belle of the Fifties: Memoirs of Mrs. Clay, of Alabama, Covering Social and Political Life in Washington and the South, 1853–1866*. New York, 1905.

Coffin, Charles Carleton. *The Boys of '61; or, Four Years of Fighting*. Boston, 1886.

Craven, John J. *Prison Life of Jefferson Davis*. New York, 1866.

Davis, Jefferson. *The Rise and Fall of the Confederate Government*. 2 vols. New York, 1881.

Davis, Varina. *Jefferson Davis, Ex-president of the Confederate States of America: A Memoir by His Wife*. 2 vols. New York, 1890.

Dowd, Clement. *Life of Zebulon B. Vance*. Charlotte, 1897.

Dowdy, Clifford and Louis H. Manarin, eds., *The Wartime Papers of R. E. Lee*. Boston, 1961.

Du Bellet, Paul Perquet. *The Diplomacy of the Confederate Cabinet of Richmond and Its Agents Abroad: Being Memorandum Notes Taken during the Rebellion of the Southern States from 1861 to 1865*. Edited by William Stanley Hoole. Tuscaloosa, 1963.

Duke, Basil W. *Reminiscences of General Basil W. Duke, C.S.A.* Garden City, N.Y., 1911.

Durkin, Joseph T., ed. *John Dooley, Confederate Soldier: His War Journal*. Washington, D.C., 1945.

Freeman, Douglas Southall, ed. *A Calendar of Confederate papers*. New York, 1969.

———, ed. *Lee's Dispatches: Unpublished Letters of General Robert E. Lee, C.S.A., to Jefferson Davis and the War Department of the Confederate States of America, 1862–65*. New York, 1957.

Gordon, John B. *Reminiscences of the Civil War.* New York, 1903.

Harrison, Mrs. Burton. *Recollections Grave and Gay.* New York, 1911.

Harrison, Fairfax, ed. *The Harrisons of Skimino.* Privately published, 1910.

Headley, John W. *Confederate Operations in Canada and New York.* New York, 1906.

Henderson, Dwight Franklin, ed. *The Private Journal of Georgiana Gholson Walker, 1862–1865, with Selections from the Post-war Years.* Tuscaloosa, 1963.

Howard, McHenry. *Recollections of a Maryland Confederate Soldier and Staff Officer under Johnston, Jackson, and Lee.* Dayton, Ohio, 1975.

Johnston, Joseph E. *Narrative of Military Operations, Directed, during the Late War between the States.* New York, 1874.

Jones, J. B. *A Rebel War Clerk's Diary at the Confederate States Capital.* Edited by Howard Swiggett. 2 vols. New York, 1935.

Jones, J. William. *The Davis Memorial Volume; or, Our Dead President, Jefferson Davis, and the World's Tribute to His Memory.* Atlanta, 1890.

———.*Life and Letters of Robert Edward Lee: Soldier and Man.* New York, 1906.

Jones, Katharine M., ed. *Ladies of Richmond, Confederate Capital.* Indianapolis, 1962.

Journal of the Congress of the Confederate States of America, 1861–1865. 7 vols. Washington, D.C., 1094–5.

Kirk, Charles H., ed. *History of the Fifteenth Pennsylvania Volunteer Cavalry, Which was Recruited and Known as the Anderson Cavalry in the Rebellion of 1861–1865.* Philadelphia, 1906.

Lee. Robert E., [Jr.]. *Recollections and Letters of General Robert E. Lee.* New York, 1904.

Life and Reminiscences of Jefferson Davis by Distinguished Men of His Time. Baltimore, 1890.

Long, A. L. *Memoirs of Robert E. Lee.* New York, 1886.

Longstreet, James. *From Manassas to Appomattox: Memoirs of the Civil War in America.* Edited by James I. Robertson, Jr. Bloomington, Ind. 1960.

Lubbock, Francis Richard. *Six Decades in Texas; or, Memoirs of Francis Richard Lubbock.* Austin, 1900.

McDonald, Cornelia. *A Diary, with Reminiscences of the War and Refugee Life in the Shenandoah Valley, 1860–1865.* Nashville, 1934.

McGuire, Judith W. *Diary of a Southern Refugee during the War.* New York, 1972.

Marszalek, John F., ed. *The Diary of Miss Emma Holmes, 1861–1866*. Baton Rouge, 1979.

Memorials of the Life, Public Services, and Character of William T. Sutherlin. Danville, 1894.

Morgan, James Morris. *Recollections of a Rebel Reefer*. London, 1917.

Official Records of the Union and Confederate Navies in the War of the Rebellion. 30 vols. Washington, D.C., 1894–1922.

Parker, William Harwar. *The Recollections of a Naval Officer, 1841–1865*. New York, 1883.

Pember, Phoebe Yates. *A Southern Woman's Story: Life in Confederate Richmond*. Edited by Bell Irvin Wiley. Jackson, Tenn. 1959.

Pollard, Edward A. *Life of Jefferson Davis, with a Secret History of the Confederacy*. Philadelphia, 1869.

———.*The Lost Cause: A New Southern History of the War of the Confederacy*. New York, 1866.

Pryor, Mrs. Roger A. *Reminiscences of Peace and War*. New York, 1904.

Ramsdell, Charles W., ed. *Laws and Joint Resolutions of the Last Session of the Confederate Congress (November 7, 1864–March 18, 1865), Together with the Secret Acts of Previous Congresses*. Durham, 1941.

Reagan, John H. *Memoirs, with Special Reference to Secession and the Civil War*. Austin, 1968.

Richardson, James D., ed. *The Messages and Papers of Jefferson Davis and the Confederacy, Including Diplomatic Correspondence, 1861–1865*. 2 vols. New York, 1966.

Roman, Alfred. *The Military Operations of General Beauregard in the War between the States, 1861 to 1865*. 2 vols. New York, 1883.

Rowland, Dunbar, ed. *Jefferson Davis, Constitutionalist: His Letters, Papers, and Speeches*. 10 vols. Jackson, Miss., 1923.

Semmes, Raphael. *Memoirs of Service Afloat, during the War between the States*. Baltimore, 1869.

Sherman, William T. *Memoirs of William T. Sherman, Written by Himself*. 2 vols. in 1. New York, 1891.

Smith, Daniel E. Huger, et al., eds. *Mason Smith Family Letters, 1860–1868*. Columbia, S.C., 1950.

Stephens, Alexander H. *A Constitutional View of the Late War Between the States*. 2 vols. Philadelphia, 1870.

Strode, Hudson, ed. *Jefferson Davis: Private Letters, 1823–1889*. New York, 1966.

Summers, Festus P., ed. *A Borderland Confederate*. Westport, Conn., 1973.

Vandiver, Frank E., ed. *The Civil War Diary of General Josiah Gorgas*. University, Ala., 1947.

War of the Rebellion: A Compilation of the Official Records of the Union and Confederate Armies. 128 vols. Washington, D.C., 1880–1901.

Welles, Gideon. *Diary of Gideon Welles.* 2 vols. Boston, 1911.

Wiley, Bell Irvin, ed. *Letters of Warren Akin, Confederate Congressman.* Athens, 1959.

Williams, Max R., and J. G. de Roulhac Hamilton, eds. *The Papers of William Alexander Graham.* 7 vols. Raleigh, 1957–85.

Wilson, James Harrison. *Under the Old Flag: Recollections of Military Operations in the War for the Union, the Spanish War, the Boxer Rebellion, etc.* 2 vols. New York, 1912.

Wise, John S. *The End of an Era.* Boston, 1900.

Withers, Robert Enoch. *Autobiography of an Octogenarian.* Roanoke, 1907.

Woodward, C. Vann, ed. *Mary Chesnut's Civil War.* New Haven, Conn., 1981.

Younger, Edward, ed. *Inside the Confederate Government: The Diary of Robert Garlick Hill Kean, Head of the Bureau of War.* New York, 1957.

Articles

Abbott, Martin, ed. "A Southerner Views the South, 1865: Letters of Harvey M. Watterson." *Virginia Magazine of History and Biography* 68 (Oct. 1960): 478–89.

"Atchison's Father." Atchison *Daily Globe* clippings, July 16, 1894. Kansas State Historical Society, Topeka.

Averill, J. H. "Richmond Virginia: The Evacuation of the City and the Days Preceding It." *Southern Historical Society Papers*, 25 (1897): 267–73.

Bean, W. G., ed. "Memoranda of Conversations between General Robert E. Lee and William Preston Johnston, May 7, 1868, and March 18, 1870." *Virginia Magazine of History and Biography* 73 (Oct. 1965): 474–84.

Boom, Aaron M., ed. " 'We Sowed & We Have Reaped': A Postwar Letter from Braxton Bragg." *Journal of Southern History* 31 (Feb. 1965): 75–79.

Booth, R. V. "Last Address of President Davis, C.S.A." *Confederate Veteran* 22 (July 1914): 304.

Bradwell, I. G. "Making Our Way Home From Appomattox." *Confederate Veteran* 29 (March 1921): 102–3.

Bringhurst, W. R. "Survivor of President Davis's Escort." *Confederate Veteran* 34 (Oct. 1926): 368–69.

Brown, William LeRoy. "The Red Artillery: Confederate Ordnance during the War." *Southern Historical Society Papers* 26 (1898): 365–76.

Bruce, H. W. "Some Reminiscences of the Second of April, 1865." *Southern Historical Society Papers* 9 (May 1881): 206–11.

Campbell, John A. "Evacuation Echoes." *Southern Historical Society Papers* 24 (1896): 351–53.

Clark, Micajah H. "The Last Days of the Confederate Treasury and What Became of Its Specie." *Southern Historical Society Papers* 9 (December, 1881): 542–56.

————. "Retreat of Cabinet from Richmond." *Confederate Veteran* 6 (July 1898): 293–94.

————. "Retreat of the Cabinet." *Southern Historical Society Papers* 26 (1898): 96–101.

Colyar, A. S. "When Gen. Lee Lost Hope of Success." *Confederate Veteran* 1 (Nov. 1893): 324–25.

"Confederate Gold." *Southern Historical Society Papers* 39 (April 1914): 23–30.

Cox, Jacob D. "The Surrender of Johnston's Army and the Closing Scenes of the War in North Carolina." In *Sketches of War History, 1861–1865: Papers Read before the Ohio Commandery of the Military Order of the Loyal Legion of the United States, 1886–1888*, edited by Robert Hunter. Cincinnati, 1888, 2:247–76.

Davis, Jefferson. "Autobiography of Jefferson Davis." *Confederate Veteran* 15 (May 1907): 217–22.

————. "The Peace Commission—Letter from Ex-President Davis." *Southern Historical Society Papers* 4 (Nov. 1877): 208–12.

"Dr. Stringfellow Dead." Atchison *Daily Globe*, 24 July 1905. In Kansas Scrapbook, Biography, vol. 162, Kansas State Historical Society, Topeka.

Duke, Basil W. "Last Days of the Confederacy." In *Battles and Leaders of the Civil War*, edited by Robert U. Johnson and Clarence C. Buel. New York, 1956, 4:762–66.

"Evacuation of Richmond." *Southern Historical Society Papers* 13 (1885): 247–59.

Ewell, R. S. "Evacuation of Richmond," *Southern Historical Society Papers* 13 (1885): 247–49.

An Eyewitness. "The Capture of President Jefferson Davis." *Register of the Kentucky Historical Society* 64 (Oct. 1966): 270–76.

Ferguson, S. W. "Escort to President Davis." *Confederate Veteran* 16 (June, 1908): 263–64.

Fiveash, Joseph G. "When Mr. Davis Heard of Lincoln's Death." *Confederate Veteran* 15 (Aug. 1907): 366.

Gilliam, Robert. "Last of the Confederate Treasury Department." *Confederate Veteran* 37 (Nov. 1929): 423–25.

Goode, John. "The Peace Conference in Hampton Roads." *Southern Historical Society Papers* 29 (1901): 177–93.

Hampton, Wade. "An Effort to Rescue Jefferson Davis." *Southern Historical Society Papers* 27 (1899): 132–36.

Hanna, A. J. "The Confederate Baggage and Treasure Train Ends Its Flight in Florida: A Diary of Tench Francis Tilghman." *Florida Historical Quarterly* 17 (Jan. 1939): 159–80.

Harris, John W. "Confederate Naval Cadets." *Confederate Veteran* 12 (April 1904): 170–71.

———. "The Gold of the Confederate States Treasure." *Southern Historical Society Papers*, 32 (1904): 157–63.

Harrison, Burton N. "The Capture of Jefferson Davis." *Century Magazine* 27 (Nov. 1883): 130–45.

Haw, Joseph R. "The Last of the C.S. Ordnance Department." *Confederate Veteran* 34 (Dec. 1926): 450–52, 35 (Jan. 1927): 15–16.

Hoole, W. Stanley, ed. "Admiral on Horseback: The Diary of Brigadier General Raphael Semmes, February–May 1865." *Alabama Review* 28 (April 1975): 129–50.

Hunter, R. M. T. "The Peace Commission of 1865." *Southern Historical Society Papers* 3 (April 1877): 168–76.

Johnson, Bradley T. "The Peace Conference in Hampton Roads, January 31, 1865." *Southern Historical Society Papers* 27 (1899): 374–77.

Jones, James P., ed. " 'Your Left Arm': James H. Wilson's Letters to Adam Badeau." *Civil War History* 12 (Sept. 1966): 230–45.

Juvenis [pseud.]. "The Last of the Confederacy." New York *Times*, 7 Jan. 1866.

Knobel, Casper. "The Capture of President Davis." *Confederate Veteran* 19 (May 1911): 224–25.

"The Last Days of the Confederate Government." *Illustrated London News*, 22 July 1865, 70.

"Last Days of the Southern Confederacy." *Southern Historical Society Papers* 19 (1891): 329–33.

"Last Letters and Telegrams of the Confederacy—Correspondence of General John C. Breckinridge." *Southern Historical Society Papers* 12 (March, 1884): 97–105.

Leyburn, John. "The Fall of Richmond." *Harper's New Monthly Magazine* 33 (June 1866): 92–96.

McAllister, L. C. "Disbanding President Davis's Escort." *Confederate Veteran* 13 (Jan. 1905): 25.

Mallory, Stephen R. "Last Days of the Confederate Government." *McClure's Magazine* 16 (Dec. 1900): 99–107, 239–48.

Mason, Frank H. "Stoneman's Last Campaign, and the Pursuit of Jefferson Davis." In *Sketches of War History, 1861–1865: Papers Prepared for the Ohio Commandery of the Military Order of the Loyal Legion of the United States, 1888–1890,* edited by Robert Hunter. Cincinnati, 1890. 3:21–43.

Mullen, James M. "Last Days of Johnston's Army." *Southern Historical Society Papers* 18 (1890): 97–113.

Overly, Milford. "Escort to President Davis." *Confederate Veteran* 16 (March 1908): 121–23.

Packard, Joseph. "Ordnance Matters at the Close." *Confederate Veteran* 16 (May 1908): 227–29.

"Papers of Convention between Sherman and Johnston." *Southern Historical Society Papers* 39 (April 1914): 45–53.

"Papers of Hon. John A. Campbell, 1861–1865." *Southern Historical Society Papers* 42 (Oct. 1917): 3–81.

Parker, William H. "The Gold and Silver in the Confederate States Treasury." *Southern Historical Society Papers* 21 (1893): 304–13.

"Petition for Mr. Davis' Release." *Southern Historical Society Papers* 24 (1896): 240–42.

Pickett, Mrs. George E. "Words from Jefferson Davis." *Confederate Veteran* 21 (March 1913): 108.

Polignac, C. J. "Polignac's Mission." *Southern Historical Society Papers* 35 (1907): 326–34.

"President Davis in Concord." Charlotte *Daily Observer,* 3 Feb. 1901.

"Resources of the Confederacy in February 1865." *Southern Historical Society Papers* 2 (July, Aug., Sept. 1876): 56–63, 85–105, 113–28.

"Resources of the Confederacy in 1865—Report of General I. M. St. John, Commissary General." *Southern Historical Society Papers* 3 (March 1877): 97–111.

Robertson, Mrs. M. E. "President Davis's Last Official Meeting." *Southern History Association Publications* 5 (July 1901): 291–99.

Russell, D. H. "Last Issue of Confederate Money." *Confederate Veteran* 22 (March 1914): 131.

Shepherd, Lewis. "The Confederate Treasure Train." *Confederate Veteran* 25 (June 1917): 257–59.

[Stuart, C. E. L.] "Davis' Flight." New York *Herald,* 4 July 1865.

Swallow, W. H. "Retreat of the Confederate Government from Richmond to the Gulf." *Magazine of American History* 15 (June 1886): 596–608.

Taylor, Richard. "The Last Confederate Surrender." In *The Confederate Soldier in the Civil War*, edited by Benjamin LaBree. Louisville. 1897, 318.

"Terms of Capitulation of the Command of Lieutenant-General Richard Taylor." *Southern Historical Society Papers* 16 (1888): 215–18.

Terry, F. G. "Last Official Escort of President Davis." *Confederate Veteran* 17 (Jan. 1909): 10.

Townsend, Harry C. "Townsend's Diary—January–May 1865." *Southern Historical Society Papers* 34 (1906): 99–127.

Tucker, Dallas. "The Fall of Richmond." *Southern Historical Society Papers* 29 (1901): 152–63.

Walmsley, James Elliot, ed. "Some Unpublished Letters of Burton N. Harrison." *Publications of Mississippi Historical Society* 8 (1904): 81–85.

Walthall, W. T., ed., "The True Story of the Capture of Jefferson Davis." *Southern Historical Society Papers* 5 (March 1878): 97–126.

Wellford, B. R. "Mr. Goode Sustained as to the Historic Hampton Roads Conference." Richmond *Dispatch*, 18 May 1902.

Wheeler, Joseph. "An Effort to Rescue Jefferson Davis." *Century Magazine* 56 (May 1898): 85–91.

Wheless, John F. "The Confederate Treasure—Statement of Paymaster John F. Wheless." *Southern Historical Society Papers* 10 (March 1882): 137–41.

Wight, Willard E., ed. "Some Letters of Lucius Bellinger Northrop, 1860–1865." *Virginia Magazine of History and Biography* 68 (Oct. 1960): 456–77.

SECONDARY SOURCES

Books

Andrews, J. Cutler. *The South Reports the Civil War*. Princeton, 1970.

Arnett, Ethel Stephens. *Greensboro, North Carolina: The County Seat of Guilford*. Chapel Hill, 1955.

Avery, I. W. *The History of the State of Georgia from 1850 to 1881*. New York, 1881, 1972.

Barrett, John G. *The Civil War in North Carolina*. Chapel Hill, 1963.

Bettersworth, John K. *Confederate Mississippi: The People and Policies of a Cotton State in Wartime*. Baton Rouge, 1943.

Bill, Alfred Hoyt. *The Beleaguered City: Richmond, 1861–1865.* New York, 1946.

Black, Robert C., III. *The Railroads of the Confederacy.* Chapel Hill, 1952.

Bledsoe, Albert Taylor. *Is Davis a Traitor, or Was Secession a Constitutional Right Previous to the War of 1861?* Baltimore, 1866.

Blythe, LeGette, and Charles Raven Brockmann. *Hornets' Nest: The Story of Charlotte and Mecklenburg County.* Charlotte, 1961.

Boynton, H. V. *Sherman's Historical Raid: The Memoirs in the Light of the Record.* Cincinnati, 1875.

Brubaker, John H., III. *The Last Capital: Danville, Virginia, and the Final Days of the Confederacy.* Danville, 1979.

Bryan, T. Conn. *Confederate Georgia.* Athens, 1953.

Buck, Paul H. *The Road to Reunion.* Boston, 1937.

Burger, Nash K., and John K. Bettersworth. *South of Appomattox.* New York, 1959.

Catton, Bruce. *The Centennial History of the Civil War,* vol. 3: *Never Call Retreat.* Garden City, N.Y., 1965.

Cauthen, Charles Edward. *South Carolina Goes to War, 1860–1865.* Chapel Hill, 1950.

Clark, James C. *Last Train South: The Flight of the Confederate Government from Richmond.* Jefferson, N.C., 1984.

Connelly, Thomas Lawrence. *Autumn of Glory: The Army of Tennessee, 1862–1865.* Baton Rouge, 1971.

———. *The Marble Man: Robert E. Lee and His Image in American Society.* Baton Rouge, 1977.

Connelly, Thomas, and Barbara L. Bellows. *God and General Longstreet: The Lost Cause and the Southern Mind.* Baton Rouge, 1982.

Conway, Alan. *The Reconstruction of Georgia.* Minneapolis, 1966.

Crook, D. P. *The North, the South, and the Powers, 1861–1865.* New York, 1974.

Davis, Burke. *The Long Surrender.* New York, 1985.

Davis, William C. *Breckinridge: Statesman, Soldier, Symbol.* Baton Rouge, 1974.

DeLeon, T. C. *Belles, Beaux, and Brains of the 60s.* New York, 1909.

Durden, Robert F. *The Gray and the Black: The Confederate Debate on Emancipation.* Baton Rouge, 1972.

Durkin, Joseph T. *Stephen R. Mallory: Confederate Navy Chief.* Chapel Hill, 1954.

Eaton, Clement. *Jefferson Davis.* New York, 1977.

Escott, Paul D. *After Secession: Jefferson Davis and the Failure of Confederate Nationalism.* Baton Rouge, 1978.

Evans, W. McKee. *Ballots and Fence Rails: Reconstruction on the Lower Cape Fear.* Chapel Hill, 1966–67.

Fischer, Roger A. *The Segregation Struggle in Louisiana, 1862–1867*. Urbana, 1974.

Fleming, Walter L. *Civil War and Reconstruction in Alabama*. New York, 1905.

Flood, Charles Bracelen. *Lee: The Last Years*. Boston, 1981.

Freeman, Douglas Southall. *Lee's Lieutenants: A Study in Command*. 3 vols. New York, 1942–44.

Hanna, A. J. *Flight into Oblivion*. Richmond, 1938.

Hattaway, Herman, and Archer Jones. *How the North Won: A Military History of the Civil War*. Urbana, 1983.

Hendrick, Burton J. *Statesmen of the Lost Cause: Jefferson Davis and His Cabinet*. New York, 1939.

Hoeling, A. A., and Mary Hoeling. *The Day Richmond Died*. San Diego, 1981.

Hoge, Peyton Harrison. *Moses Drury Hoge: Life and Letters*. Richmond, 1899.

Hoole, W. Stanley. *Vizetelly Covers the Confederacy*. Tuscaloosa, 1957.

Hughes, Nathaniel Cheairs, Jr. *General William J. Hardee: Old Reliable*. Baton Rouge, 1965.

Humphreys, Andrew A. *The Virginia Campaign of '64 and '65: The Army of the Potomac and the Army of the James*. New York, 1937.

Johns, John E. *Florida during the Civil War*. Gainesville, 1963.

Jones, James Pickett. *Yankee Blitzkrieg: Wilson's Raid Through Alabama and Georgia*. Athens, 1976.

Jones, Virgil Carrington. *The Civil War at Sea*. 3 vols. New York, 1960–62.

Kerby, Robert L. *Kirby Smith's Confederacy: The Trans-Mississippi South, 1863–1865*. New York, 1972.

Long, E. B. *The Civil War Day by Day: An Almanac, 1861–1865*. Garden City, N.Y., 1971.

Lonn, Ella. *Desertion during the Civil War*. Gloucester, Mass., 1928.

McElroy, Robert. *Jefferson Davis: The Unreal and the Real*. 2 vols. New York, 1937.

Meade, Robert Douthat. *Judah P. Benjamin: Confederate Statesman*. New York, 1943.

Nelson, Larry E. *Bullets, Ballots, and Rhetoric: Confederate Policy for the United States Presidential Contest of 1864*. University, Ala., 1980.

Nixon, Raymond B. *Henry W. Grady: Spokesman of the New South*. New York, 1943.

Noll, Arthur Howard. *General Kirby Smith*. Sewanee, Tenn., 1907.

Osterweis, Rollin G. *The Myth of the Lost Cause, 1865–1900*. Hamden, Conn., 1973.

Owsley, Frank Lawrence. *State Rights in the Confederacy.* Chicago, 1925.

Parks, Joseph H. *General Edmund Kirby Smith, C.S.A.* Baton Rouge, 1954.

———. *Joseph E. Brown of Georgia.* Baton Rouge, 1977.

Patrick, Rembert W. *The Fall of Richmond.* Baton Rouge, 1960.

———. *Jefferson Davis and His Cabinet.* Baton Rouge, 1944.

Patton, James Welch. *Unionism and Reconstruction in Tennessee, 1860–1869.* Chapel Hill, 1934.

Pollock, Edward. *Illustrated Sketchbook of Danville, Virginia.* Danville, 1885.

Romine, Dannye, *Mecklenburg: A Bicentennial Story.* Charlotte, 1975.

Rywell, Martin. *Judah Benjamin: Unsung Rebel Prince.* Asheville, NC., 1948.

Seitz, Don C. *Braxton Bragg: General of the Confederacy.* Columbia, S.C., 1924.

Shaw, Arthur Marvin. *William Preston Johnston: A Transitional Figure of the Confederacy.* Baton Rouge, 1943.

Shingleton, Royce Gordon. *John Taylor Wood: Sea Ghost of the Confederacy.* Athens, 1979.

Simpkins, Francis B., and Robert H. Woody. *South Carolina during Reconstruction.* Chapel Hill, 1932.

Soley, James Russell. *The Blockade and the Cruisers.* New York, 1883.

Spencer, Cornelia Phillips. *The Last Ninety Days of the War in North Carolina.* New York, 1866.

Stern, Philip Van Doren. *An End to Valor: The Last Days of the Civil War.* Boston, 1958.

Strode, Hudson. *Jefferson Davis: Tragic Hero, 1864–1889.* New York, 1964.

Thomas, Emory M. *The Confederacy as a Revolutionary Experience.* Englewood Cliffs, N.J., 1971.

———. *The Confederate Nation, 1861–1865.* New York, 1979.

———. *The Confederate State of Richmond: A Biography of the Capital.* Austin, 1971.

Todd, Richard Cecil. *Confederate Finance.* Athens, 1954.

Tompkins, D. A. *History of Mecklenburg County and the City of Charlotte from 1740 to 1903.* 2 vols. Charlotte, 1903.

Tucker, Glenn. *Zeb Vance: Champion of Personal Freedom.* Indianapolis, 1965.

Vandiver, Frank E. *Ploughshares into Swords: Josiah Gorgas and Confederate Ordnance.* Austin, 1952.

Wakelyn, Jon L. *Biographical Dictionary of the Confederacy.* Westport, Connecticut, 1977.

Warner, Ezra J. *Generals in Gray: Lives of the Confederate Commanders*. Baton Rouge, 1959.

Weaver, Richard. *The Southern Tradition at Bay: A History of Post-bellum Thought*. Edited by George Core and M. E. Bradford. New Rochelle, N.Y., 1968.

Weddell, Elizabeth Wright. *St. Paul's Church, Richmond, Virginia: Its Historic Years and Memorials*. 2 vols. Richmond, 1931.

White, William W. *The Confederate Veteran*. Tuscaloosa, 1962.

Williams, T. Harry. *P. G. T. Beauregard: Napoleon in Gray*. Baton Rouge, 1955.

Wilson, Charles Reagan. *Baptized in Blood: The Religion of the Lost Cause, 1865–1920*. Athens, 1980.

Winters, John D. *The Civil War in Louisiana*. Baton Rouge, 1963.

Woodward, C. Vann. *Origins of the New South, 1817–1913*. Baton Rouge, 1971.

Yates, Richard E. *The Confederacy and Zeb Vance*. Tuscaloosa, 1958.

Yearns, Wilfred Buck. *The Confederate Congress*. Athens, 1960.

Yearns, Wilfred Buck, and John G. Barrett, eds. *North Carolina: Civil War Documentary*. Chapel Hill, 1980.

Articles

Alexander, Violet G., comp. "The Confederate States Navy Yard at Charlotte, N.C., 1862–1865." *Southern Historical Society Papers* 40 (Sept. 1915): 183–94.

Anderson, Mrs. John H. "The Confederate Cabinet." *Confederate Veteran* 37 (May 1931): 178–83.

Ashmore, Otis. "The Story of the Confederate Treasury." *Georgia Historical Quarterly* 2 (Sept. 1918): 119–38.

———. "The Story of the Virginia Banks Funds." *Georgia Historical Quarterly* 2 (Dec. 1918): 171–97.

Aull, John K. "Jefferson Davis Met Cabinet at White's Mansion in Fort Mill." Columbia, S.C. *The State* 27 Sept. 1931.

———. "Journey of Mrs. Jefferson Davis across South Carolina Retraced." Columbia, S.C. *The State*, 13 Sept. 1931.

Ballard, Michael B. "Cheers for Jefferson Davis." *American History Illustrated* 16 (May 1981): 8–15.

Barbee, David Rankin. "Dr. Craven's 'Prison Life of Jefferson Davis'—an Exposé," *Tyler's Quarterly Magazine*, 32 (April 1951): 282–95.

Bobbitt, B. Boisseau. "Last Hours of the Confederacy Here." Danville *Register*, 13 April 1919.

———. "Our Last Capital: Danville's Part in the Closing Hours of the Confederacy." *Southern Historical Society Papers* 31 (1903): 334–39.

Bradley, Chester D. "Dr. Craven and the Prison Life of Jefferson Davis." *Virginia Magazine of History and Biography* 62 (Jan. 1954): 50–94.

———. "Was Jefferson Davis Disguised as a Woman When Captured?" *Journal of Mississippi History* 36 (Aug. 1974): 243–68.

Brumgardt, John R. "Alexander H. Stephens and the State Convention Movement in Georgia: A Reappraisal." *Georgia Historical Quarterly* 59 (Spring 1975): 38–49.

Callahan, J. Morton. "The Confederate Diplomatic Archives—the 'Picket Papers,'" *South Atlantic Quarterly* 2 (Jan. 1903): 1–9.

Davis, Nora Marshall. "Jefferson Davis's Route from Richmond, Virginia, to Irwinville, Georgia, April 2–May 10, 1865." *The Proceedings of the South Carolina Historical Association* (1941), 11–20. Copy in Monroe Fulkerson Cockrell Papers, Manuscript Department, William R. Perkins Library, Duke University.

Escott, Paul D. "Joseph E. Brown, Jefferson Davis, and the Problem of Poverty in the Confederacy." *Georgia Historical Quarterly* 61 (Spring 1977): 59–71.

Fore, Mrs. James A. "Cabinet Meeting in Charlotte." *Southern Historical Society Papers* 41 (Sept. 1916): 61–67.

———. "Cabinet Meeting Was Held Here," Charlotte *Daily Observer*, 26 April 1915.

Goodwyn, Lawrence. "Hierarchy and Democracy: The Paradox of the Southern Experience." In *From the Old South to the New: Essays in the Transitional South*, edited by Walter J. Fraser, Jr., and Winfred B. Moore, Jr. Westport, Conn., 1981.

Gorham, George C. "General Johnston's Surrender." *Southern Historical Society Papers* 20 (1892), 205–12.

Hall, James O. "The Dahlgren Papers: A Yankee Plot to Kill President Davis." *Civil War Times Illustrated* 22 (Nov. 1983): 30–39.

Hanchett, William. "Reconstruction and Rehabilitation of Jefferson Davis: Charles G. Halpine's *Prison Life*." *Journal of American History* 56 (Sept. 1969), 280–89.

Harris, William C. "Formulation of the First Mississippi Plan: The Black Code of 1865." *Journal of Mississippi History* 29 (May 1967): 181–201.

Holladay, Florence Elizabeth. "The Powers of the Commander of the Confederate Trans-Mississippi Department." *Southwestern Historical Quarterly* 21 (Jan. 1918), 279–98, (April 1918): 333–39.

Irvine, Dallas D. "The Fate of Confederate Archives." *American Historical Review* 44 (July 1939): 823–41.

"The Jefferson Davis Monument." *Confederate Veteran* 15 (May 1907): 198.

Johnson, Ludwell H. "Lincoln's Solution to the Problem of Peace Terms, 1864–1865." *Journal of Southern History* 34 (Nov. 1968), 576–86.

"Lamar's Defense of Jefferson Davis," *Confederate Veteran*, 29 (April, 1921), 125–26.

"Last Capital of the Confederacy at Danville." *Southern Historical Society Papers*, 31 (1903): 80.

Mobley, Joe A. "The Siege of Mobile, August, 1864–April, 1865." *Alabama Historical Quarterly* 38 (Winter 1976): 250–70.

Montgomery, Walter A. "What Became of Seal of Confederate States of America," Richmond *Times-Dispatch*, 15 Oct. 1911.

Moore, John Hammond. "The Rives Peace Resolution—March 1865." *West Virginia History* 26 (April 1965): 153–60.

Nelson, Bernard H. "Confederate Slave Impressment Legislation, 1861–1865." *Journal of Negro History* 31 (Oct. 1946): 392–410.

Nichols, Roy Franklin. "United States vs. Jefferson Davis, 1865–1869." *American Historical Review* 31 (Jan. 1926): 266–84.

Parks, Joseph H. "State Rights in a Crisis: Governor Joseph E. Brown versus President Jefferson Davis." *Journal of Southern History* 32 (Feb. 1966): 3–24.

Pollock, Edward. "President Davis' Stay in Danville." Danville *Register*, 17 May 1914.

"President Davis in Concord." Charlotte *Daily Observer*, 3 Feb. 1901.

Rabun, James Z. "Alexander H. Stephens and Jefferson Davis." *American Historical Review* 58 (Jan. 1953): 290–321.

Raper, Horace W. "William W. Holden and the Peace Movement in North Carolina." *North Carolina Historical Review* 31 (Oct. 1954): 493–516.

Reagan, John H. "The Truth of History." *Southern Historical Society Papers* 25 (1897): 68–77.

Reed, Wallace Putnam. "Last Forlorn Hope of the Confederacy." *Southern Historical Society Papers* 30 (1902): 117–21.

Reid, Bill G. "Confederate Opponents of Arming the Slaves, 1861–1865." *Journal of Mississippi History* 22 (Oct. 1960): 249–70.

Robbins, Peggy. "Jim Limber and the Davises." *Civil War Times Illustrated* 17 (Nov. 1978): 22–27.

Schwab, John Christopher. "Prices in the Confederate States, 1861–1865." *Political Science Quarterly* 14 (June 1899): 281–304.

Sloan, James P. "Jefferson Davis Slept Here—and Here—and Here: An Account of South Carolina's Hospitality to the President of the Confederacy." Columbia, S.C., *State Magazine*, 31 Jan. 1954, 4–5. Copy in the Monroe Fulkerson Cockrell Papers, Manuscript Department, William R. Perkins Library, Duke University.

Sparks, Randy J. "John P. Osterhaut: Yankee, Rebel, Republican." Forthcoming in the *Southwestern Historical Quarterly.*

Stephenson, N. W. "The Question of Arming the Slaves." *American Historical Review* 18 (Jan. 1913): 295–308.

Talmadge, John E. "Peace-Movement Activities in Civil War Georgia." *Georgia Review* 7 (Summer 1953): 190–203.

Trexler, Harrison A. "The Davis Administration and the Richmond Press, 1861–1865." *Journal of Southern History* 16 (May 1950): 177–95.

Van Noppen, Ina W. "The Significance of Stoneman's Last Raid." *North Carolina Historical Review* 38 (Jan. 1961): 1–18 (April 1961): 149–72 (July 1961): 341–61 (Oct. 1961): 500–526.

Walker, Mrs. [?]. "The Federals in Greensboro." Charlotte *Daily Observer,* 27 Jan. 1901.

Walmsley, James Elliott. "The Last Meeting of the Confederate Cabinet." *Mississippi Valley Historical Review* 6 (Dec. 1919): 336–49.

Yates, Richard E. "Zebulon B. Vance as War Governor of North Carolina, 1862–1865." *Journal of Southern History* 3 (Feb. 1937): 43–75.

Yearns, Wilfred B. "The Peace Movement in the Confederate Congress." *Georgia Historical Quarterly* 41 (March 1957): 1–18.

Zingg, Paul J. "John Archibald Campbell and the Hampton Roads Conference: Quixotic Diplomacy, 1865." *Alabama Historical Quarterly* 36 (Spring 1974): 21–34.

Thesis and Dissertations

Ballard, Michael B. "Editorial Opinions of Jefferson Davis during the Civil War." M.A. thesis, Mississippi State University, 1976.

Kaufman, Janet E. "Sentinels on the Watchtower: The Confederate Governors and the Davis Administration." Ph.D. dissertation, American University, 1977.

Robbins, John Brawner. "Confederate Nationalism: Politics and Government in the Confederate South, 1861–1865." Ph.D. dissertation, Rice University, 1964.

Index

Abbeville, GA, 138, 139, 141, 149
Abbeville, SC, 102, 120, 121, 124, 125, 127
Akin, Warren, 16
Anderson, Archer, 84
Army and Navy Journal, 155
Army of Northern Virginia, 8, 59, 70
Army of Tennessee, 6, 85–86

Bailey, Edward, 170
Barksdale, Ethelbert, 12–13
Barnwell (Confederate officer), 143
Barringer, Victor, 98
Bates, Lewis, 100, 101, 102, 163
Beauregard, P. G. T., 6, 8, 9, 60, 61–62, 66, 88, 89, 93, 105, 107, 168; and Greensboro, NC, conferences, 78–82 *passim*
Beauvoir, postwar home of Jefferson Davis, 157
Benedict House, Danville, VA, 55, 65
Benjamin, Judah P., 10, 40, 42, 48, 52–55 *passim*, 60, 65, 67, 68, 78, 80, 82, 88, 95, 100, 104–5, 127, 157; and Hampton Roads Peace Conference, 31n; described, 38–39; and Danville proclamation authorship controversy, 71n; leaves government, 128–29; escape of, 154. *See also* Confederate cabinet; Confederate government.
Bentonville, Battle of, 24
Blair, Francis P., Sr., 18
Bledsoe, Albert Taylor, 168
Booth, John Wilkes, 112, 161
Bragg, Braxton, 28, 49, 107, 120, 122, 123, 131
Breckinridge, John C., 4, 21, 25, 35, 36, 62, 63, 64, 79, 80, 88, 89, 93–98 *passim*, 103–8 *passim*, 111, 118–19, 122–28 *passim*, 131, 134, 173; and Campbell and Rives peace proposals, 22–23; described, 38;

role in Richmond evacuation, 44–46; at Johnston-Sherman conference, 95, 96–97; dissolves War Department, 136; escape of, 154. *See Also* Confederate cabinet; Confederate government.
Breckinridge, W. C. P., 88, 122, 123, 136
Britannia, 154
Brock, Sallie Ann, 34, 37, 44
Brown, Joseph E., 7–8, 9, 17, 120, 134, 173
Brownell, William J., 42
Bruen, C. T., 110
Burt, Armistead, 120, 121, 122

Campbell, Given, 88, 99, 133, 135, 137, 138, 141, 143
Campbell, John A., 3, 18–19, 22, 57–58, 112
Canby, E. R. S., 23
Charleston, SC, *Daily Courier*, 160
Charlotte, NC, 55, 75, 98, 99–100, 101, 106–11 *passim*
Chesnut, James, Jr., 119
Chesnut, Mary Boykin, 119
Clark, Micajah H., 41, 42, 87, 125, 133, 134, 136, 137, 154–55; appointed Acting Treasurer of Confederacy, 131
Clay, Clement C., 45, 152, 153, 158
Clay, Virginia, 152, 153
Cleburne, Pat, 10
Cobb, Howell, 103
Cokesbury, SC, 121
Concord, NC, 97, 98
Confederacy: general military affairs of, 3–4, 6, 8, 23–24, 60, 70, 79, 86, 90, 103, 132, 140, 175n
Confederate archives, 41–43, 66, 88, 110, 127, 133, 147n, 154–55
Confederate cabinet: members of, 38–40; meetings of, 40–41, 56, 64, 65, 80, 81–82, 84, 104, 106, 109, 118, 132; opinions of Johnston-Sherman agreement, 104–5;